M000121796

Responsive Reading Instruction:

Flexible Intervention for Struggling Readers in the Early Grades

Word Work

Fluency

Assessment

Supported Reading

Supported Writing

Sopris West™
EDUCATIONAL SERVICES
A Cambium Learning™ Company

Carolyn Denton, Ph.D., and Jennifer Hocker

Copyright 2006 by Sopris West Educational Services. All rights reserved.

12 11 10 09 08 07 06   2 3 4 5 6

Permission is granted to the purchasing teacher to reproduce the lists and forms
from the Appendix for use in his or her classroom only. No other portion of this
work may be reproduced or transmitted in any form or by any means, electronic
or mechanical, including photocopying or recording, or by any information storage
and retrieval system, without the express written permission of the publisher.

ISBN 1-59318-592-8

Printed in the United States of America

Published and Distributed by

Sopris West™
EDUCATIONAL SERVICES

A Cambium Learning™ Company

4093 Specialty Place • Longmont, CO 80504 • 303-651-2829

www.sopriswest.com

227RRTE/128303/2-03

We dedicate this book to our friend and colleague
Daraugh Meyers-Turner, who spent two years
teaching Responsive Reading Instruction. Her teaching
talents, generosity with her time, and endless
encouragement helped us become better teachers and
helped this intervention program take shape.
She will be greatly missed.
C.D. and J.H.

To my dear husband, Barry.
C.D.

To my parents, Dennis and Julie.
J.H.

Acknowledgments

This book would not have been written without the support of many people.

First, I would like to thank my parents, Lou and Georgia, who have always taught me to be the best I can be and to use my time for things that matter.

I owe so much to my husband, Barry, who has always believed in me and is incredibly supportive, loving, and patient. I would like to thank my daughters, Christy and Laura, who had to put up with having a mother who worked way too much, and who taught me much of what I know about working with children. I also want to thank Christy's husband, Ignacio Jr., and my beautiful granddaughter Bella, just for being there.

I have been extremely lucky to have had two important mentors in my professional life: Jan Hasbrouck and Jack Fletcher. Jan and her colleague Richard Parker were the ones who first saw potential in me and urged me to pursue a doctorate. Jan was my first professional role model, and I continue to learn from her. I had the great privilege to work on a research project with Jack for three years, and learned a great deal from him about conducting rigorous research, and about keeping things in perspective. Both of these people are leaders in the field of reading education, and I have been truly blessed to have had the chance to know them and learn from them.

My thanks go to many other outstanding persons with whom I have worked and from whom I have learned—Sharon Vaughn, Barbara Foorman, Patricia Mathes, Chris Schatschneider, David Francis, Jason Anthony, Louisa Moats, Susan Sekaquaptewa, and many others.

Finally, I sincerely thank all of the students who I have been privileged to teach over the years, especially the children for whom learning to read was a challenge. You taught me as much as I taught you.

C.D.

I want to thank all my family and friends, and the educators who have supported me. Especially I would like to thank Carolyn Denton for mentoring me to grow to be a better teacher and reading coach. I am still learning from you!

J.H.

We would both like to thank the project directors, research assistants, and teachers who have contributed so much to our research efforts, and thus to Responsive Reading Instruction (RRI), especially Eleanor Boyce, Gloria Hanson, Jennifer Griffin, Gaye Thornton, Teresa Taylor-Partridge, Carolyn Buss, Melinda McGrath, Paige Ware, Elizabeth Swanson, and

Caroline Kethley. Also thanks to all the teachers and principals who have worked with us on the RRI research projects and given us feedback over the years

We owe many thanks to Candace Kiene, who gave this book an "extreme makeover," always keeping her sense of humor when asked to revise and revise more. Her expert editing, patience, and organization have helped turn this book into something to be proud of.

Finally, we thank the good people at Sopris West, especially Holly Bell, Steve Mitchell, Louisa Moats, and Sarah Beatty, for their support of *Responsive Reading Instruction: Flexible Intervention for Struggling Readers in the Early Grades.*

C.D. and J.H.

About the Authors

Carolyn Denton, Ph.D., is an assistant professor in the Department of Special Education at the University of Texas at Austin and serves on the board of directors of the Vaughn Gross Center for Reading and Language Arts at the University of Texas. A former teacher, Dr. Denton conducts research in school settings and works with educators across the US to translate research to practice. She is the co-author with Dr. Jan Hasbrouck of *The Reading Coach: A How-To Manual for Success.*

Jennifer Hocker is an instructional developer and a Responsive Reading Instruction (RRI) trainer and coach for the Institute for Reading Research at Southern Methodist University in Dallas. She is a former first grade and RRI intervention teacher.

Contents

Introduction

What Is Responsive Reading Instruction?

Since the mid-1980s, there has been a dramatic increase in our understanding of what constitutes effective reading instruction. This knowledge includes some truly exciting findings in several disciplines, such as brain imaging, genetics, cognitive development, and instruction (Denton, Vaughn, & Fletcher, 2003). Research in early reading intervention has demonstrated that, with appropriate instruction, nearly all students—including those from low-income backgrounds and those with mild to moderate disabilities—can become competent readers. Prevention studies have demonstrated that 75 to 90 percent of at-risk children (bottom 20 percent) in kindergarten through Grade 2 can learn to read in the average range (see Mathes & Denton, 2002). Virtually all of the effective interventions used by researchers provide students with explicit instruction in the alphabetic principle, along with opportunities to apply the strategies they are learning while reading and writing text.

One literacy intervention program that has successfully supported student growth in this kind of research is Responsive Reading Instruction (RRI). Designed for primary-grade students who struggle to learn to read, RRI is delivered daily in small groups of three to four students for 40-minute periods.

What Does Research Say?

Scientifically based research has demonstrated the effectiveness of RRI for first-graders who are at risk for reading difficulties (Mathes et al., 2005). The first study that evaluated RRI took place in an urban area of Texas over a two-year period. Six schools, six reading intervention teachers, and 300 at-risk first-graders participated in the study. Students for the study were selected in a two-step process. First, they were screened for reading difficulties using the Texas Primary Reading Inventory (TPRI) (Foorman, Fletcher, & Francis, 2004) at either the end of their kindergarten year or the beginning of their first-grade year. Second, measures of word reading and an oral reading sample were taken to ensure that the students identified by the TPRI were truly at risk for developing serious reading problems. Once students were identified, they were randomly assigned to one of three reading instruction groups:

- **Group 1**. *Quality classroom reading instruction with RRI intervention* (92 students).
- **Group 2**. *Quality classroom reading instruction with an alternate early literacy intervention* (92 students) (Mathes & Torgesen, 2004).
- **Group 3**. *Quality classroom reading instruction* with whatever intervention the schools were typically providing to struggling readers (114 students). In four of the six schools, students received no intervention outside of their regular classrooms; in the other two schools students received supplemental intervention provided by their schools.

Students in Groups 1 and 2, who received one of the two interventions, were tutored in small groups with a ratio of three students to one teacher. They met five days a week, 40 minutes a day, from October through April. Student progress was measured using several standardized tests such as the TPRI, the Comprehensive Test of Phonological Processing (Wagner, Torgesen, & Rashotte, 1999), the Test of Word Reading Efficiency (Torgesen, Wagner, & Rashotte, 1999), and the Woodcock-Johnson III Tests of Achievement (Woodcock, McGrew, & Mather, 2001). Additionally, students' growth in oral reading fluency was monitored every three weeks. Graphs showing each student's progress in fluency were distributed to the students' intervention teachers, classroom teachers, principals, and parents or guardians.

The results of the Texas study were significant. Students in both intervention groups performed better than the students in Group 1 who only received quality classroom instruction. Students who received the

RRI intervention performed significantly better than Group 3 students in multiple key reading components, including phonemic awareness, reading words in lists, recognizing sight words instantly, spelling, and accurate and fluent oral reading. *Students in RRI made quicker progress than normally developing readers in the same schools in phonemic awareness, word reading, and oral reading fluency.* This means that the RRI students were "closing the gap" with the students who did not have reading problems. These findings indicate that classroom instruction alone, even when it is of a high quality, is not enough for the small number of children who require higher-intensity instruction. The interventions used in Groups 1 and 2 differed in several ways, but they shared a systematic approach to explicit instruction in phonemic awareness, phonics, fluency, and comprehension, with an emphasis on teaching the students to sound out unknown words and identify sounds in words in order to spell them. This supplemental intervention complemented quality classroom reading instruction.

By the end of their first-grade year, all but a very small percentage of the at-risk first-grade readers in the six schools participating in the study could read at grade level. At the end of the school year, fewer than 1.5 percent were still poor readers (Mathes et al., 2005).

Who Can Teach RRI?

The effectiveness of RRI is supported by research in which certified teachers provided daily small-group reading intervention outside of the regular classroom. However, RRI can be adapted for use by classroom teachers or other educators. The teaching activities included in RRI can be integrated into instructional programs for at-risk and struggling readers in a variety of settings. It must be noted, however, that results are not likely to be as strong as those obtained in the original research if students receive only parts of RRI, receive RRI only a few days a week, or receive RRI instruction in a setting that has many distractions. Teachers should receive adequate professional development to enable them to effectively use the program.

Overview of the RRI Lesson

The daily RRI lesson includes (1) direct and explicit instruction in decoding, (2) instruction and practice designed to support the development of fluent reading, (3) continuous monitoring of student growth through frequent assessment, and (4) large amounts of engaged practice in reading and writing connected text.

Each child in the RRI group receives an individual assessment on reading or key reading skills at least once a week, and teachers record their observations of the students' reading and writing in Anecdotal Records each day. Teachers provide instruction designed specifically to meet the needs of individual children based on the results of the assessments. Although teachers are provided with guidelines suggesting the order of instruction in early reading skills, such as letter-sound correspondences, they have the flexibility to plan each lesson with students' specific needs in mind, based on assessment results.

RRI teachers provide explicit instruction based on a routine of modeling followed by guided and independent practice. The practice activities normally take the form of games that engage the students and ensure that each child is actively involved in learning to read. A large part of each lesson is spent reading and writing connected text as children apply the skills and concepts they have been taught with feedback and support from the RRI teacher.

The daily RRI lesson has five components. Each of these components is included in every 40-minute lesson, as follows:

1. **WORD WORK** (10 minutes). The primary objective is accurate and efficient word recognition. **WORD WORK** includes explicit instruction and many opportunities to practice skills related to phonemic awareness and phonics.

2. **PRINT CONCEPTS AND FLUENCY** (10 minutes for both **PRINT CONCEPTS AND FLUENCY** and **ASSESSMENT**). This component focuses primarily on strategies to increase oral reading fluency. **PRINT CONCEPTS** are taught in the early lessons if needed.

3. **ASSESSMENT**. An assessment is administered to one of the students in the group. A different student is assessed each day.

4. **SUPPORTED READING** (10 minutes). Students are supported as they apply decoding and comprehension strategies and skills while reading connected text.

5. **SUPPORTED WRITING** (10 minutes). Students are supported as they apply strategies and skills while writing connected text.

Before the RRI lesson, the teacher must select appropriate text and activities to meet the students' needs. Responsive Reading Instruction contains a "menu" of activities for each part of the RRI lesson from which the teacher chooses activities based on a suggested progression of instruction and the students' needs based on the results of assessments. During the lesson, the teacher makes constant decisions about the need to scaffold students to facilitate their success. After the lesson, the teacher analyzes data from assessments and Anecdotal Records to help plan future lessons.

RRI teachers should use a timer to make sure every lesson begins and ends within five minutes of the scheduled time. When teachers first implement RRI, it is helpful to set a timer for each of the 10-minute lesson segments. Within each lesson segment, the pace of the instruction is quick but not rushed. Students should be engaged actively throughout the lesson. Teachers should devote a minimum amount of time to "teacher talk." Much of an RRI lesson is devoted to practice and the application of skills in reading and writing connected text.

Books Students Read in RRI

In the Texas study of RRI described earlier, students read books leveled according to Fountas and Pinnell's (1999) *Matching Books to Readers*. Levels A–M were used in the study. These leveled books are not meant to be decodable using the phonic elements students have learned. Researchers selected Benchmark Books for each of the levels in order to monitor student progress. It is important to realize that the levels in this system are not equidistant. For example, there is little difference between Levels A and B but at least half a grade level of difference between Levels N and M.

Leveled books provide a framework that can help the RRI teacher provide text to students at an appropriate level of difficulty and increase the level of difficulty systematically as students progress through the program. If decodable texts are available, the teacher may also use these in RRI instruction, as long as they are at the students' instructional reading levels. Teachers are encouraged to include what are called "semi-decodable" texts, books that contain many examples of a phonic element being taught (such as the /a/ sound or the *ai* vowel pattern). Using books with a relatively high degree of decodability, particularly at the beginning of the program, can be helpful in lessening children's tendency to guess words by looking at pictures in the books. These books give students many opportunities to apply the skills they are learning while reading connected text. If RRI is used with older struggling readers or adapted for classroom use, any text may be used as long as it is on students' instructional reading levels.

Teaching Students to Read Words

In RRI, students are taught to use phonics to read and spell unknown words and to focus on the meaning of the text to self-monitor, making sure that what they have read makes sense. *RRI emphasizes sounding out words from the earliest lessons in order to prevent overreliance on pictures or guessing to identify words. Many students who are taught to overrely on pictures and context in the earliest lessons develop guessing habits that persist even when they are reading more advanced text in which the pictures and context are only minimally supportive.* It is, frankly, easier for struggling readers to look at a picture or use context to guess a word than to sound out and use phonics patterns to decode. *This is not to say that students should ignore the meaning of the text. Quite the contrary: It is the students' responsibility to constantly monitor their reading to be sure that it makes sense.* The purpose of reading is, after all, to comprehend the meaning of the text! RRI teachers consistently emphasize comprehension through discussions before, during, and after reading.

The use of nondecodable texts presents challenges in the early stages of RRI because students typically know few letter-sound associations and recognize few words on sight. At this stage, RRI teachers use a modeling routine when students encounter unknown words. The teacher first points out any phonemes in the word the student knows, then models sounding out the word, saying the word first in a slow, connected fashion, then as an intact word. Thus, students are encouraged to use their limited letter-sound knowledge and are simultaneously supplied with words they are not yet able to decode as their teacher models efficient word identification. If the problem word is irregular or very complex, the teacher simply tells the child the word. After the word is supplied to the child via modeling the strategy or telling the word, the child is instructed to reread the sentence with the word in it to be sure that it makes sense.

Reading and Writing Text

In RRI, students read and write connected text with daily scaffolding and support from the teacher, beginning on the very first day of instruction. In the earliest lessons, students read books that include the limited words and sounds the students know. These books are typically written in a rebus format, with pictures integrated into the text to represent words the student cannot read. As students' skills increase, the text they read becomes progressively more challenging. A critical job of the RRI teacher is to select text for the students on their instructional levels, text that is challenging enough for the students to learn from but not so difficult that it frustrates them.

In the SUPPORTED READING and SUPPORTED WRITING components of the RRI lesson, students read and write with their teacher's support. One student in the group composes a sentence each day in response to the teacher's questions related to the book that was just read, and all students write the same sentence in their journals. When students encounter difficult words or make errors in reading or writing, the RRI teacher provides scaffolding and instruction to teach them to apply the reading and spelling skills and strategies they have learned.

Fluency and Comprehension

RRI emphasizes the development of reading fluency and comprehension. In PRINT CONCEPTS AND FLUENCY, students practice the repeated reading of familiar text with support and feedback from the teacher, and they engage in oral partner reading of familiar books. The teacher models fluent and expressive reading, explicitly teaches the meaning of punctuation marks, and prompts students to read smoothly and in phrases, rather than focusing on one word at a time.

As students read new and familiar books, teachers continually refer to the meaning of the text. Before students read a new book, teachers pre-teach potentially difficult vocabulary words, discuss potentially confusing subject matter, and encourage students to make predictions to link the book's subject matter to prior knowledge and to establish a purpose for reading. Before, during, and after reading, teachers ask questions focused on specific facets of comprehension, including the main ideas of expository (nonfiction) text and elements of story structure such as characters, problems, and solutions. Teachers may also ask students to retell or summarize portions of the book. Teachers provide feedback and they support students as they discuss the meaning of text. After the students progress from the earliest stages of reading, they are taught to write brief text summaries, identify story structure characteristics, and answer other kinds of comprehension questions in their journals during the SUPPORTED WRITING portion of the lesson.

Three Phases of RRI

The activities in this book are designed to be used in three phases (see Table I.1):

- **Phase 1**. The activities in Phase 1 are appropriate for students in the earliest stages of reading acquisition. The objectives include the understanding of 1:1 correspondence between the written and spoken word, the meaning of terms such as *word*, *sentence*, and *letter*, and left-to-right directionality. At this stage, students may recognize only a few letters and may be unable to write their names or simple words correctly. *They may not fully understand the alphabetic principle—that letters stand for sounds, can be combined to make words, and can be recombined to make other words.*

- **Phase 2**. This phase represents most of the intervention period. This is the phase in which the child learns to identify words and to read and write progressively more complex text. Older struggling readers will normally begin at Phase 2. Students gain facility with:
  – Letter-sound correspondences and word patterns.
  – Automatic recognition of high-frequency words.
  – Reading text with increasing accuracy and fluency.
  – Spelling words by listening for letter-sound correspondences and remembering common spelling patterns.
  – Implementing basic comprehension strategies.

- **Phase 3**. This phase occurs in the last months of first grade for students who are making adequate progress. In Phase 3, students can focus on more advanced decoding strategies, including knowledge of more advanced letter combinations and reading and writing multisyllabic words. They should be reading longer texts with minimal support and scaffolding. Building oral reading fluency is a major goal for this phase. The student's writing should reflect increasing control of more advanced elements, including multisyllabic words.

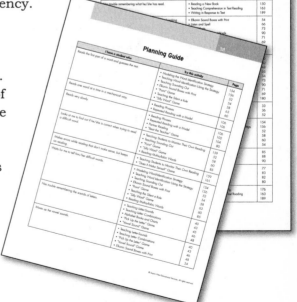

Only a sensitive and observant teacher can determine when a child has moved from one phase to the next. In RRI, the teacher relies on assessments for guidance in selecting appropriate texts and activities to meet students' changing needs. (See the Planning Guide provided in the Appendix.)

TABLE I.1

Responsive Reading Instruction Activities: Overview

		Phase 1	Phase 2	Phase 3
Word Work		**Phonological Awareness** • Syllable Identification • Stretching Words • Mystery Word Game • Elkonin Sound Boxes Without Print **Letter-Sounds and Letter Combinations** • Teaching Letter-Sounds • Alphabet Books and Charts • Pick Up the Letter Game • Teaching Letter Formation **Sounding Out and Spelling Words** • Teaching Sounding Out **High-Frequency Words** • Teaching High-Frequency Words • Teaching Students' Names • "Beat the Teacher" Game • Word Building • Writing High-Frequency Words	**Phonological Awareness** • Syllable Identification • Stretching Words • Mystery Word Game • Elkonin Sound Boxes Without Print **Letter-Sounds and Letter Combinations** • Teaching Letter-Sounds • Teaching Letter Combinations • Alphabet Books and Charts • Pick Up the Letter Game • Vowel Sound Game • Teaching Letter Formation **Sounding Out and Spelling Words** • Teaching Sounding Out • Elkonin Sound Boxes with Print • Point Game • Silly Word Game • Teaching the Silent *e* Rule • Listen and Spell • Word Linking • Word Pattern Charts • Word Sorts **High-Frequency Words** • Teaching High-Frequency Words • "Beat the Teacher" Game • Word Building • Writing High-Frequency Words **Multisyllabic Words** • Reading Multisyllabic Words • Flexing Words • Writing Multisyllabic Words	**Letter-Sounds and Letter Combinations** • Teaching Letter-Sounds • Teaching Letter Combinations • Vowel Sound Game **Sounding Out and Spelling Words** • Teaching Sounding Out • Point Game • Silly Word Game • Listen and Spell • Word Linking • Word Pattern Charts • Word Sorts **High-Frequency Words** • Teaching High-Frequency Words • "Beat the Teacher" Game • Word Building • Writing High-Frequency Words **Multisyllabic Words** • Reading Multisyllabic Words • Flexing Words • Writing Multisyllabic Words
Print Concepts and Fluency		• Teaching Left-Right Directionality • Teaching Print-Related Vocabulary • Teaching 1:1 Correspondence	• Repeated Reading with a Model • Partner Reading • Reading Phrases	• Repeated Reading with a Model • Partner Reading • Reading Phrases

	Phase 1	Phase 2	Phase 3
Assessment	• Anecdotal Records • Assessment of Reading Accuracy • Benchmark Book Assessment • Letter-Name Assessment • Letter-Sound Assessment • High-Frequency Word Assessment	• Anecdotal Records • Assessment of Reading Accuracy • Benchmark Book Assessment • Letter-Name Assessment • Letter-Sound Assessment • High-Frequency Word Assessment • Oral Reading Fluency Assessment	• Anecdotal Records • Assessment of Reading Accuracy • Benchmark Book Assessment • Letter-Sound Assessment • High-Frequency Word Assessment • Oral Reading Fluency Assessment
Supported Reading	• Introducing a New Book • Reading a New Book • Modeling the Word Identification Strategy • Teaching Students to Monitor Their Own Reading • "Does It Make Sense?" Game	• Introducing a New Book • Reading a New Book • Modeling the Word Identification Strategy • Teaching Word Identification Using the Strategy • Teaching Students to Monitor Their Own Reading • "Does It Make Sense?" Game • Teaching Comprehension in Text Reading: Questioning • Teaching Comprehension in Text Reading: Story Structure	• Introducing a New Book • Reading a New Book • Teaching Word Identification Using the Strategy • Teaching Students to Monitor Their Own Reading • Teaching Comprehension in Text Reading: Questioning • Teaching Comprehension in Text Reading: Story Structure
Supported Writing	• Supported Group Writing • Teaching Sound Analysis	• Supported Independent Writing • Teaching Sound Analysis • Teaching Students to Edit Their Writing • Writing in Response to Text	• Supported Independent Writing • Teaching Sound Analysis • Teaching Students to Edit Their Writing • Writing in Response to Text

The Foundations of RRI

RRI is based on six characteristics that research has shown are important for effective instruction of struggling readers. These characteristics are the foundations of RRI. They are: (1) instruction in key domains of reading, (2) explicit instruction, (3) opportunities to practice, (4) targeted instruction based on assessments, (5) scaffolding and feedback, and (6) the home-school connection.

Instruction in Key Domains of Reading

The National Reading Panel (2000) identified five key elements of effective reading instruction in the primary grades:

- **Phonemic awareness**. An auditory skill that involves the ability to notice, identify, and manipulate the sounds in spoken words.
- **Phonics**. Understanding that the sounds in spoken words are represented in print by letters and combinations of letters, and application of the knowledge of the English "code" to read unknown words.
- **Fluency**. The ability to read text accurately, quickly, and with good expression.
- **Vocabulary**. Knowledge of word meanings.
- **Reading comprehension**. The ability to make meaning of written text.

The main focus of RRI in the early lessons is on phonemic awareness and phonics—the tools students need to accurately decode words. RRI also emphasizes fluency and comprehension. It does not explicitly teach vocabulary, although teachers pre-teach key vocabulary before reading a new book and discuss word meanings during Supported Reading.

Explicit Instruction

Students with reading problems are often easily confused. They need to be directly or explicitly taught the knowledge and skills involved in learning to read (National Reading Panel, 2000). When a teacher provides explicit instruction, students do not have to guess or infer what they should learn. The teacher models, demonstrates, or clearly explains the concept or skill and guides the students as they practice it. For example, a teacher who is explicitly teaching the sound of the letter combination *oa* might point to these two letters written on a card and say, "The sound of these letters is usually /ō/ [the long o sound]. When you see *oa* together in a word you will usually say /ō/. What sound do these letters usually make? Let's read some words that have *oa* in them."

A teacher who does not provide explicit instruction might show the students a sentence in a book that includes a word with the *oa* pattern. For example, a page in a book may have a picture of a small boat in the middle of a lake, with the words, "The boy was in the *boat*." The teacher might ask students to look at the word *boat*, look at the picture, think about what would make sense in the sentence, and try to read the word.

After the students have used picture cues to help them identify the word, the teacher might point out that the *oa* in the word *boat* makes the sound /ō/. This nonexplicit approach is not as effective for many struggling readers. RRI teachers provide explicit instruction by consistently using an instructional format designed to directly teach students what they need to learn.

Instructional Format. Each time a new skill, strategy, or element (e.g., a letter-sound, new word, etc.) is introduced or a difficult activity is practiced, follow this instructional sequence:

1. *Model and teach.* Show the students what to do. Be explicit. Teach the students what you want them to learn. Don't make them learn by trial and error. Practicing errors is harmful, especially for a child who has learning difficulties.

2. *Provide guided practice.* Carefully monitor and scaffold the students as they practice the skill. This may include performing the skill along with them to lead them through the steps. Provide feedback if errors occur. This may include scaffolding or modeling the skill again.

3. *Provide independent practice.* Observe students closely while they practice the skill alone, providing scaffolding and feedback if necessary. Provide many opportunities for practice.

4. *Provide cumulative practice.* Integrate the new learning with past learning. For example, if students have recently learned the sound of the letter combination *sh*, present the *sh* along with other letters or letter combinations they have learned in the past, and have the students practice discriminating between the new element and others that they already know.

5. *Assess and reteach as necessary.*

Table I.2 provides *one* example of the RRI instructional format for each of the five lesson components. The table provides *examples* only. In any part of an RRI lesson, you can teach and practice multiple activities using RRI's instructional format.

Modeling "Today we are going to practice some high-frequency words. Let's look at the first word—*could* [magnetic letters are arranged on a burner cover]. Everyone say the word *could*. Good! Now watch me. First I'm going to look very closely at the word *could*. Then I'll mix up the letters. Then I'll say the word *could* and make the word quickly by placing the letters in the correct order. Then I will say the word again, running my finger under the word—*could*. Now watch. I'm going to change the word *could* into the word *would*. What sound do you hear at the beginning of *would*? Yes, it's the /w/ sound. Since I want to change *could* to *would*, I will take off the *c* at the beginning of *could* and put in a *w* for the /w/ sound in *would*. Now I'm going to read my new word and run my finger under the word to be sure it is right." The teacher says the word slowly, then fast: "*woooood, would.*" "Monica, am I right? Did I make *would*?"

Guided and Independent Practice *Guided practice:* "Now it's your turn. Hands in your lap while I pass out the burner covers. The word on your burner cover is *could*. Take a good look at it. Now mix up the letters. Are you ready to make it say *could* again? Now begin. Say the word *could* first, then make the word quickly, then read the word. Show me the word."

Isaac has made *coudl*. "Isaac, check your letters. What sound do you hear at the end of *could*? Good. You figured out that there is a /d/ sound at the end of the word. Now make the word quickly and then read the word. Everyone pass your burner cover to your neighbor. Make *could* again. Look at it closely, Isaac, and make sure it looks right. Everyone made the word correctly. Now I am going to give you the letter *w* to change the word *could* to *would*. Now change the word to *would*."

Students mix up letters and make the word one or two times. "Now let's change the word *would* to *should* by changing the beginning sound. Think about what letters you will need to make the first sound in should."

Independent practice: "I'm going to give you each a different word to make on your burner cover. Make it quickly. Isaac, make *could*. Monica, make *would*. Lamont, make *should*. Good, you remember the words."

Cumulative Practice Another day: "We are going to quickly read some words we have been working on by playing 'Beat the Teacher.'" Students read words from note cards: *there, could, little, find, would, come, my, now, should.*

TABLE I.2

How to Apply the Instructional Format

	Example of Activity	Modeling and Teaching	Guided Practice	Independent Practice	Cumulative Practice
Word Work: Introducing new letter-sounds.	Teacher writes letter or letter combination on whiteboard or card, or makes it with magnetic letters. Teacher tells students the sound of the letter(s).	Students say the new sound with the teacher as the teacher shows them the written form.	Students take turns saying the new sound individually.	Students identify the new letter-sound along with other sounds they have previously learned.
Print Concepts and Fluency: Teaching students how to observe punctuation while reading.	Teacher explicitly tells the students to pause after each period in the text. Teacher demonstrates what this sounds like.	Teacher scaffolds students as they apply the skill while reading a section of text.	Teacher observes and provides feedback to individual students as they apply the skill in reading.	Students learn to respond to other forms of punctuation and practice each new skill integrated with previously learned skills.
Supported Reading: Teaching a strategy for decoding unknown words.	Teacher explicitly models three-part strategy: (1) Look for known word parts, (2) sound out word, and (3) make sure resulting word makes sense in sentence.	Teacher scaffolds students as they apply the strategy while reading words and/or text.	Teacher observes and provides feedback to individual students as they apply the strategy when they encounter an unknown word.	Students learn to apply the strategy to increasingly more complex words.
Supported Writing: Teaching a strategy for spelling unknown words.	Teacher explicitly models the strategy of saying a word slowly, listening for its phonemes, and recording them.	Teacher scaffolds students as they apply the strategy while writing.	Teacher observes and provides feedback to the students as they independently apply the strategy.	Students learn to apply the strategy to increasingly more complex words.

Opportunities to Practice

It is important to provide your students with many opportunities to practice the elements (e.g., sounds, words) and skills you have taught. Students who are having difficulty learning to read need extended practice in order to master new knowledge and skills. WORD WORK lessons should be as much as 75 to 80 percent practice and only 20 to 25 percent new learning. Students should also practice applying skills in increasingly challenging ways, such as decoding increasingly complex words.

How to Know When the Student Has Truly Learned Something. Consider the five different levels of learning adapted with permission from Killoran, Templeman, Peters, & Udell (2001):

1. *Unknown.* A skill or knowledge is new to the student. The student may not know the most common sound of the letter *r* or may not be aware of what it means to sound out a word. Example: Rachel doesn't know what a sentence is.

2. *Awareness.* The skill is familiar to the student, but more instruction and practice are needed to be able to use it. The student may be aware of what it means to blend sounds to identify words but still be unable to do it. Example: Jennifer seems to understand the process of stretching words (phonemic awareness activity) but is unable to perform it correctly.

3. *Knowledge.* The student is able to use the skill but needs more practice and feedback. The student may forget what was learned and need scaffolding and/or reteaching. One day, the student seems to know how to read the word *what* but is unable to remember the word a few days later. Example: A student stops on or misidentifies a high-frequency word that he previously read correctly.

4. *Application.* The student is able to apply the skill in a variety of situations and settings at a satisfactory level but needs more practice to become fluent in it. The student applies the sounding-out word reading strategy most of the time but does it slowly and is sometimes inconsistent. Example: Sarah sounds out two-syllable words correctly, but she does it very slowly.

5. *Mastery.* The student can successfully, independently, and consistently apply the skill in multiple situations with a high level of competence; applying the skill has become a habit and is automatic (fluent). The student very quickly employs word identification skills and strategies "on the run" while reading unfamiliar text with high fluency and accuracy. The student uses a sound analysis strategy efficiently to spell words in the regular classroom, at home, and in other settings. It has become a habit for the student to pay attention to what he or she is reading, and correcting errors independently has also become a habit. Example: Jason can read grade-level stories fluently in his classroom without help.

Teachers of struggling young readers seem to make two common mistakes. First, they assume that children know things that they don't know. For example, RRI teachers have heard colleagues remark that a child is not paying attention because he or she won't follow directions to put a finger under the first word on a page. In actuality, the student may not know what *first* or *word* mean. Second, teachers tend to stop teaching a skill or item of knowledge when it is at a student's knowledge level. Once the student has demonstrated that he or she knows a letter-sound correspondence or knows how to write the word *said*, the teacher moves on to other objectives. If the student is at the knowledge level for that skill, the student needs more practice, support, and possibly more instruction to be able to perform it consistently. If the teacher doesn't supply ample opportunities for practice over time, it should be no surprise if the student forgets how to write the word.

In short, students need to practice skills and apply knowledge until it becomes a habit. The teacher's task isn't done until students have mastered the material. This really is the only chance that the struggling reader has to continue to make progress on his or her own after the supplemental intervention is discontinued.

Targeted Instruction Based on Assessments

Providing targeted instruction means teaching what students need to learn. It means assessing students' strengths and needs to find out what they need to learn, designing instruction based on the assessment results, monitoring students' progress as they apply what they are learning, and reteaching as needed.

Assessment is the essence of targeted instruction. Teaching struggling readers effectively means continuously monitoring and assessing their strengths and needs. RRI teachers conduct assessments of one individual student in each lesson (on a rotating basis). Every student in the group is assessed at least once a week.

In the research demonstrating the effectiveness of RRI, students were tutored in groups of three. This is the optimum group size and should be maintained whenever possible. Studies of reading intervention in the early grades have demonstrated that students made substantial progress when tutored in groups of three (Rachotte, MacPhee, & Torgesen, 2001; Vaughn et al., 2003).

RRI may be just as effective in groups of four, although this has not been substantiated by research. Targeted instruction is based on the needs of individual students, but it can be hard to individualize instruction, even when teaching small groups.

Star Reader. To develop individualized instruction, each daily RRI lesson is planned with a focus on one member of the small group. Each day, one of the three children is designated the Star Reader (rotating through the children in the same order). The teacher plans the lesson and selects new text with the particular strengths and needs of the Star Reader in mind.

The Star Reader sits next to the teacher (side by side) and receives the most concentrated attention from the teacher that day. The nature of this individualization in each part of the lesson is as follows:

- The Star Reader works one-on-one with the teacher during the **FLUENCY** segment of the lesson while the other two children partner read.
- Each day the teacher conducts an assessment with the child who was the Star Reader the day before.
- The teacher chooses a new book appropriate for the Star Reader. The Star Reader reads a part of this book alone while the teacher prompts the student for accurate and fluent reading with comprehension. This initial reading is followed by a second (and sometimes third) reading in which all students participate.
- The Star Reader composes the sentence for the **SUPPORTED WRITING** activity, and all of the students write the same sentence.

RRI teachers keep track of which student is the Star Reader each day by writing the names of all the students in a group on a small poster and moving a clothespin or paper clip next to the name of the student on the poster each day. (See the Star Reader Poster in the Appendix.) Students develop the routine of entering the room each day and checking the poster to find out who is the Star Reader for the day. Then students walk to the RRI table, and the Star Reader sits next to the teacher's chair. If the Star Reader for that day is absent, the next student becomes the Star Reader for the day.

Scaffolding and Feedback

Providing scaffolding and feedback to students is an essential characteristic of RRI. It is so important that a teacher is not actually using the RRI approach to teach reading unless he or she is skillful at providing students with the supportive environment they need to take risks, apply what they know, and reach mastery. Many young students who are at risk for learning to read have already experienced failure, and some already have poor self-concepts regarding their ability to be successful readers.

RRI is designed to enable children to feel successful. This does not mean that the lessons are overly easy but that students encounter challenges that are manageable with the teacher's support. People grow in feelings of self-efficacy (a belief in your ability to do something well) through recognizing that challenges have been met and overcome. If students have this experience repeatedly, their self-confidence tends to grow, resulting in a willingness to take even more risks and exert even greater effort to overcome challenges.

Just as young children who are learning to swim must trust that the person teaching them will keep them safe and provide them with support until they are able to swim independently, children who are learning to read must trust that their teacher will not allow them to be hurt emotionally while they are learning to be independent readers.

Star Reader

Carlina

Marquis

Justin

Scaffolding. Scaffolding is defined by Graves, Graves, and Braaten (1996) as "providing a support to help learners bridge the gap between what they know and can do and what they need to accomplish in order to succeed in a particular learning task" (p. 169). In other words, instructional scaffolding enables a student to be successful with support from the teacher at a task that he or she could not successfully accomplish without help. To provide effective scaffolding, the teacher must be able to determine the abilities and needs of the learner and design what Larkin (2001) calls "tailored assistance" (p. 31). Effective scaffolding requires close observation of the student. It is always individualized, built on each student's strengths and needs.

In RRI, the goals of scaffolding are to provide a "safety net" to ensure student success, support students' developing skills and problem-solving processes, and teach students effective and efficient strategies to apply when they encounter difficulty while reading or writing.

A very important characteristic of scaffolding is that it is temporary. As students become more proficient at a task, they need less and less support. Typically, teachers raise the level of skills or text difficulty to provide students with the opportunity to continue to make progress, and students are once again scaffolded at the more difficult level. Each activity included in this book includes suggestions for scaffolding. Some examples of the forms of scaffolding included in RRI are:

- Choosing books for students that are at their instructional levels, books that are just difficult enough to provide challenges but that students can read successfully with the support of the teacher.
- Providing prompts such as, "What sound does this letter make? Now can you sound out the word?"
- Using Elkonin Sound Boxes to help students isolate sounds they hear in words.
- Breaking tasks into smaller steps and prompting students as they execute one step at a time.
- Teaching only two to three new letter-sounds in a week and giving students ample opportunities to practice these before adding more.

Specific Praise. Feedback in RRI takes two forms: *specific praise* and *corrective feedback*. Research has demonstrated that positive feedback is more effective in promoting change and growth in a person than criticism. RRI teachers consistently offer praise when students apply the strategies and skills they have been taught. In fact, RRI teachers often praise students' attempts even when these efforts are not successful.

There are two very important considerations in offering praise. First, it has to be *authentic*. Never say that a student did something well if he or she did not. This "fake praise" does more damage than good. Students see through it and get the message that the teacher could not think of something in the student's performance that was truly worth praising and had to make something up. Second, the praise must be *specific*. Simply saying "good job" repeatedly begins to sound empty and has little effect in promoting student growth. Some examples of specific praise are:

- "You figured out that word all by yourself. That's what good readers do."
- "You made a mistake on that word, but you went back and fixed it. Well done!"
- "You read that fast and smooth, just like a grown-up would read."
- "Great job of remembering how to write that hard word."
- "When you got to that new word, I saw you trying to sound it out. You nearly had it. It's so important that you try hard even if you sometimes don't quite get it. Let's go back and take a look at that word."
- "What a great sentence you made up for us to write today! You used an extra word in your sentence that really tells us what the dog in the story was like—bouncy. Good writers use extra words like that so their readers can imagine just what things are like."
- "Julia, nice job of sitting tall and listening while I was talking."

Corrective Feedback. It is important to provide students with information about their errors, or *corrective feedback*. This statement comes with a large caution: Corrective feedback in RRI must always be provided in a *neutral* tone, with the attitude of simply providing information. It should never be deriding or punitive in tone.

Why is corrective feedback important? Students who don't realize they made an error are likely to repeat it, and when students practice their mistakes, the mistakes become habits. To a large extent, what a teacher says or does when a student makes an error determines what the student will do in the future and, ultimately, whether the student will learn to read successfully. Student errors can be powerful opportunities for teaching, especially when the students are partially right—when the errors show that they have partial knowledge or partially developed skills, but they can't quite apply what they know successfully without support. Some examples of corrective feedback are:

- "Try this word again."
- "You almost had this word. This word is *train*."
- "You made a mistake in this part. Can you find it?"
- "The word you wrote is *was*. Can you write *what*?"
- "That's not quite right. Let's take another look."
- [As student is trying to write the word:] "You heard all the sounds in *lady*. It does sound like there is an *e* at the end of the word. But sometimes the /ē/ at the end of a word is spelled with the letter *y*. Can you change the *e* at the end of *lady* to *y*? Great. You made it look right."

One of the goals of RRI is to assist students in developing strategies for monitoring their own reading and writing and correcting their own errors. Try waiting a few seconds before you give the feedback, to see whether the student will notice the error on his or her own. Be sure you have carefully read the information on scaffolding in this section, and also take note of the suggestions for scaffolding provided in the descriptions of each of the RRI activities throughout this book.

The Home-School Connection

A common characteristic of successful schools is that teachers work closely with parents to support student growth, the development of a positive self-image, and a positive attitude toward reading. In RRI, the home-school connection is established early in the school year, as teachers connect with parents through notes and phone calls, as well as invitations to school to observe lessons or meet with the teacher. In addition, once a week the RRI teacher sends home with each student a certificate photocopied on colorful paper titled "Read All About It!" (adapted from Mathes & Torgesen, 2004). This certificate (provided in the Appendix) is a brief report that summarizes some of the things the students learned during the week and books that have been read. There is also a space for comments if the teacher needs to communicate something to the parent.

RRI teachers encourage parents to listen to students read books that are sent home for practice. Sometimes teachers may also send students home with word cards or games to practice skills already learned in the RRI lesson. It is important that any activity done at home must have already been taught and practiced in school. Students must always be set up for success in their home practice activities.

Book Checkout. Before the beginning of each lesson, devote a few minutes to checking out books to students. This should be done quickly and efficiently, and it should become a standard routine when the students enter the group space.

Students can place the books they have checked out under their chairs or in another predetermined place where they are unlikely to be a distraction during the lesson. Encourage students to return the books each day and then check out new books. It is helpful to have a large ziplock bag for each student, labeled with the student's name, to use when transporting books to and from school. This protects the books, keeps them together, and helps keep them from being misplaced.

At the beginning of the year, send a note to parents to tell them the purpose of the book checkout and ask that a parent or family member be a "reading partner" to the student. Parents and students should expect to spend 10 to 20 minutes each night reading these books. The books should be familiar and should have already been read in a lesson. They should be at the student's instructional or independent level so that the home reading practice is enjoyable for the student and parents. Parents should not be expected to teach their child to read a book that is too difficult for the child to read independently.

Some students may have difficulties with taking books home and returning them. They may not be able to read each evening at home. (Many parents work two jobs, and all family situations are different.) In this case, the RRI teacher may talk to the classroom teacher and arrange for the student to read the books he or she has checked out during free reading time in the regular classroom. The student can keep the books in the classroom but still participate in the daily book checkout. It may be possible to arrange for an older student or volunteer to be the student's "reading buddy" at school.

Planning the Daily RRI Lesson

It is important to remember that RRI is supported by research *when it is implemented according to the instructions in this book.* (See the Implementation Guide provided in the Appendix.) Therefore, as you plan your daily RRI lesson, you must select activities from the lists provided in each of the five lesson components. (See the Responsive Reading Instruction Lesson Plan provided in the Appendix.) Additionally, always use the following steps to guide you when planning the RRI lesson:

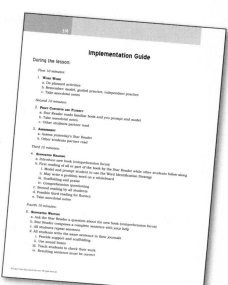

1. Look at assessment data and Anecdotal Records from previous lessons to determine the reading level, strengths, and needs of the Star Reader for the lesson you are planning. As you plan, imagine the lesson activities from the Star Reader's point of view. What will be hard? What will be easy? Select the objectives for your lesson.

2. For each lesson component, choose those activities that are designed to meet the objectives you have identified and are most appropriate for the Star Reader and the group. Note that some activities, such as those in **Supported Reading**, occur in some format during every lesson.

3. Plan the **Word Work** component by first determining the objectives for the lesson (what you want the students to learn) and then choosing the activities that are likely to support the students in meeting the objectives. Plan both instruction and practice activities. The choices of objectives for **Word Work** (such as learning the sound of the letter *m*) are based on two things: your assessments of the students' strengths and needs; and your knowledge of which phonemic awareness activities, phonic elements, and/or high-frequency words are more useful at that point in the students' development. Guidelines for the sequencing of instruction are provided in the **Word Work** chapter.

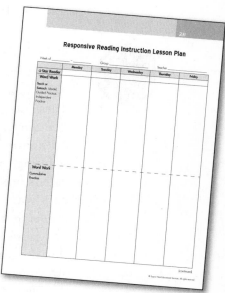

4. Select one to two familiar books the Star Reader will read during the **Fluency** component, and plan your focus for this part of the lesson (Phases 2 and 3).

5. Select the assessment you will administer to the student who was the Star Reader in the *previous* lesson. Choose the assessment that will give you the most beneficial information as you plan future lessons for this student.

6. Choose the new book for the Star Reader to read during supported reading. Guidelines for book selection are provided in the **Supported Reading** chapter. Plan the book introduction and your comprehension focus.

7. Plan the question you will ask the Star Reader to guide him or her in composing a sentence during **Supported Writing**.

8. Assemble and organize your materials and forms.

You will probably find that, at first, it is challenging to pack all the RRI components into a 40-minute lesson. Having all of your materials and forms organized in advance will help you achieve this goal. It is much easier to keep students engaged in learning when the lesson moves smoothly at a brisk pace from one activity to the next. If you copy the Implementation Guide (found in the Appendix) on card stock and keep it in front of you during your lessons, you will find it easier to follow the RRI lesson sequence.

How This Book Is Organized

Each of the next five chapters focuses on one of the five components of the RRI lesson. Each chapter begins with an overview of the component, including a description of the research on which it was based. The rest of the chapter is devoted to detailed descriptions of the activities to be used. The concluding chapter, Putting It All Together, contains more information about implementing RRI. Reproducible forms, instruction materials, and a list of materials used in RRI are located in the Appendix. References and other resources that may be helpful to RRI teachers are also provided.

The DVD

The "Multimedia" icon appears with activities for which supporting video is available on the DVD which, optionally, accompanies this book. The footage was filmed as we worked with groups of actual students and demonstrates how many of the RRI activities are implemented. Because authentic teaching is a process of making decisions "on the run," while reacting to sometimes unpredictable things that students do or say, these videos are not always perfect; however, they provide good examples that can help you understand what RRI "looks like" in practice. Teachers who have implemented RRI in our ongoing research report that having video footage has made a world of difference for them as they have learned to teach using this program. We encourage you to watch these videos as you implement the activities described in the next few chapters. We developed this book with the idea of making it as "teacher friendly" as possible, and the DVD was a big part of this design.

Word Work

In the **WORD WORK** component of the Responsive Reading Instruction (RRI) lesson, teachers use a variety of strategies to develop students' understanding and skills in phonemic awareness, the alphabetic principle, letter-sound correspondences, sight word recognition, decoding, and spelling.

Key Terms and Abbreviations

The following list provides definitions of some of the key terms used when talking about **WORD WORK** instruction:

- **Phonological awareness**: The ability to hear and manipulate units of spoken language such as words, syllables, and sounds; an auditory skill that does not involve print.
- **Phoneme**: The smallest unit of sound in the language. One phoneme can be represented by more than one letter. (The word *eight* has two phonemes: /ā/ and /t/. The letters *eigh* together represent one sound.)
- **Phonemic awareness**: One kind of phonological awareness; the ability to hear and manipulate the individual sounds within spoken words; an auditory skill that does not involve print.
- **Phonics**: The relationship between the sounds of language and print.
- **Alphabetic principle**: The understanding that letters represent sounds in words and can be recombined to spell other words.
- **Continuous sound**: A letter-sound that can be held for several seconds without distorting it (such as /m/, /a/, /f/, and /r/).
- **Stop sound**: A letter-sound that cannot be held without distorting it (such as /b/, /p/, /t/, and /h/).
- **Segmenting phonemes**: Pronouncing the individual phonemes, or sounds, in a word separately, either by saying a word in a smooth, stretched-out way (*mmmmaaaannnn*) or by separating each sound in a word with an instant of silence (/m/ /a/ /n/).
- **Blending phonemes**: Combining individual phonemes, or sounds, to form words. This can be an auditory activity, in which students hear a segmented word and blend the sounds to produce the word. Students also blend the phonemes in a word when they sound out the word.
- **Multisyllabic words**: Words with more than one syllable.
- **Onset**: The initial consonant or consonant blend in a one-syllable word (*pl-* in *play*).
- **Rime**: The portion of a one-syllable word that follows the onset (*-ay* in *play*).

Abbreviations are used to describe different spelling patterns in words. These are:

- **C**: Consonant.
- **V**: Vowel.
- **CVC word**: A word with a consonant–short vowel–consonant pattern (*tap*). The same system is used to describe words with beginning or ending consonant blends (CCVC: *trip*, CVCC: *past*, CCCVC: *split*, CCVCC: *blend*).
- **CVC-E word**: A word with a silent *e* signaling a long vowel sound (*tape*).
- **CVVC word**: A word made up of a consonant, two vowels, and a final consonant (*beat*).

What Does Research Say?

Students who are at risk for reading difficulties often lack skills in *phonemic awareness* and *alphabetic knowledge*, two essential foundational skills needed for reading (Foorman & Torgesen, 2001). Early reading interventions that focus on building these foundational skills and that provide for the application of these skills in reading and writing connected text have been shown to have the greatest impact on struggling readers (National Reading Panel, 2000). Instruction that builds phonemic awareness, alphabetic knowledge, and phonics skills will support the successful development of reading, in the early grades.

Phonemic Awareness

Phonemic awareness, the ability to hear and manipulate individual sounds within spoken words, is critically important in the development of early reading skills (National Reading Panel, 2000). Phonemic awareness is an auditory skill. It builds on the more general awareness of words and syllables in speech, known as phonological awareness. Before students can identify sounds they hear in words (in order to spell) or blend together the sounds (in order to decode the words), they must be able to isolate and manipulate the sounds of letters in spoken words. This ability to isolate and manipulate sounds is one of the strongest predictors of success in early reading acquisition (Scarborough, 1998), and research has indicated that most people with dyslexia have difficulties in this area (see Lyon, 1995). The good news, however, is that phonemic awareness can be taught through systematic instruction and practice, enabling students who struggle with the most basic components of decoding and spelling to be successful. Research has also shown that there is a continuum along which phonological awareness skills develop; typically, some of these skills develop before others. Students normally become aware of words and syllables before they are able to identify and manipulate phonemes within words.

Phonics

Phonics builds on phonemic awareness by mapping sound to print. Phonics includes an understanding of sound-symbol relationships and how sounds and symbols are combined to make words. Students develop phonics skills through activities that include learning letter-sound relationships, sounding out words, and listening for the sounds within words in order to spell them. Students should also learn a few useful phonics rules, such as the silent *e* rule, but research has shown that students benefit more from learning to recognize common word patterns than from memorizing a long list of rules. Phonics skills should be applied to reading and writing connected text (Snow, Burns, & Griffin, 1998). Lessons that provide explicit phonics instruction have been shown to be crucial for struggling readers in the primary grades (National Reading Panel, 2000; Snow et al., 1998).

Phonics instruction has been found to improve growth in spelling and comprehension, as well as in decoding (National Reading Panel, 2000).

In RRI, students learn the alphabetic principle by mapping sounds to print. Using explicit instruction, the teacher teaches students to segment, blend, decode, and spell words. The intervention provides many opportunities to practice, using a variety of games that support the development of the understanding of written language. Throughout the intervention, students apply their decoding and spelling skills to reading and writing text.

Planning the Word Work Part of the RRI Lesson

Word Work activities are planned in advance. Using the results of assessments and observations from previous lessons, the teacher chooses three to five activities from those presented in this chapter. In choosing the focus of **Word Work**:

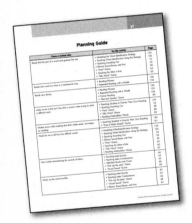

1. Teach the most useful or frequently occurring letters, words, and concepts first. Consult Table 1.1 for guidance.
2. Consider the needs of the students as recorded in Anecdotal Records and assessments.
3. Teach easier skills before more difficult skills. Table 1.2 provides additional guidance for planning **Word Work**. Plan lots of cumulative practice. Do not assume that once you have taught something, the students have mastered it. Provide practice over time in the same skills or phonics elements using a variety of activities from this book.
4. Provide variety *within* the **Word Work** component of each lesson. Include a balance of decoding and spelling activities.
5. Provide variety *across* lessons. It is fine to use the same activities multiple times, but try not to include the same sequence of activities in every lesson. Keep students' attention by providing instruction and practice using different activities from this book.

The concluding chapter, Putting It All Together, provides detailed directions for planning **Word Work** and other RRI lesson segments. The Planning Guide (found in the Appendix) can guide you as you as you respond to your students' needs.

General Instructional Format for Word Work

Follow the instructional format outlined here each time a new element (e.g., a new letter-sound or new word) is introduced or a new skill is taught:

1. *Model and teach.* Show the students what to do. In teaching letter-sounds or words, this means showing the students the letters or words and pronouncing them. Be explicit. Teach the children what you want them to learn. Don't make them learn by trial and error. Practicing errors is extremely detrimental, especially for a child who is at risk.
2. *Provide guided practice.* Have the students do it with you. They say the new sound with you or practice the new skill with you as a group.

Sound	Key Word	Sound Type*
m	mad	continuous
a	ask	continuous
t	top	stop
s	sell	continuous
i	if	continuous
r	rat (rrrr not er)	continuous
d	dog	stop
n	net	continuous
o	off	continuous
f	fat	continuous
c	cat	stop
p	park	stop
l	log	continuous
h	hat	stop (breath only)
g	go	stop
u	up	continuous
b	big	stop
th	that/thing	continuous
j	jump	stop
k	kick	stop
y	yes (yyyyyy)	continuous
e	egg	continuous
ck	sock	stop
ar	car	
ing	sing	
w	wet	continuous
er	her	
x	fox (kssss)	continuous
sh	she	continuous
v	very	continuous
ch	chair	stop
ee	feet	continuous
ow	cow	
oa	toad	continuous
ai	rain	continuous
ay	play/crayon	continuous
ur	hurt	
ir	bird	
or	corn	
z	zoo	continuous
oo	boom	continuous
qu	quit (kw)	stop
oo	look	continuous

TABLE 1.1

Sound Pronunciation Guide

(continued)

(continued)

TABLE 1.1

Sound Pronunciation Guide

Sound	Key Word	Sound Type*
a_e	late	continuous
ee/e_e	tree; Pete	continuous
ea	seat	continuous
ue/u_e	blue/rude	continuous
ou	out	
ow	yellow	continuous
i_e	kite	continuous
oe/o_e	toe/bone	continuous
igh	night	continuous
au/aw	haul, saw	continuous
al/all	palm; fall	
ew	chew	continuous
oi/oy	boil, boy	
tch	watch	stop
le	able	continuous
ea	head	continuous
dge	judge	stop
ge/gi	gentle/giant	stop
ce/ci	century/circle	continuous
_y (1-syllable)	try	continuous
_y (2-syllable)	baby	continuous
a-	above/about	continuous
nk	sank	
wr	write	continuous
kn	knot	continuous
augh	caught	continuous
ough	fought	continuous
ph	phone	continuous
mb	lamb	continuous
ture	picture	continuous
tion	action	
sion	mission	
tial	partial	
cial	special	
cious	precious	
tious	cautious	
ion	billion	

* Continuous sounds can be held for two seconds without distorting them. Stop sounds cannot be held without distorting them. They are pronounced very quickly. Some combination sounds do not fit clearly into the continuous/stop categories. These are left blank in the table.

Source: Adapted with permission from a Sound Pronunciation Guide developed by Jan Hasbrouck, Ph.D.

TABLE 1.2

Level of Difficulty for Word Work Activities

Skill/Element	Activity	Characteristics
Phonological Awareness	Syllable Identification	• Clap 2-syllable words. • Distinguish 1- and 2-syllable words. • Clap 3- and 4-syllable words. • Distinguish 1-, 2-, and 3-syllable words. *Discontinue the activity when students can consistently do the hardest tasks.*
Phonological Awareness	Stretching Words	• 2 phonemes, initial continuous sound. • 2 phonemes, initial stop sound. • 3 phonemes, initial continuous sound. • 3 phonemes, initial stop sound. • 4 phonemes, initial continuous sound. • 4 phonemes, initial stop sound. • 5 phonemes. *Discontinue the activity when students can consistently do the hardest tasks.*
Phonological Awareness	Mystery Word Game	• 2 phonemes, initial continuous sound. • 2 phonemes, initial stop sound. • 3 phonemes, initial continuous sound. • 3 phonemes, initial stop sound. • 4 phonemes, initial continuous sound. • 4 phonemes, initial stop sound. • 5 phonemes. *Discontinue the activity when students can consistently do the hardest tasks.*
Phonological Awareness	Elkonin Sound Boxes Without Print	• 2 phonemes, initial continuous sound. • 2 phonemes, initial stop sound. • 3 phonemes, initial continuous sound. • 3 phonemes, initial stop sound. • 4 phonemes, initial continuous sound. • 4 phonemes, initial stop sound. • 5 phonemes. *Discontinue the activity when students can consistently do the hardest tasks.*
Letter-Sounds and Letter Combinations	Teaching Letter-Sounds, Teaching Letter Combinations	See the Sound Pronunciation Guide (Table 1.1).
Letter-Sounds and Letter Combinations	Alphabet Books and Charts, Pick Up the Letter Game	Use these activities to practice letter-sounds and letter combinations you have already taught.
Letter-Sounds and Letter Combinations	Vowel Sound Game	Use this activity to practice identifying vowel sounds represented by letters and letter combinations you have already taught. Begin with vowels in VC and CVC words.

Note: V = vowel; C = consonant.

(continued)

(continued)

TABLE 1.2

Level of Difficulty for Word Work Activities

Skill/Element	Activity	Characteristics
Letter-Sounds and Letter Combinations	Teaching Letter Formation	See the Sound Pronunciation Guide (Table 1.1).
Sounding Out and Spelling	Teaching Sounding Out, Teaching the Silent *e* Rule, Listen and Spell, Word Pattern Charts	• VC and CVC words. • CVCC and CCVC words. • Silent *e* (CVC-E) words. • Follow the Sound Pronunciation Guide (Table 1.1) to add vowel and consonant combinations. • Multisyllabic words (2, 3, more).
Sounding Out and Spelling	Elkonin Sound Boxes With Print	• VC and CVC words (start with initial continuous sounds). • CVCC and CCVC words. • Silent *e* (CVC-E) words. • Follow the Sound Pronunciation Guide (Table 1.1) to add vowel and consonant combinations.
Sounding Out and Spelling	Point Game, Silly Word Game, Word Sorts, Word Linking	Use these activities to practice word types with letter-sounds and letter combinations you have already taught.
High-Frequency Words	Teaching Students' Names	Use this activity only in the earliest lessons when needed.
High-Frequency Words	Teaching High-Frequency Words, Writing High-Frequency Words	See the High-Frequency Word List (Table 1.10).
High-Frequency Words	"Beat the Teacher" Game, Word Building	Use these activities to practice high-frequency words you have already taught.
Multisyllabic Words	Reading Multisyllabic Words, Flexing Words, Writing Multisyllabic Words	• 2-syllable words with no flexing. • 2-syllable words with flexing. • 3-syllable words with no flexing. • 3-syllable words with flexing. • Words with more than 3 syllables.

Note: V = vowel; C = consonant.

3. *Provide independent practice.* Give each student a turn. Observe students closely while they practice the skill alone. Provide many opportunities for practice. Scaffold or reteach as necessary. If errors occur, model again, and support the students as they try again.
4. *Provide cumulative practice.* Integrate the new items or skills with those previously learned. Provide large amounts of cumulative practice each day.
5. *Assess and reteach as necessary.*

Table 1.3 illustrates the **WORD WORK** activities appropriate in each of the three phases of instruction.

TABLE 1.3

Responsive Reading Instruction Activities: Word Work

Phase 1	Phase 2	Phase 3
Phonological Awareness • Syllable Identification • Stretching Words • Mystery Word Game • Elkonin Sound Boxes Without Print	**Phonological Awareness** • Syllable Identification • Stretching Words • Mystery Word Game • Elkonin Sound Boxes Without Print	**Letter-Sounds and Letter Combinations** • Teaching Letter-Sounds • Teaching Letter Combinations • Vowel Sound Game
Letter-Sounds and Letter Combinations • Teaching Letter-Sounds • Alphabet Books and Charts • Pick Up the Letter Game • Teaching Letter Formation	**Letter-Sounds and Letter Combinations** • Teaching Letter-Sounds • Teaching Letter Combinations • Alphabet Books and Charts • Pick Up the Letter Game • Vowel Sound Game • Teaching Letter Formation	**Sounding Out and Spelling Words** • Teaching Sounding Out • Point Game • Silly Word Game • Listen and Spell • Word Linking • Word Pattern Charts • Word Sorts
Sounding Out and Spelling Words • Teaching Sounding Out	**Sounding Out and Spelling Words** • Teaching Sounding Out • Elkonin Sound Boxes with Print • Point Game • Silly Word Game • Teaching the Silent e Rule • Listen and Spell • Word Linking • Word Pattern Charts • Word Sorts	**High-Frequency Words** • Teaching High-Frequency Words • "Beat the Teacher" Game • Word Building • Writing High-Frequency Words
High-Frequency Words • Teaching High-Frequency Words • Teaching Students' Names • "Beat the Teacher" Game • Word Building • Writing High-Frequency Words	**High-Frequency Words** • Teaching High-Frequency Words • "Beat the Teacher" Game • Word Building • Writing High-Frequency Words	**Multisyllabic Words** • Reading Multisyllabic Words • Flexing Words • Writing Multisyllabic Words
	Multisyllabic Words • Reading Multisyllabic Words • Flexing Words • Writing Multisyllabic Words	

Word Work

Word Work

Teaching and Practicing Phonological Awareness

Syllable Identification

Objective

Students will clap for each syllable in words.

Implement Activity

When students need to learn that longer words have "chunks," or syllables, and to practice orally dividing words into syllables.

Materials

- Individual cards with pictures or photographs of objects (such as *duck*, *airplane*, *flower*, *magazine*). The names of the objects should have from one to four syllables.

Procedures

1. Model the process of identifying the chunks, or syllables, in a spoken word. (This activity does *not* involve print.) Show students a picture card, say the word, and then clap the syllables while repeating the word.
2. Next, provide guided group practice. Show students a picture card. Have them name the picture, then clap the syllables while repeating the word.
3. For independent practice, have students take turns naming and clapping the syllables in a word from a picture card.
4. The students may also clap words without the picture prompt. The teacher gives the word prompt; then the students clap it. It's also fun to clap students' names.

- Begin with one-syllable and two-syllable words first, then move on to three- and four-syllable words (see Table 1.4). Starting with a three-syllable word can confuse students.
- If a student has difficulty with a word, model the correct segmentation and then try group practice. Finally, have the student clap the word independently.
- Adjust the activity for individual students in the group. Use words with one or two syllables for students who are still learning this skill while providing words with more syllables to more proficient students.

SCAFFOLDING

Notes

❑ Remember that this is an auditory activity. Students do *not* look at the printed words. They listen to hear the parts of words.

❑ Remember that each syllable has a vowel sound in it. For example *peanut* (pea-nut) has two syllables, *toad* has one syllable, *telephone* (tel-e-phone) has three syllables.

❑ Write down word prompts in advance if you are not using picture cards.

❑ Note the examples of one-, two-, three-, and four-syllable words provided in Table 1.4.

❑ Remember to include the names of students in the group.

TABLE 1.4

Words for Syllable Identification

1 Syllable	2 Syllables	3 Syllables	4 Syllables
zoo	rabbit	dinosaur	television
dog	robot	animal	alligator
sun	mother	bicycle	calculator
pan	table	computer	motorcycle
door	pencil	banana	watermelon
shirt	apple	elephant	caterpillar
toy	sister	video	rollercoaster

Stretching Words

Objective
Students will segment words into their individual sounds.

Implement Activity
When students need practice saying the individual sounds (phonemes) in words separately.

Materials
- Slinky toy (available from Poof-Slinky®, Inc.)
- *Optional:* Cards with pictures or photographs of objects

Procedures
1. Place a picture card of an object (for example, mop) in front of the students. The pictures should represent words with continuous sounds (letter-sounds that can be held for several seconds without distorting them). Or you may simply pronounce the words for the students without using picture cards. See Table 1.5. (Also use the words in Table 1.5 for the next two activities, Mystery Word Game and Elkonin Sound Boxes Without Print.) The Stretching Words activity does not include print. The students should *not* see the printed words.
2. Model the activity. Say the word normally: *mop*. Then say the word slowly, stretching the word so that each phoneme can be heard (*mmmmoooopppp*).
3. Show students how to use the Slinky to stretch the word. To stretch the word, say it slowly (*mmmmoooopppp*) while pulling open the Slinky. Then say the word normally (*mop*) while pushing the Slinky back together.
4. For guided practice, have the students practice the stretching hand movements with you. Have them pretend to hold a Slinky while they stretch a word.
5. Give the students independent practice by passing the Slinky around to each child in the group. Do this activity with different picture cards or words. Keep all students in the group actively involved by having them pretend to stretch a Slinky and "think" the stretched-out words in their heads when it is not their turn.
6. In other lessons, teach students these additional methods to indicate each sound in a word (and use the same methods for modeling, guided practice, and independent practice):
   - *Holding up fingers.* Make a fist with the back of your hand facing the children and hold up one finger to correspond with each sound, beginning with the pointer finger.

– *"Chopping."* Stretch out one arm and use the other hand (fingers out, hand flattened) to "chop" (like a "karate chop") on the outstretched arm for each sound.

7. A more advanced version is to segment the sounds completely (rather than saying them in a smooth, connected way). Students say a word with an instant of silence between each phoneme (/m/ /o/ /p/). Then they blend the word (saying the word normally: *mop*).

Prompts
- "Say the word slowly."
- "Can you stretch the word?"
- "Can you 'hum' the word?" Demonstrate stretching the word by humming the sounds on one tone.

> - Begin with words with two sounds; move to words with three, four, or five sounds.
> - Start with words that are made up of two to three continuous sounds (sounds that can be held for several seconds without distorting them).
> - Practice one method of segmenting for several days before introducing a different method.

SCAFFOLDING

Notes
❑ It's helpful to use all three of the segmenting strategies at different times because individual children may be able to understand the process better using one strategy over another.

❑ Don't stretch words that have more than one syllable or more than five sounds.

❑ Remember that words can have more letters than sounds (phonemes). Practice segmenting the words before the lesson so that you are comfortable with the number of phonemes in each word and are sure that you can demonstrate the process correctly:
   - *Eight* has two phonemes: /ā/ and /t/.
   - *Ship* has three phonemes: /sh/ /i/ /p/.
   - *Split* has five phonemes: /s/ /p/ /l/ /i/ /t/.
   - *Crunch* has five phonemes: /c/ /r/ /u/ /n/ /ch/.
   - *Stopped* has five phonemes: /s/ /t/ /o/ /p/ /t/.
   - *Reach* has three phonemes: /r/ /ē/ /ch/.

TABLE 1.5

Words for Phonemic Awareness Activities

Two Phonemes, Initial Continuous Sound	Two Phonemes, Initial Stop Sound	Three Phonemes, Initial Continuous Sound	Three Phonemes, Initial Stop Sound	Four Phonemes, Initial Continuous Sound	Four Phonemes, Initial Stop Sound	Five Phonemes
am	be	and	back	fast	black	blend
at	boo	face	bat	find	clean	crept
ate	by	fan	big	flap	club	crisp
eat	day	feet	book	frog	crash	crunch
egg	do	like	bus	last	cried	dressed
if	go	look	cat	lamp	dance	front
is	he	man	chop	mask	desk	plant
it	hi	mom	game	nest	dream	print
me	tea	mop	gave	ranch	great	scream
moo	to	much	get	rest	held	spend
my		name	good	rust	help	split
no		net	got	sleep	hunt	stamp
see		night	home	slide	jump	stomp
up		not	hen	slip	just	street
us		old	hit	smooth	pest	trunk
zoo		rain	kick	smash	plane	twist
		red	pig	snail	plus	
		ride	play	snack	track	
		rock	take	snap	train	
		sell	team		trap	
		zip	top		treat	
			tip		trick	
			tub		truck	

Two-Phoneme Sound Boxes	Three-Phoneme Sound Boxes	Four- and Five-Phoneme Sound Boxes

a	m
e	gg
i	n
t	ea
s	ee

a	n	d
g	oo	d
m	u	ch
sh	a	k	e
n	igh	t

r	i	v	er
s	p	ea	k
f	r	o	g
s	c	r	ea	m
d	r	e	ss	ed

The "Mystery Word" Game

Objective

When given a segmented "mystery word" by the teacher, students will blend the phonemes to identify the word.

Implement Activity

When students need practice in blending phonemes to say words. This may be noticeable particularly when a student is trying to sound out words and is able to say each individual sound but is unable to blend the sounds to identify the word.

Materials

- List of words that have two, three, four, or five sounds

Procedures

1. To model the activity say, "Listen carefully. I'm going to say a word slowly." Stretch the word: *mmmmaaaannnn.* Then say, "That word is *man.*"
2. For guided and independent practice, say a word slowly (*mmmmaaaaannnnn*). First as a group, and then individually, have students say the word normally (*man*).
3. For more advanced practice, say the word with an instant of silence between the phonemes. Do this while "chopping" phonemes on the arm or holding up one finger for each phoneme (/m/ /a/ /n/), as described on pages 33 and 34. Students identify the word.

Prompt

"If I say *mmmmaaaaannn,* what is the word?"

Note

Plan and write down the words you will use in advance. This will help keep the pace of the game moving quickly.

- Begin with words with two sounds; then move to words with three, four, or five sounds.
- Start with words that are made up of two to three continuous sounds (sounds that can be held for several seconds without distorting them). See Table 1.5 on page 35.
- Use the Slinky toy, arm chopping, or fingers while stretching the word.
- Provide many opportunities to practice with fully blended sounds before going into the more advanced method of segmenting the phonemes fully.
- Emphasize certain phonemes if the students are having difficulty hearing them as they try to blend the word: /ssss/ /t/ /oooo/ /p/.

SCAFFOLDING

Elkonin Sound Boxes Without Print

Objective

Students will segment words into phonemes as they pull plastic markers into sound boxes (Elkonin, 1973).

Implement Activity

When students need practice hearing individual sounds in words.

Materials

- Sheets with two, three, four, or five Elkonin Sound Box Cards (provided in the Appendix)
- Plastic markers (squares, disks, or other manipulatives)
- *Optional:* Sound Pronunciation Guide (provided in the Appendix)
- *Optional:* Magnetic letters

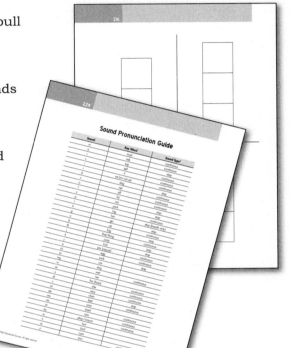

Procedures

1. To model, say, "We're going to play Sound Boxes." Place a two-phoneme (two boxes) Elkonin Sound Box Card on the table. Place a plastic marker above each box. Say, "I am going to pull down the sounds in the word *an*." Next, say the word *an* slowly, *aaaannnn*. While you say each phoneme, use one index finger to pull one marker into each sound box to match the sound. Start with the box on the left and move toward the right (just as you read). Your finger should move the marker into the box at *exactly* the same time your voice begins each phoneme. As soon as you start saying the /a/ in *aaaannnn*, move the first marker into the box. At exactly the same time you start saying the /n/ in *aaaannnn*, move the second marker into its box. Try not to break between the two sounds. After you have pulled the markers into the boxes, run your index finger under the boxes quickly and say the word *an*.

2. For guided practice, give each student a sound box sheet with two boxes on it. Place a marker above each box. Say, "Let's all pull down the sounds in *an*." As a group, have the students say the word slowly, stretching the phonemes while pulling the plastic markers into the boxes exactly as each phoneme is sounded. Students use one index or "pointer" finger to move the markers. It is important that students move each marker into the sound box at the same time they make each sound. Then the students will say the word quickly as they run

their fingers under the boxes. Try several words this way. The number of boxes on the card and number of markers must match the number of phonemes in the word.

3. Next have each student try the activity independently. Give each one a new word. Keep all the students in the group actively involved when it is not their turn by having them pull down imaginary markers while "thinking" the stretched-out word silently or by giving each of them Elkonin Sound Box Cards and markers but having them do the activity silently when it is not their turn.

4. Extension: When students can consistently perform the skill with the markers, replace the markers with magnetic letters that represent the sounds in the word (see the Elkonin Sound Boxes with Print activity, page 54). Research has shown that this kind of phonemic awareness activity is especially beneficial when letters are used.

Prompts

- "Make it match."
- "Say it smoothly."

Teaching Sound Boxes Activity

The teacher says, "I'm going to pull down the sounds in the word *sun*. I am going to pull each marker into a box as I say each sound."

The teacher says *sss* and moves the first marker. The teacher says *uuu* and moves the middle marker. The teacher says *nnn* and moves the last marker.

"Next, I am going to run my finger under the word and say the word *sun* quickly. Now that I have shown you an example, it's your turn."

The teacher places one Elkonin Sound Box Card in front of each student. Each student practices segmenting the same word before the teacher gives each student an individual word. If needed, the teacher models again so students learn the correct procedure.

- Start with words that have two or three phonemes. Start with the easier CV and CVC words that begin with continuous consonants (for example, *man* or *sun*). Later move to more complex words that have stop sounds (such as *top*) or blends (such as *slide*). It will be helpful to refer to the list of words shown in Table 1.5 (page 35).
- If a student has difficulty with a particular word, model the word and have the student try the word again.
- If the student continues to have difficulty, emphasize each sound as you model or as you gently guide the student's hand.

Many students initially need a lot of modeling and patience. If a student has trouble moving the markers to match the sound, politely ask the student if it is all right to gently guide the student's hand.

As soon as a student becomes familiar with sound boxes, begin to use words that contain stop sounds as well as continuous sounds (for example, *tan*). Always take care to blend the continuous sounds together without stopping between the sounds. Stop sounds, of course, cannot be stretched out, so the break between the stop sound and the next sound should be short. The Sound Pronunciation Guide in the Appendix can help you identify which sounds are continuous and which are stop sounds.

When a student seems to be resisting, it is usually because the activity is too difficult. Remember to try to make it easy, and always praise students for what they can do. If this activity is very difficult for a student, be sure the student can successfully perform Stretching Words (page 33) and can blend the phonemes in Mystery Word Game (page 36).

Word Work

Teaching and Practicing Letter-Sounds and Letter Combinations

Teaching Letter Sounds

Objective

Students will identify the most common sound of each letter.

Implement Activity

When the students need instruction and practice in identifying letter sounds.

Materials

- Sound Pronunciation Guide (provided in the Appendix)
- Letter-Sound Cards (set of 54 cards provided in the Appendix)
- Magnetic letters
- Burner covers
- Small whiteboards
- Dry-erase markers and erasers
- Magnetic whiteboard or cookie sheet
- Chart tablet or note cards
- Small ziplock bags

General Guidelines

- Before the lesson, look at the students' Letter-Sound Assessment Forms (see the Letter-Sound Assessment on page 126 in **ASSESSMENT**) to see which letter sounds they do not know or are confused about. These letters should be taught first.
- Introduce only two new letter sounds per week. Refer to the Sound Pronunciation Guide in the Appendix for the order in which letters should be introduced. If all students in the group have shown (on their assessments) that they already know certain letter sounds, skip these and move to the next letter on the Sound Pronunciation Guide that they do not know.
- When you introduce letters, keep in mind that letters that are similar to each other can be very confusing. Separate by at least a week (preferably more) letters that are visually similar, such as (*f, t*), (*d, b*), (*v, w*), (*p, q*), and those with similar sounds, such as (*d, p, b*), (*m, n*), (*i, e*).

- Introduce one letter-sound correspondence at a time. Keep reviewing the sounds by integrating cumulative practice into lessons.
- Teach short vowels before long vowels.
- Make words and teach sounding out as soon as students know two or three letter sounds that can be combined to form words.

Procedures

1. Model and teach the letter-sound. Hold up a Letter-Sound Card. Say, "The sound of this letter is /___/. What's the sound of this letter?"

2. Then provide guided and independent practice in which you scaffold students as they supply the letter-sound. Finally, provide cumulative practice in which the new letter-sound is combined with other letter-sounds students have already learned.

3. During the lesson, you can practice letter sounds in many different ways:
   - Practice letter sounds using the Letter-Sound Cards, a whiteboard, or magnetic letters.
   - Students trace or write a letter on whiteboards and make the sound of the letter.
   - Write a list of simple words made of letters the students already know and the letter you have most recently taught. Write the words on a chart tablet or on note cards and have students practice reading the words from the list.
   - Draw a circle on a magnetic whiteboard or cookie sheet with a dry-erase marker. Place several magnetic letters on the board for each of the sounds you are practicing. (For example, you may have four magnetic m's and four magnetic t's next to the circle.) Students move the magnetic letters into the circle while making the sounds of the letters. Do not have students select from more than three different letter sounds at one time.
   - Try to select a new book that contains examples of the new letter-sound. Observe students as they read a portion of the text aloud to find out whether they are able to apply the new sound. Provide scaffolding as needed.

Teaching a Letter Sound

"Today we are going to learn a new sound." The teacher holds up a card with the letter p written on it. The teacher points to the letter and says the sound /p/. "Whenever you see p you will say /p/. What is the sound of this letter? [/p/] Good. Julie, what is the sound? [/p/] Good. Nisa, what is the sound? [/p/] Good. Isabella, what is the sound? [/p/] Right. When you see this letter, most of the time you will say /p/. Now I am going to give you some magnetic letters."

The teacher passes out burner covers with magnetic letters on them. "When I say a sound, you repeat it, and then hold up the letter for that sound. Here are the sounds [one at a time]: /m/, /p/, /t/, /p/, /s/, /m/, /p/. Nice job of saying each sound as you hold up the letter. Now I am going to give each one of you a different sound. Let's begin. Julie, please hold up the letter for the /m/ sound. Good. Tomorrow I will add more sounds."

4. Extensions include having the students write words containing the new letter sound. This will help teach them to apply the skill in writing. Provide scaffolding as needed.

- If one of the students makes an error, provide feedback by making the correct sound, having all students do it together, and then having the original student provide the sound independently. Later, return to this student with the same sound to make sure the student has learned the sound firmly.

SCAFF

Notes

❑ It is important that teachers follow a sequence when they introduce letters and letter combinations so that students do not have "holes" in their knowledge. The Sound Pronunciation Guide is not the only sequence that can be followed in RRI. It is a guide that is useful in choosing a progression of letters and letter combinations, from the most useful to the least useful, but teachers may follow a sequence from the student's classroom reading program instead of the Sound Pronunciation Guide.

❑ The final selection of letters to teach is made in response to students' needs, as observed in assessments.

IN OUR CLASSROOM

It can be easy to overplan the number of new sounds introduced in one week. Keep in mind that this confuses struggling readers. Try to introduce only two new sounds a week.

Be sure to incorporate sounds that the students already know. Practice sounds that have been taught daily. Don't assume that if you cover the sound in one week, the students will know the same sound the next week. Keep reviewing sounds through cumulative practice.

Students sometimes pronounce a sound incorrectly because that is the way they originally learned it. For example, students sometimes pronounce the letters b, d, and c as /bu/, /du/, and /cu/, adding the sound /u/ to each letter. The sounds /b/, /d/, /c/ are stop sounds and should be pronounced with as little vowel attached as possible. RRI teachers have found that adding just a very brief /i/ sound to the consonant stop sounds

is best. We have had students who learned that the letter b says /bu/ and tried to sound out a word such as bat as /b/ /u/ /a/ /t/ instead of /b/ /a/ /t/. When students tried to combine the sounds to make a word, it came out bu-at! Correct students who are adding an extra sound to letters. By addressing this early, you can help them master the correct sounds through repetition.

Placing the magnetic letters you will use in each lesson in small ziplock bags (one for each student with the letters he or she will need for the activity) before the lesson helps with time management. If there are enough burner covers to have one for each child, the letters can be placed on the burner covers in advance and the burner covers placed in a basket with the other materials for the group (see page 208 in Putting It All Together for tips on organizing materials). Having supplies at your fingertips during the lesson keeps students engaged by keeping up the lesson pace.

Teaching Letter Combinations

Objective

Students will be able to apply the sounds of letter combinations when reading and writing.

Implement Activity

When students need to learn and practice the sounds associated with letter combinations.

Materials

- Sound Pronunciation Guide (provided in the Appendix)
- Letter-Combination Cards (set of 51 cards provided in the Appendix)
- Prepared word lists

Procedures

1. Before the lesson, identify the letter combinations the student needs to learn, such as *r*-controlled vowels (*ar*, *ir*, etc.) and vowel teams (*ai*, *ea*, etc.), using students' Assessments (see Letter-Sound Assessment on page 126 in Assessment) and your Anecdotal Records. Refer to the Sound Pronunciation Guide in the Appendix for help in selecting an order in which letter combinations may be introduced.

2. Prepare a list of words that contain the target letter combination. This should include words from the text the students will read. Underline the target letters in each word.

3. Prepare a second list of words that is a mixture of words with the new target letter combinations and two or three words with elements that have already been taught (to provide cumulative practice). Underline the target letters in each word.

4. During the lesson, model the sound of the new letter combination. Point to the letter combination on the Letter-Combination Card, and tell students how that sound is usually pronounced in words. Consult the Sound Pronunciation Guide for words that illustrate each letter combination's most common sound.

5. Ask the students to repeat the sound back to you. Ask individual students to tell you how the sound is usually pronounced. Then have the students practice with Letter-Combination Cards containing the new letter combination mixed in with letter combinations they have already learned.

6. Show students the first word list you have prepared. Point to each word and ask students to read the underlined part, then the whole word. Give feedback and scaffolding if errors are made (model the sound again).

7. Repeat the procedure for the cumulative practice list.

8. Try to select a new book that contains examples of the new letter combination. Observe students as they read a portion of the text orally to find out whether they are able to apply the target combination. Provide scaffolding as necessary.

9. Extensions include having the students write words with the new letter combination to teach them to apply the skill in writing. Provide scaffolding as necessary.

Snapshot of Teaching a New Letter Combination

The teacher has prepared a list of words with the new target sound /ar/ and a second list of /ar/ words mixed in with words with the /ay/ and /ee/ patterns, which were taught in previous weeks.

List 1: c<u>ar</u>, c<u>ar</u>t, f<u>ar</u>, f<u>ar</u>m, f<u>ar</u>mer, st<u>ar</u>, st<u>ar</u>t, p<u>ar</u>k, d<u>ar</u>k, sp<u>ar</u>k, t<u>ar</u>get.

List 2: sl<u>ee</u>p, c<u>ar</u>t, d<u>ay</u>, st<u>ar</u>t, tod<u>ay</u>, f<u>ar</u>m, str<u>ee</u>t, p<u>ar</u>k, gr<u>ee</u>n, f<u>ar</u>mer, sp<u>ar</u>k, st<u>ar</u>, aw<u>ay</u>, m<u>ee</u>t, k<u>ee</u>ping, d<u>ar</u>k, t<u>ar</u>get, tod<u>ay</u>.

The teacher shows the students the *ar* Letter-Combination Card and says, "The sound of these letters is /ar/. You've seen this pattern in the word car. What's the sound?" [/ar/] "Right. When you see these letters together you will usually say /ar/. Julie, what sound?" [/ar/] "Right. Jason, what's the sound?" [/ar/] "Right. Let's practice the new sound along with some we have learned before."

The teacher uses Letter-Combination Cards for cumulative practice. "Good job of remembering the sounds. Let's read some words with the *ar* pattern in them."

The teacher has students practice List 1, pointing out the *ar* pattern in each word and scaffolding as needed. Students read the list together first for guided practice. Then the teacher chooses a few words for each student to read for independent practice. They practice until all answers are correct and students seem confident reading all the words. Then the teacher has the students read List 2 to practice the new pattern, along with others they have learned.

Alphabet Books and Charts

Objective

Students will identify letter-sounds.

Implement Activity

When students need practice identifying letter-sound correspondences.

Materials

- Alphabet book or chart
- *Optional:* Plastic disks or buttons

Procedures

1. Provide an alphabet book or an alphabet chart (either checked out from the library or purchased). You might be able to borrow an alphabet chart from another teacher, such as a kindergarten teacher at your school.
2. Play the "Point to the Letter" game. Say, "Point to the letter that makes the sound /_/."
3. Point to letters and ask students to supply the sounds. Alphabet books and charts normally have pictures representing words that begin with each letter. Have students try to supply the sound before looking at the picture, if possible (you may cover it up). Then refer to the picture to check the sound.

> - Provide a key word that begins with the difficult letter.
> - When students have problems remembering letter-sounds, it sometimes helps to prompt them to think about what their mouths are doing when they make the sound of the letter. Have them look at your mouth while you say a sound. For example, when making the short /o/ sound, the students' mouths should be open, forming an O.

SCAFFOLDING

Notes

☐ Be sure all students take a turn supplying the letter-sounds.

☐ When using the alphabet chart, plastic disks or buttons can be placed by the students on each letter as you practice it. This helps keep track of which letter-sounds you have practiced.

The "Pick Up the Letter" Game

Objective

When given the *sound* of a letter or letter-combination, students will identify the corresponding letter or letters.

Implement Activity

When students need practice identifying the letters that represent letter-sounds they are learning. This skill is necessary for spelling words phonetically.

Materials

- Magnetic letters
- Burner covers
- Scotch™ tape

Procedures

1. Before the lesson, select two to four letters for which the students have learned the corresponding sounds. At first, include only lowercase letters, but later you may include uppercase letters as well. Select the magnetic letters and prepare a burner cover for each student.
2. Explain to the students that:
   - You will be asking them to pick up a letter that makes a sound they have learned.
   - You will make the sound of a letter, and then they will repeat the sound and pick up the letter that makes the sound.
   - When they pick up the letter, they should hold it inside their fists until you say, "Show me." Then they should open their hands.
3. To demonstrate the procedure, say, "Pick up the letter that makes this sound." Make the sound of one of the letters. Model picking up the letter associated with that sound, holding it inside your fist. Then say, "Show me," and open your fist to show the letter. Show the students that the letter you picked makes the sound you said.
4. Provide guided and independent practice. Give gentle feedback or scaffolding if students have errors. You may ask individual students to give you a peek before they show their letter to the group, to prevent embarrassment.
5. Extensions include changing the directions to "Pick up the capital letter that makes this sound" or "Write the letter that makes this sound."

6. Later, repeat this activity using letter combinations. Join letters using Scotch tape on the backs of the letters. Place two to four letter combinations on the students' burner covers (such as *ing*, *ai*, and *ow*) and say, "Pick up the letters that make this sound."

- Give hints to students who are unsure, but later return to the same sound and give them an opportunity to perform independently.
- Have students select from fewer letters. Choosing between two letters will be appropriate for some students for a while. More advanced students may choose from several letters.

Note

❑ Try not to always use the same colors for individual letters. Students might focus on the color rather than the letter's sound.

The "Vowel Sound" Game

Objective

When given letter-sounds or words that contain vowel sounds, students will identify the corresponding sound by holding up a letter card or magnetic letter.

Implement Activity

When students are confusing vowel sounds with each other.

Materials

- Magnetic letters and burner covers *or* small note cards with letters written on them (one set for each student in the group)
- Small ziplock bags
- *Optional:* Scotch® tape

Procedures

1. Before the lesson, select two to four vowel sounds that the students are confusing. At first, use only lowercase letters. Choose magnetic letters and prepare a burner cover or prepare small note cards with the letters written on them and place them in a ziplock bag. Prepare one set of letters for each student in the group.
2. Explain to the students that:
   - You will say a word that has one of the sounds they have learned. Students will repeat the word.
   - You will say, "Show me the letter that makes the vowel sound (*a, e, i, o, u*) in the word ____ ," and students will be given a minute to think about the vowel sound they hear in the word.
   - The students must hold up the magnetic letter or letter card to represent the vowel sound in the word and make the sound.
3. Demonstrate the procedure.
4. Now say a word that has a short vowel sound, like *fan.* Have students repeat the word to you.
5. Say, "Hold up the letter that makes the vowel sound in *fan.*" Students should hold up the letter *a.*
6. Give students feedback or scaffold if they have errors.
7. As an extension, have students select from letter combinations that represent vowel sounds, such as *ai, oa, ee,* and *ea,* when you say words that contain these patterns (i.e., boat). You will need to tape the magnetic letters for the letter combinations together or write them on small note cards.

- Have students "stretch" the word (as in the Stretching Words activity, page 33) to isolate the vowel sound before they try to identify the vowel. It is not necessary to provide Slinkies. Students can pretend they are holding Slinkies and make the motion of pulling them apart as they say the sounds in the words in a stretched-out way.

SCAFFOLDING

Notes

❑ Use only two vowel sounds at first, and be sure they have been previously taught and practiced by the students. When students have mastered the game with two sounds, add more vowel sounds, one at a time.

❑ Teachers have found it useful to follow the Vowel Sound Game with the Silly Word Game (see page 60) using nonsense words containing the same vowels practiced in the Vowel Sound Game.

Teaching Letter Formation

Objective
Students will write letters correctly.

Implement Activity
When students need practice writing letters.

Materials
- Dry-erase markers and erasers
- Large whiteboard
- Small whiteboards
- Chart paper or individual pieces of paper

General Guidelines
- Before the lesson, look at the Anecdotal Records and students' journals to see which letters the students need to practice.
- Find out which handwriting method is being taught in the school, and use the same method.

Procedures
1. Model the formation of the letter on the whiteboard. Then provide guided practice in which you scaffold students as they learn how to write the letter. Next, provide independent practice and observe each student writing the letter on a whiteboard. Finally, give cumulative practice in which the letters the students have been practicing are combined with other letters that they already know how to write.
2. Use phrases to prompt students to remember correct letter formation. The handwriting method used in your school may include such phrases. If so, use the same phrases that are used in the students' classrooms. If the students' teachers do not use any specific phrases to prompt students, you can make up your own. You might use "Up and around, down" for the letter *a*. Use language that will direct the students to form the letter correctly. If you make up your own phrases, it is important to be consistent and use the same phrase every time to prompt students to form a specific letter.
3. Gently guide students' hands for guided practice, if needed.
4. For independent practice, students may:
   - Write letters on small whiteboards.
   - Write letters on chart paper.
   - Write letters on individual pieces of paper.

Word Work

Teaching and Practicing
Sounding Out and Spelling Words

Teaching Sounding Out

Objective

Students will sound out unknown words correctly.

Implement Activity

When students need to *learn* the process of sounding out and blending sounds into words. The purpose of this activity is to teach students *how* to sound out words.

Materials

- Large whiteboard
- Dry-erase marker and eraser
- Magnetic letters and cookie sheet

Procedures

1. Select a list of CVC words with sounds the students have been taught. Be sure that the words you choose are *decodable* words—words in which the letters make the sounds the students know. (Don't use *was*, for example.) Choose words you think the students will be able to blend and read.
2. Explain to students that when they come to a hard word, they must look for letters or parts of the word they know and then sound out the word. Tell them that sounding out a word means to say each of the sounds in the word and then put the sounds together to make the word. Model the process.
3. Provide guided and independent practice. Have students sound out words by saying them slowly, connecting each sound to the others as much as possible rather than having silence in between the sounds (*mmmmaaaannnn* rather than /m/ /a/ /n/). It is easier for most students to blend the sounds into a word as they sound out the word slowly and smoothly, rather than chopping up the sounds.

- As students sound out a word, explain, "Say the sounds slowly first, then read the word fast."
- Remind students of sounds they forget. If they are concentrating on the process of sounding out, they may temporarily forget other things they have learned.
- Model and reteach as many times as needed.

4. Once the students can sound out words, push them to sound out faster. Model for the students how to move a finger quickly under a word.

5. Encourage students to process word parts, or chunks, rather than individual letters. These chunks may include rime patterns. Show the students that they can look at a part they know, such as letter combinations or a rime, and then sound out the word.

6. Once students know both the long and short sounds of vowels, tell them that sometimes they might try one vowel sound in a word, say the word, and find that it doesn't make sense. Tell them they should then try another vowel sound and see whether it makes sense or sounds like a real word. This is also true for sounds such as the "hard and soft" *g* (*go*, *giant*) and *c* (*cat*, *circus*).

"Trying Out" Sounds

With a whiteboard handy, the teacher demonstrates how students can try out both long and short vowel sounds in a word. "Sometimes when I try to sound out a word, the word I say doesn't make sense. Then I try the other way of saying the vowel in the word."

The teacher shows students the word *have* on a whiteboard. "Listen. I'm going to sound out this word. I notice that there is an *e* at the end of the word, so I think that I should say the *name* of the vowel in the word."

The teacher sounds it out with a long /a/. "Hmmm. That doesn't sound right. Let me try the other sound of the letter *a*, /hav/. Now, that makes more sense! The word is *have*. Sometimes words may not follow the silent *e* rule we have learned. Most of the time, when there is a silent *e* at the end of a word, the vowel in the word says its name, but some words, like *have*, just don't like to follow the rules. Now you try these words." The teacher writes the words *live* and *give* on the whiteboard.

Note

❑ Research has shown that children who use analogies or related word parts to identify words must *also* be able to sound out the phonemes within those word parts. Example: Students who can read *sock*, *clock*, *block*, and so on must also be able to sound out the *ock* pattern, phoneme by phoneme.

| Sounding Out and Spelling Words | Phase 2 |

Elkonin Sound Boxes with Print

Objective

Students will segment words into their sounds while moving the corresponding letters into Elkonin Sound Boxes.

Implement Activity

When students need practice segmenting sounds in order to spell words.

Materials

- Magnetic letters and small ziplock bags
- Markers that can be erased with water (to draw on burner covers, cookie sheets)
- Burner covers with sound boxes drawn with erasable marker
- Cookie sheet with sound boxes drawn with erasable marker
- *Optional*: Elkonin Sound Box Cards (provided in the Appendix)
- *Optional*: Scotch tape
- *Optional*: Paper and pencils
- *Optional*: Large whiteboard and dry-erase marker

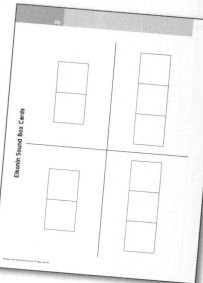

Procedures

1. When students can consistently perform the skill of segmenting words using Elkonin Sound Boxes (described in the Elkonin Sound Boxes Without Print activity, page 37), use magnetic letters in place of plastic markers to represent sounds in words.

2. Before the lesson, make a list of words that contain letter-sounds that the students know and that can be sounded out using sound boxes. Start with simple CVC words (see Table 1.6). Select the magnetic letters needed to spell these words and put a set of letters for each child in a ziplock bag. Prepare burner covers by drawing three sound boxes on them using a marker that can be erased with water. (An alternative is to draw the sound boxes on paper and tape the paper to the top of the burner covers if your magnetic letters will stick "through" the paper.) Place the magnetic letters for the first word the students will make on the burner covers, with one letter above each corresponding sound box. (On the day you introduce this activity, do only one or two words.)

TABLE 1.6
CVC Word List

CVC Words with Short a										
cat	sad	bad	mad	tag	bag	rag	fax	tax	yam	ham
ram	jam	zap	rap	cap	hat	rat	fat	mat	bat	fan
tan	van	ban	can	man	pan	pal	dad			

CVC Words with Short e										
pet	let	jet	net	bet	set	wet	den	pen	hen	fed
bed	red	led	gem							

CVC Words with Short i										
fin	kid	lid	lip	sip	hip	dip	tin	bin	win	pin
sit	kit	fit	pig	dig	jig	big	wig	dim	rim	

CVC Words with Short o										
job	hop	mop	pop	top	dot	hot	not	box	fox	sob
dog	log	hog	jog	fog	mom					

CVC Words with Short u										
cub	mud	fun	sun	run	bun	hut	nut	cut	gum	sum
dug	rug	hug	bug	bus	rub	tub	pup	cup		

3. Draw sound boxes on a cookie sheet (or tape a paper with sound boxes drawn on it to the cookie sheet). Select a word to demonstrate, and place the magnetic letters on the cookie sheet to spell the word. Put one letter above each corresponding sound box.

4. Model the process. Say, "You know how to pull down the sounds in a word by saying the word slowly and moving markers into sound boxes for each sound you hear. Today, I'm going to show you how to put in the letters for each sound." Say the word slowly, segmenting its sounds, and move one magnetic letter into each box, exactly when you say the sound associated with that letter. Finally, run your finger underneath the boxes and say the word quickly.

5. Pass out burner covers with sound boxes drawn on them and magnetic letters to spell the first word in position above the sound boxes.

6. Provide guided practice and independent practice. Say a word. Have students repeat the word. Then have them say the word

Teaching Elkonin Sound Boxes with Print

Students are at the reading table, and their burner covers are in front of them. The teacher says, "We are going to pull down the sounds in some words. You will use the magnetic letters to pull the sounds into the boxes. Watch me. As you move the letters, say the sounds: /mmm/ /eee/ [pronounced with a short /e/] /t/, then say the word quickly: *met*. Now you try it."

Students pull down the letters for the sounds in *met* on their burner covers.

"Let's have you practice some other words." Place magnetic letters students will need for the word *rat* on their burner covers. "The first word is *rat*. Say the word *rat*. Now say it slowly and pull down the letters." Students move the letters and say sounds slowly: *rrraaat*.

slowly while moving each letter into the appropriate box, one for each phoneme in the word. After "pulling down the sounds" in the word, the students run their fingers under the word and say it fast.

7. Once the students master this process, provide several magnetic letters from which they can choose letters that will correctly represent the sounds in the words. For example, students may be given the magnetic letters *a*, *c*, *r*, *m*, *o*, *n*, and *t* and a burner cover with three boxes on it. Ask the students to pull down the sounds in the word *mat*. Have them do this *without* letters at first (pretending they are pulling plastic markers into the boxes) as they say the word slowly. Then have them decide which letter is needed to represent each sound they hear in the word *mat*. Have them move the magnetic letters they select into the boxes and check to find out whether the letters they picked have the sounds they hear in *mat*. Provide scaffolding as needed. For example, you may need to pull down the sounds in a word for a student (without letters) and emphasize a sound the student is having problems with, such as the short /a/ sound. Or, you may need to gently guide the student's hand while saying the word slowly along with the student, pausing on the difficult letter.

8. When students have practiced selecting magnetic letters to spell words using sound boxes, you may follow this by having them do the activity with sound boxes drawn on paper. *To demonstrate the procedure*: Draw three sound boxes on a piece of paper (or on a large whiteboard). Say a CVC word slowly while *pretending* to pull a plastic marker into each box for each sound in the word. You will not actually use the manipulatives, but pull with one pointer finger into each box as though you were moving markers. After pulling down the sounds for the word, demonstrate listening for each sound and deciding which letter would make the sound. Write each letter in its corresponding sound box. (See the Teaching Sound Analysis activity on page 180 in SUPPORTED WRITING.) Give each student a piece of paper with sound boxes drawn on it and a pencil, and provide guided and independent practice pulling down the sounds in a word with the pointer finger and recording the letter or letters for each sound in the corresponding sound box.

Prompt

- "Say the sounds slowly and smoothly."

- If students have trouble, be sure to model again for them. You may also need to guide their hands gently once or twice.
- Model and reteach as needed.
- Say the word slowly with the students, stressing any sounds they have trouble hearing.

Note

❑ In this activity, the sounds in the words are stretched but not broken. Begin with words with two phonemes and with continuous sounds (i.e., *am*). Take care when demonstrating words with initial stop sounds (i.e., *tan*). The break between the stop sound and the next sound should be very short. Work up to words that begin with consonant blends (*cr*, *tr*, *bl*, and so on) and require four sound boxes.

❑ To implement this activity with words that contain letters combinations (i.e., *ship*), use Scotch tape to tape magnetic letters together for each letter combination so students can move them as a unit.

The "Point" Game

Objective

Students will sound out words to decode them.

Implement Activity

When students need *practice* sounding out words. The skill of sounding out words should first be taught using the Teaching Sounding Out activity on page 52. The Point Game is a way to provide practice in the skill.

Materials

- Word list
- Whiteboard
- Dry-erase marker and eraser
- *Optional:* Magnetic letters and burner cover

Procedures

1. Before the lesson, look at your Anecdotal Records for letter-sounds or letter combinations the students need to practice, or examine your lesson plans for letter-sounds or combinations that you have covered on previous days.
2. Be sure that the words you choose are *decodable* words—words in which the letters make the sounds the students have been taught. (Don't use *was*, for example.) Choose words you think the students will be able to blend and read.
3. Write a word on the whiteboard, or make a word with magnetic letters on a burner cover. Start with CVC words (*can, man, fun*), and then add blends (*grand, brown, frog*).

Modeling the Point Game

The teacher and students are at the reading table, with their attention on the whiteboard. "Today we are going to play a game in which you will be sounding out words by running your finger under them and saying them slowly, and then saying them fast. If you figure out a word, you get a point. Watch me as I show you what to do. I am going to write a word on the board."

The teacher writes *rag* on the board. "Now I am going to point to the sounds and sound it out slowly, *rrraaag*, and then read the word quickly, *rag*. You must point to the sounds in order to get the point. You can hold up a finger for each point you get for reading a word correctly. Let's begin."

4. Students take turns sounding out words you write on the whiteboard or make with magnetic letters on a burner cover. They must point to the letters and say the word slowly, then say the word correctly to get a point. Provide enough scaffolding so that students rarely miss words. The objective is not to stump the students but to provide practice in sounding out words successfully!

5. Students keep track of points they earn on their fingers, or you can keep a tally of words read correctly.

6. At first, choose words that share common patterns you have taught (*now, how, pow, power, shower, plow, flower*). If you have students read words with common rimes, be sure that they sound out the entire word and do not just read the rime as a unit (*paaaannnn, pan; raaaannnn, ran*). It can be helpful to begin with a word the students know and build other words from it (*and, sand, hand, stand, standing; out, pout, shout, shouted*).

7. At other times, have the students sound out words that are *not* in word families and vary the patterns (*band, slip, town*).

Note

❑ Use words with only two to three sounds at first, and be sure these sounds have been previously taught and practiced by the students. When students have mastered the game with two or three sounds, add more sounds one at a time.

It may seem that earning points and keeping track of them by holding up fingers is not very motivating, but first-graders have consistently liked this game. Teachers have sometimes told children they will get a sticker at the end of the lesson if they win the game (in which case teachers always make sure that the game ends in a tie so that *all* the children get stickers), but students can have fun just keeping track of the number of points they have. By the way, this game got its name from a youngster named Joseph who asked every single day before his lesson whether they could play "that pointing game"!

Students catch on quickly to this game. It is easy for a child to forget to point to the sounds and sometimes they just say the word the "fast way" without saying it slowly first. Make sure you clearly define the rule that they must point under the word, sound it out slowly, and then say the word quickly.

Sometimes students can get caught up in the points, but the goal is for them to use a sounding-out strategy to figure out words. Remind them they are playing against the teacher and should not worry about how many points other students have.

Many teachers try to make every game come out as a tie among students. They give each student words to sound out that are at their own levels. Some students can sound out more complex words, such as *slim* or *swim*, while others may be given a word like *him*. These teachers also provide enough support and scaffolding for students to be successful with each word.

IN OUR CLASSROOMS

The "Silly Word" Game

Objective

Students will correctly sound out nonsense words to prepare them for sounding out words they have never seen before.

Implement Activity

When the students need to *practice* decoding unfamiliar words. When students need to gain confidence in their abilities to sound out words they have never seen.

Materials

- Whiteboard
- Dry-erase marker and eraser
- *Optional:* Note cards with "silly words" written on them

Procedures

Before the lesson, consult Table 1.7 to identify silly words that contain word patterns and letter-sounds you have already taught, starting with VC words with two sounds, then moving to CVC words with three sounds, and so on.

1. Write a list of nonsense words that are made up of these patterns and letters. For example, for the CVC pattern with the short /a/ sound, you may include such "silly words" as *cam*, *bap*, and *dat*.
2. Explain to students that you are going to ask them to read silly words that are not real words.
3. Model for the students how they should run a finger under each silly word as they sound out the word. Say the sounds slowly and smoothly. Then say the word fast. (You can also use the Point Game strategies during this activity; see page 58.)
4. Provided guided and independent practice.

Prompt

- Tell students to "say the sounds slowly and smoothly." Students should not say the sounds in a choppy way, but in the same manner as stretching a word (*caaaammm*).

TABLE 1.7
Silly Words

VC Words, Two Sounds	CVC Words, Three Sounds
ap	sim
et	fid
ib	gaz
im	hap
op	lis
ip	rep
ep	ses
ud	tib
	wef

CCVC Words, Four Sounds	CVCC Words, Four Sounds
brop	bimp
drun	telt
frap	dest
frig	gomp
frum	hest
glet	hond
glop	junt
plen	posk
slet	rast
smif	sant
swek	tesk
swom	welf
swip	yelt
trab	zomp
trif	
trin	
trud	
twip	
twam	

CCCVC Words, Five Sounds	CCCVCC Words, Six Sounds
scrit	scramp
scrop	scromp
splam	spresk
splug	sprest
spres	strant
sprim	strimp
sprog	stromp
straf	
stret	
strup	

- Use letter-sounds that the students know, not sounds that students are confused about or that have not been taught.
- Start with VC and CVC words, and then add blends to words (*fr, br, tr, sn, sp, dr, cl, pl, gr, sk, sm*).
- If students forget the sounds of some letters, remind them. As they concentrate on the new activity of sounding out nonsense words, they may forget some of the sounds they have learned.

Notes

❑ This activity helps the students practice decoding skills so that when they come to an unknown word, they will use a sounding-out strategy to read the word.

❑ Be sure that you clearly explain that these are not real words so that students do not become confused.

Sounding Out and Spelling Words | **Phase 2**

Teaching the Silent *e* Rule

Objective

Students will apply the silent *e* rule to read words with the consonant-vowel-consonant-E pattern (CVC-E; silent *e* words).

Implement Activity

When students need to learn to read words with the CVC-E pattern (silent *e* words).

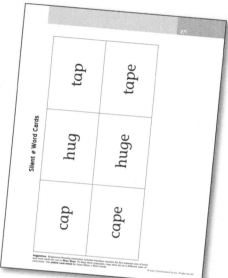

Materials

- Magnetic letters
- Burner cover or cookie sheet
- Silent *e* Word Cards with CVC and CVC-E words (set of 30 cards included in the Appendix)
- Small whiteboards
- Dry-erase markers and erasers
- Note cards

Procedures

1. Teach the rule that when a short word ends with an *e*, the *e* is usually silent and the vowel in the word usually says its name.
2. Demonstrate by making the word *kit* with magnetic letters on a burner cover or cookie sheet. Ask the students to read the word with you. Then add an *e* at the end of the word to form *kite*. Point to the *i* and ask the students for the name of the letter. Repeat the rule and model sounding out the word with the long i sound.
3. Provide guided practice with other words made on the burner cover, consistently starting with a CVC word and then adding an *e* to change it into a CVC-E word. Ask individual students to read words. You can find words for this activity on the Silent *e* Word Cards included in the Appendix and in Table 1.8. Ask individual students to read words.
4. After a few days of practice, when students are confident going from a CVC word to a CVC-E word, provide some mixed practice using the word cards. Mix up words with and without the silent *e* pattern.
5. Have students write CVC words and CVC-E words that you dictate. Begin with the words that are on the Silent *e* Word Cards.
6. Observe students as they read and write CVC-E words, and prompt and scaffold them to apply the rule.

TABLE 1.8

Examples of Silent e Words

Silent e Words That Can Be Formed From "Real" CVC Words				
cap—cape	bit—bite	can—cane	cut—cute	con—cone
cop—cope	mad—made	dim—dime	dot—dote	fad—fade
cub—cube	man—mane	fat—fate	hop—hope	fin—fine
hat—hate	mat—mate	gap—gape	nod—node	pan—pane
nap—nape	mop—mope	hug—huge	pal—pale	rip—ripe
pop—pope	not—note	kit—kite	pin—pine	sit—site
tap—tape	rat—rate	win—wine	rod—rode	tub—tube

Silent e Words						
/a/		/i/		/o/	/u/	
bake	late	bike	pipe	bone	cute	
base	made	bite	nice	code	fuse	
cage	make	dice	rice	cone	huge	
cake	male	dime	ride	cope	mule	
came	name	dine	ripe	cove	mute	
cane	pace	dive	rise	dome	rude	
cape	page	file	side	hole		
case	pale	fine	site	home		
cave	race	fire	size	hope		
daze	rage	five	tide	joke		
face	rake	hide	tile	nose		
fade	rate	hike	time	note		
fake	sage	hive	vine	poke		
fame	sale	kite	wide	pole		
fate	same	life	wife	rode		
gage	sane	like	wine	role		
game	save	lime	wise	rope		
gate	take	line		rose		
gave	tale	mice		tone		
gaze	tame	mile		vote		
jade	vase	mime		woke		
lace	wage	mine		yoke		
lake	wave	pine		zone		
lane						

Prompts

- "Is there an *e* at the end?"
- "What's the name of that letter?" Point to the vowel as you give the prompt.

- Reteach the rule and model as necessary.
- Break the task into small steps. ("Is there an *e*?" [*yes*] "Find the vowel. Say its name. Is there an *e*?" [*no*] "Read the word.")
- Write silent *e* words on note cards. Underline the silent *e* and highlight the vowel in each word.

Note

- ❑ When students demonstrate solid understanding of this rule, show them that it also applies to some syllables within longer words (*awake, milkshake, lively, sunshine, makeup*).

Listen and Spell

Objective

Students will attend to the sounds within words as they attempt to write them.

Implement Activity

When the students need to practice the strategy of segmenting a word into its sounds and recording the sounds. This activity should follow the activity Elkonin Sound Boxes with Print on page 54. Introduce the Listen and Spell activity before expecting the students to implement it during the **SUPPORTED WRITING** component of RRI.

> **LISTEN AND SPELL STRATEGY**
> 1. Stretch the word.
> 2. Write the sounds as you say the word slowly.
> 3. Check it.

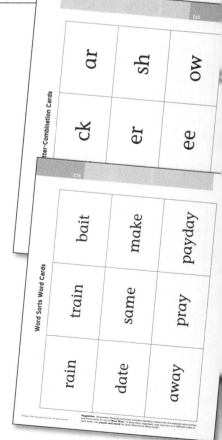

Materials
- Whiteboard or chart tablet
- Dry-erase marker and eraser
- Letter-Combination Cards (set of 51 cards provided in the Appendix)
- *Optional*: Small whiteboards, dry-markers, and erasers for students
- *Optional*: Sticky notes
- *Optional*: Note cards with words written on them or words selected from the Word Sorts Word Cards (set of 190 cards provided in the Appendix)

Procedures
1. Tell the students that they will learn a strategy, or plan, called Listen and Spell, to help them spell words.
2. Using a whiteboard or chart tablet, model saying a word slowly, stretching it sound by sound, and then write the sounds in the order you hear them. Begin with simple words that contain letter-sounds and letter combinations the students know.

3. Provide guided practice, leading students through the process with a simple word.

Teaching the Listen and Spell Strategy

To model how to apply the listen and spell strategy, the teacher says, "I'm going to show you a strategy to use when you are trying to write a word you don't know how to spell. It's called Listen and Spell. Watch me first. My first word is *map*. I'm going stretch the word first, sound by sound. Watch my mouth: *mmmaaap*. Then I am going to write the sounds in the order I hear them on my whiteboard, saying the sounds as I write them." The teacher demonstrates. "Now let's do a word together. I'll say the word first, *Sam*. Stretch the word with me: *Sssaaammm*. Now we are going to write the sounds we hear on our whiteboards. Good job of saying your sounds as you write!" Continue with more CVC words.

---

4. Provide many opportunities for independent practice in both **WORD WORK** and **SUPPORTED WRITING**.
5. Show students that they must recognize that sometimes parts of words do not follow the rules and that these parts must be memorized (for example, ha*s*, c*ome*).
6. As students become adept at this process, teach them through demonstration that *sometimes one letter or letter combination can spell more than one sound* (such as *oo* as in *look* and in *tool*). Many children need to be explicitly taught this concept. They also need to know that when they are sounding out words, they may need to try more than one sound if the first one they try doesn't work in the word.
7. Later, as students learn different patterns that spell the same sounds (like *ow* and *ou*), teach them that *sometimes the same sound can be spelled in more than one way* and that they must memorize which way these sounds are spelled in different words. Again, it is very important to teach this fact explicitly and to provide practice in remembering how to spell the same sound in different words. See Teaching Sounds That Can Be Spelled in Different Ways (page 68) for the procedure to use in teaching this concept and a strategy for recalling details about how words are spelled. For this procedure, you may substitute selected Letter-Combination Cards for sticky notes and selected Word Sorts Word Cards for words written on note cards.
8. Provide additional guided practice. Repeat the procedure often as students are introduced to new word patterns.

Teaching Sounds That Can Be Spelled in Different Ways

Before the lesson, the teacher prepares three sticky notes with the letter combinations *ay*, *ai*, and *a_e* written on them (after these patterns have been learned by the students) and a set of word cards with words that contain these three patterns. During the lesson, the teacher holds up each sticky note and asks students to supply the sounds.

The teacher says, "What do you notice about the sounds for these three letter combinations? Yes—all of them make the long a sound. Often, there is more than one way to spell the same sound. That can make spelling kind of tricky. You have to memorize the way the sound is spelled in different words. We're going to work on that today. Watch me. I'm going to pick up a word card and look at it very carefully for a few seconds, noticing how the long a sound is spelled in the word. Then I'm going to read the word, spell it out loud, and read it again. Finally, I'm going to place the word card underneath the sticky note with the letter combination that is in the word."

The teacher picks up a word card with the word *play* written on it. The teacher looks at it intently for a few seconds and runs an index finger under the *ay* pattern. Then the teacher says the word *play*, spells it, and says it again: *play, p-l-a-y, play*. Finally, the teacher places the card on the table under the sticky note that says *ay*. The teacher says, "Now it's your turn. Julie, will you take a card from the stack?"

Prompts

- "Say it slowly and listen to the sounds."
- "Stretch the word."
- For words that have sounds that can be spelled in more than one way: "Think about what would make the word look right."
- "Think about what your mouth is doing."

- Say the word slowly with the student, and emphasize sounds that the student finds difficult to isolate.
- Supply letters or letter combinations if needed.

Note

❏ Be *sure* the students say the sounds as they write each letter of the words.

Word Linking

Objective

Students will write or form new words using known words and word patterns.

Implement Activity

When students need practice reading and spelling new words by recognizing patterns in words.

Materials

- Magnetic letters and burner covers
- Phonograms list (provided in the Appendix)
- *Optional*: Large magnetic whiteboard or cookie sheet
- *Optional*: Chart tablet and standard markers

Procedures

1. Use this activity to provide practice in recognizing and spelling words with letter combinations you have taught and with words or word parts that the students know. Prepare magnetic letters and burner covers for a beginning word and the letters needed to form other words from this beginning word. See the Phonograms list in the Appendix, which contains words that share common patterns.

2. Explain to students that they will be changing letters in words to form new words. They will listen to the sounds in the words and decide which letters need to be changed, added, or taken away to form new words. Demonstrate by forming words on a burner cover, large magnetic whiteboard, or cookie sheet.

Word Linking

The teacher is seated at the table with three students. The teacher says, "Today we are going to be making words that have the pattern *and* in them. Let's look at the word *and*. Now I am going to change *and* to the word *sand* by adding a letter to the beginning of the word. Jimmy, what do you hear at the beginning of *sand*? What letter should I put at the beginning of *and* to make it say *sand*?"

The teacher places the *s* before *and*. "Let's read the word and see if we were right: *sssssaaaannnnd, sand*. Were we right? Now you will be adding different beginning sounds to make new words. I am going to pass out burner covers and magnetic letters. Hands in your lap until I ask you to make the word. OK, let's make the first word: *and*. Run your finger under it and say it slowly to check it: *aaaannnnd*. Good, now make the next word, *sand*. Good. Now change sand to *band*. Make sure you say the word slowly and check it."

Students continue making more words: *land, hand, band, brand, gland*.

3. On another day, demonstrate starting with a word such as *bar*. Have the students say the word and change or add letters to make words such as *tar, star, start, park, chart, target*. Another option is to add endings such as *-ing* or *-ly* to words in order to make new words.

4. Make sure students run their pointer fingers under the letters to read and check each new word after they make it.

5. Give feedback when students make errors by helping them sound out the word (or nonword) they make and discover the error, as illustrated in Error Correction Procedure below.

> ### Error Correction Procedure
>
> "Jimmy, the word I want you to make is *brand*. Run your finger under the word you made and check it carefully. Here, I'll help you sound out the word you made: *baaaannnnd*. What word did you make?" [*band*] "Now stretch the word *brand*. What sound do you hear after the /b/? Can you fix your word? Now, run your finger under the word and check it again. Were you right this time?"

6. Extensions include writing a word on a chart tablet and underlining a letter combination or phonogram in the word. Say another word with the same pattern or phonogram. Students take turns writing the words on the chart. Throughout the year, when students find words that have the same pattern in books they are reading, they can add the words to the chart. (See the activity Word Pattern Charts, page 71.)

Prompts

- "Say the sounds slowly and check your letters."
- "What do you hear at the beginning [or end] of the word ____?"
- "What do you hear after the sound /__/?" Use when students leave out a sound or substitute an incorrect letter.

Note

- ❑ It is not important to teach a lesson on each phonogram. The point is to show students how words they already know are similar to other words and how students can use common spelling patterns to read and spell new words. Sometimes phonograms are referred to as "word chunks." Students should be able to sound out the individual phonemes in each "chunk" as well as recognize them as a unit.

Word Pattern Charts

Objective

Students create wall charts of word families, classifying words according to phonetic patterns.

Implement Activity

To provide practice in identifying phonetic patterns in words.

Materials

- Chart paper
- Colored markers
- Phonograms list (provided in the Appendix)
- Mounting tape

Procedures

1. Before the lesson, look at your lesson plans to see what letter combinations and word patterns have been taught. Refer to the Phonograms list in the Appendix for sample patterns and words.

2. Tape a piece of chart paper on the wall. Give each student a different color of marker.

3. Explain to students that they will make a list of words that have the same letter-sound patterns, such as words with the /sh/ sound. Write the first word on the list, and underline the target pattern in the word.

4. Students take turns thinking of words to add to the word pattern chart. If a student suggests a word that is spelled with a different pattern, show the difference in the patterns and provide scaffolding as the student thinks of another word.

5. Leave the word pattern chart on the wall so you can add more words with the same pattern that you encounter in texts or that the students think of at another time. By the end of the school year, you should have charts with several different spelling patterns on the walls of your teaching space.

6. Have students practice reading the charts periodically. This is an excellent way to provide cumulative practice with the letter-sounds and letter combinations the students have learned.

- Students may need hints to think of words that fit the pattern.
- Supply words for the chart if students have problems thinking of them on their own. Don't let the pace of the lesson drag.
- Look for examples of words containing the patterns in books that the group reads and the sentences they write in the following weeks. Point these out to the students if they don't notice them.

SCAFFOLDING

Some teachers who travel from one teaching space to another or share a space with other teachers make word charts using a computer and printing out on 8½" × 11" card stock. These are more portable than pieces of chart tablet paper.

IN OUR CLASSROOMS

Word Sorts

Objective

Students will classify words according to spelling patterns.

Implement Activity

When students need practice recognizing word patterns. This is the first step in the three-step RRI word-reading strategy, "Look for a part you know," and is also important for the development of spelling. This activity should provide practice for word study skills that have already been taught.

Materials

- Word Sorts Word Cards (set of 190 cards provided in the Appendix)
- Chart paper
- Phonograms list (provided in the Appendix)
- *Optional*: Note cards or sticky notes

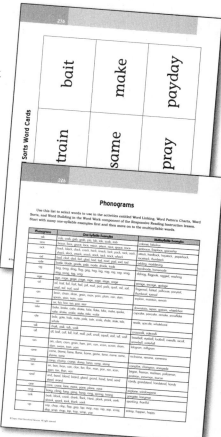

Procedures

1. Prepare a set of cards or sticky notes with words that contain word study patterns that have features in common, or select from the Word Sorts Word Cards provided in the Appendix (see Table 1.9)

2. Explain to students that they will be sorting words according to word patterns. When you introduce the activity, model the procedure and practice as a group, with students placing the word cards or sticky notes in categories. Students should read the words and notice word patterns that are alike and different. Provide independent practice. (Bear, Invernizzi, Templeton, & Johnston, 1996.)

3. Examples of types of word sorts:
   - Sort words with different spelling patterns that spell the same sound (such as words with *er*, *ir*, and *ur* or words with *ay*, *ai*, and *a_e*).
   - Sort words from different word families (*car*, *star*, *start*, *rain*, *train*, *drain*).
   - Sort words ending with *-ed* according to whether the *-ed* is pronounced as /d/ (as in *played*), as /ed/ (as in *painted*), or as /t/ (as in *jumped*).
   - Sort words in which the same letter combination is pronounced differently (*cook* versus *boot*).

- You may need to write words on sticky notes or note cards and underline the sound pattern in the words at first to direct students' attention to these patterns, but later students should be able to look for parts they know without this scaffolding.

TABLE 1.9

**Word Sorts
Word List**

ai, ay, a_e	-ed (Three pronunciations: ed, d, t)	oo	ur, er, ir	oa, o_e
rain	jumped	cook	fur	boat
train	hopped	brook	hurt	toad
bait	painted	shook	curb	foam
date	wanted	stood	purple	groan
same	played	wood	purse	oak
make	stayed	book	hurry	toast
plate	looked	wool	her	joke
say	marched	zoo	runner	bone
today	hinted	tool	river	smoke
away	trusted	boom	dinner	slope
pray	frowned	broom	perky	zone
payday	smiled	groom	shiver	hope
sway		stool	bird	float
nail		moo	stir	spoke
blade		boot	shirt	goat
			first	
			sir	
			girl	
			turn	
			water	
			birth	

ow, ou	y (long /i/ — 1 syllable) (long /e/ — 2 syllables)	silent e	ar, or	oy, oi
cow	by	cap—cape	far	toy
now	try	hug—huge	army	joy
town	fly	tap—tape	art	boy
mouse	dry	rat—rate	start	enjoy
out	sky	pan—pane	march	annoy
found	fry	hat—hate	swarm	soy
down	shy	win—wine	jar	soil
crown	lady	man—mane	mark	oink
clown	baby	fin—fine	park	moist
shout	shady	bit—bite	or	oil
loud	puppy	at—ate	torn	spoil
cloud	funny	mat—mate	born	point
around	silly	hid—hide	corn	join
found	candy	rid—ride	sort	coin
power	jelly	kit—kite	port	cowboy
			cord	
			before	
			thorn	

(continued)

(continued)

TABLE 1.9

**Word Sorts
Word List**

ee, ea	ew, aw	i_e, -igh
tree	chew	fire
seed	threw	tire
meet	grew	bite
teeth	new	write
green	blew	hide
between	stew	twice
eat	flew	pride
treat	saw	mice
team	awful	rice
cream	raw	might
seat	awning	fight
steam	crawl	tight
deep	straw	light
creep	paw	mighty
free	shawl	lightning
dream		right
cheat		midnight
easy		delight

Word Work

Teaching and Practicing High-Frequency Words

Teaching High-Frequency Words

Objective
Students will read high-frequency words quickly and accurately.

Implement Activity
When students need practice identifying high-frequency words.

Materials
- High-Frequency Word Cards (set of 120 cards provided in the Appendix)

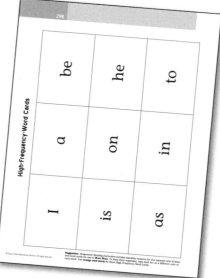

Procedures
1. Before the lesson, look at the completed High-Frequency-Word Assessment Form (see High-Frequency-Word Assessment on page 129 in **ASSESSMENT**) to see which words the students do not know or are confused about. Teach and practice one list of words at a time until the students can read most of the words fluently. For easy reference, see the lists of high-frequency words in Table 1.10.
2. During the lesson, model the new word. Point to the word on the High-Frequency-Word Card and tell students the word. Some of these words are *nondecodable*, meaning that they contain letters or combinations that don't have their most common sounds (like the words *was* and *what*) or don't follow the rules of phonics (such as the silent *e* rule) that the children have learned (like the word *some*). For these words, help the students identify any parts that *do* follow the rules of phonics that they have learned and the parts that do *not* follow the rules.
3. Ask the students to read the new word together. Ask individual students to read the word. Then have the students practice with a short stack of High-Frequency-Word Cards containing the new word mixed in with some of the words they have already learned. On the following days, increase the number of High-Frequency-Word Cards in the stack and continue to practice until all students in the group can identify them instantly (see the activity "Beat the Teacher" Game, page 80).
4. Follow up with the activity Writing High-Frequency Words, page 83.

TABLE 1.10

High-Frequency Words

List 1	List 2	List 3	List 4
I	we	should	been
a	use	so	get
be	word	two	than
is	there	up	day
on	she	them	part
he	one	look	down
as	all	about	find
in	your	will	no
to	how	more	made
you	by	out	after
for	were	write	first
are	not	time	long
have	but	go	people
of	which	other	come
at	their	see	its
they	if	many	my
from	do	has	now
and	what	make	could
the	had	him	away
with	when	then	did
that	each	her	may
his	an	would	who
was	said	into	call
this	or	these	way
it	can	some	number
am	big	blue	eat
dog	have	jump	little
like	play	going	under
me	here	our	went
run	ran	saw	must

Teaching
High-Frequency Words

The teacher shows students the High-Frequency-Word Card with the word *what* and says, "This word is *what*. Read the word." [*what*] "Good. Let's take a close look at the word. If I tried to sound out this word it would be /wh/ /a/ /t/ [pronounce with a short *a* sound]. One of these sounds didn't sound quite right in the word."

The teacher reads the word again with the short *a* sound, emphasizing this sound a little. "Right. The *a* in *what* doesn't have the sound /a/. You will have to remember that this word is *what* even though it looks like it wouldn't be pronounced that way. Please, Mary, what is this word? . . . Julio, what is this word? . . . Good. Let's read the word along with some other words we know."

Teaching Students' Names

Objective

Students will learn to recognize and write their names.

Implement Activity

When students need practice reading and writing their names.

Materials

- Magnetic letters and burner covers
- Small whiteboards
- Dry-erase markers and erasers

Procedures

1. Make each child's name with magnetic letters on burner covers. Be sure that the first letter is uppercase and all others are lowercase.

2. Mix up the letters. Have the students assemble their names quickly with magnetic letters. Practice several times, encouraging speed.

3. Directly teach students how to form the letters in their names. Insist that they begin with an uppercase letter and write the other letters in lowercase and that they form the letters correctly. (See the activity Teaching Letter Formation, page 50.)

4. Give students a whiteboard and dry-erase marker to practice writing their names. Only a few minutes should be spent on writing names each day until students have mastered the skill.

Prompt

If letters are not in correct order or are formed incorrectly say, "Does that look right?"

- First, guide the students' hands to assist them with problematic letters. Then have the students try again independently.
- You may need to write some letters in "dotted" form and have students trace over them until they are able to remember how to form them. They may need to practice repeatedly tracing over a letter.
- Model the correct spelling and letter formation as needed.

Students take pride in learning to recognize and write their names. It can be helpful to have students quickly write their names on their practice papers during **SUPPORTED WRITING** until they can write them fluently and without hesitation. Work on the students' first names, and if students can write their first names, give them an opportunity to practice their last names. If students are forming letters incorrectly, provide feedback with correct letter formation. Have them trace or practice the incorrect letters several times on another part of the page or whiteboard before trying to put the letters back into their names.

The "Beat the Teacher" Game

Objective

Students will read high-frequency words automatically and accurately.

Implement Activity

When students need practice identifying high-frequency words automatically. The purpose of this activity is to provide practice in previously taught words (see Teaching High-Frequency Words, page 77).

Materials

- High-Frequency-Word Cards (set of 120 cards provided in the Appendix)

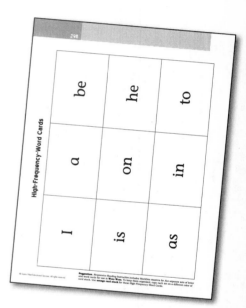

Procedures

1. Before the lesson, select a list of high-frequency words that you have already taught (Table 1.10, page 78).

2. To practice the words, show students each word card and allow three seconds for a student to give the correct response. Students must "beat the teacher" by saying the word within three seconds or the teacher keeps the card. Students who say the word correctly get to keep the card in front of them on the table.

3. As students become increasingly accurate in identifying the words in three seconds, decrease the number of seconds from three to two, then to one second. Finally, require them to pronounce the word instantly when they see the card. This is the goal for all students.

4. Reteach and provide more practice on any of the words the students missed (the ones in the teacher's pile).

Notes

❑ Maintain two stacks of High-Frequency-Word Cards throughout the year:

– *Maintenance Words*: This stack of High-Frequency-Word Cards should include words that all students in the group can recognize in one second or less. These should be practiced from time to time to be sure students remember them and can read them automatically. Don't forget to return to these Maintenance Words on a regular basis to keep them firm. If students forget or hesitate on any of these words, move the words to the New Words stack.

– *New Words*: The second stack of High-Frequency-Word Cards should include words that have been learned more recently and words that have been difficult for students to remember (including any words that students have recently missed during the High-Frequency-Word Assessment on page 129 in **ASSESSMENT**). These words need to be practiced more frequently, beginning with a three-second limit and decreasing the time to two seconds and then one second. As students learn to recognize these words automatically, put them into the Maintenance Words stack.

❑ You may make additional sets of High-Frequency-Word Cards to send home with students so that they can practice with their parents. Include some words that the students know (Maintenance Words) and some that they are still learning (New Words). Send the game home with directions after a student has played it several times with you.

Word Building

Objective
Students will spell high-frequency words correctly.

Implement Activity
When students need practice identifying and spelling high-frequency words.

Materials
- Burner covers
- Magnetic letters
- Small ziplock bags

Procedures
1. Before the lesson, select one or two words that students need to practice. These should be mainly high-frequency words that you have taught but that students are confused by when they read or write. Sometimes you may include words with spelling patterns that they are having trouble remembering (see Table 1.10, page 78). Prepare a burner cover for each child with magnetic letters for the first word. Letters to form a second word can be placed in ziplock bags for each student.

2. Explain to students that you will be asking them to make a word as quickly as possible with magnetic letters, and once they make the word and say the word, then they will mix up the letters in the word and pass the burner cover to the next student.

3. Demonstrate word building before students try it.

4. Have all students in the group make the same word on their burner covers at the same time, read the word, and then mix up the letters. Then *each student* will pass his or her burner cover to the student on the right. This sequence continues with all of the burner covers continually passed around the circle for one to two minutes.

5. Monitor and give feedback as students build the words. Remind them to look very closely at each word in order to form a mental picture of all the letters in the word.

6. Repeat with another high-frequency word if desired.

Word Building

"Today we are going to build some words that we have already learned. When you put the letters in order to make each word, look at it very carefully to be sure that it looks right. I'm going to pass out burner covers with the first word."

Teacher passes a burner cover to each student in the group. "Simon, can you read the word?" [*what*] "Yes, the word is *what*. Everyone, take a very close look at the word *what*. Look at every letter in the word. OK. Mix up the letters. Now make it say *what* again. Look at your word and check it carefully. Good job of making *what*. Now mix it up again and pass your burner cover to the person on your right. Now make it say *what* again."

High-Frequency Words	Phases 1, 2, ,3

Writing High-Frequency Words

Objective
Students will write high-frequency words accurately and quickly.

Implement Activity
When students need practice recognizing and writing high-frequency words.

Materials
- Small whiteboards
- Dry-erase markers and erasers
- Digital kitchen timer

Procedures
1. Before the lesson, refer to the High-Frequency Word Assessment Forms (completed during the High-Frequency Word Assessment on page 129 in **ASSESSMENT**) and your Anecdotal Records and lesson plans. Select one to two words that the students need to practice.
2. Show the children how to write the first word. Students copy the word on their whiteboards.
3. Set the timer for 60 seconds, and ask the students to write the word, saying the word as they write it. Tell them to cover the word with their erasers after they have written it.
4. Have the students continue to write the word until the timer goes off, covering up the word with their eraser each time they write it, so that they are not copying what they previously wrote. At the end of one minute, they can quickly count how many times they wrote the word correctly.

- Practice only one or two words during this activity.

Notes
- ❑ Students do not sound out these words unless they are *regular* words in which each letter makes a sound that the students know. Students say the words as they write them.
- ❑ During the **SUPPORTED WRITING** part of RRI, you may have the students write the same words quickly three or four times on their practice papers.

Word Work

Reading and Writing Multisyllabic Words

Reading Multisyllabic Words

Objective

Students will read multisyllabic words by sounding out each part of the word and then blending the parts to form the word.

Implement Activity

When the students need to learn to decode multisyllabic words.

Materials

- A book that students will be reading soon
- Chart tablet or whiteboard
- Dry-erase marker and eraser
- Multisyllable Strategy Poster (provided in the Appendix)

> **STRATEGY FOR READING MULTISYLLABIC WORDS**
> 1. Look for parts you know.
> 2. Find the vowels. Every chunk (word part) must have one vowel sound.
> 3. Read each chunk.
> 4. Put the chunks together.
> 5. Flex as needed.

Procedures

1. Before the lesson, preview the new book that will be read during the lesson and list multisyllabic words that may be difficult for the students, or select words from the list in Table 1.11.
2. Write these words on a chart tablet or whiteboard, and underline each syllable within each word.
3. During the lesson, model the strategy, locating the vowels, pointing to each syllable and reading it separately and then blending the syllables to read the whole word. Refer to the Multisyllabic Strategy Poster (see Appendix).
4. Guide the students as they practice the procedure. Then ask individual students to read a few of the words.

Reading Multisyllabic Words

The teacher says, "When you come to a big word that you don't know how to read, you can break the word into parts to sound them out. Let's look at the words I've written down on a list. Watch me first while I show you what to do. Look at the first word. [*pancake*] "I'm going to sound out the first chunk, *paaaannn, pan*. Now I'm going to sound out the next chunk. I notice that there is a silent *e* at the end of this part, so I'm going to make the *a* say its name: *cake*. Now I'll put the parts together, *pancake*."

5. If an error occurs, point to the syllable in which the error occurred and scaffold or tell students how to pronounce that syllable. Ask them to read the individual syllables again and then to blend the syllables into a word.

6. Teach students that sometimes parts of a word—especially the vowels—don't follow the "rules." Teach them to try the vowels in different ways until the word sounds like one they know. Teach them to pay attention to whether or not the word makes sense. This is called "flexing" the word. (See the Flexing Words activity, page 88.)

7. Observe students as they read text orally. Prompt and scaffold them as needed as they attempt to read the multisyllabic words.

- Begin with simple words with no more than two syllables. It can be helpful to begin with compound words so that the students will be aware of distinct parts of the words.

SCAFFOLDING

Note

❑ Model the procedure carefully and observe students closely to monitor their progress as they try to apply the skill while reading text. They may need a lot of support to learn to use the strategy as they are reading connected text.

TABLE 1.11

Multisyllabic Words

Compound Words		Two Syllables	Three Syllables
afternoon	homework	about	adventure
airplane	into	ago	amazing
anybody	leftover	balloon	astronaut
anywhere	lipstick	before	banana
backyard	lookout	biggest	computer
barefoot	maybe	candle	difficult
baseball	moonlight	candy	dinosaur
basketball	newspaper	cartoon	enjoying
bedroom	nightgown	contest	entertain
birthday	nobody	dinner	electric
breakfast	notebook	enjoy	eraser
bulldog	outfit	fastest	following
campfire	pancake	finger	fantastic
candlestick	paperback	insect	forever
classroom	peanut	letter	forgetful
clubhouse	playground	lovely	furniture
cookbook	playtime	midnight	horrible
cowboy	ponytail	misspell	incomplete
crosswalk	popcorn	monster	marshmallow
cupcake	postman	mother	positive
daydream	railroad	nickel	subtraction
daytime	rainbow	number	talkative
doorway	sailboat	paper	underline
downstairs	sandbox	party	understand
earring	scarecrow	pumpkin	unhappy
everyone	sidewalk	rabbit	vacation
eyeball	skateboard	robot	video
fingernail	snowball	sister	volcano
fireplace	snowman	sitting	wondering
flashlight	sometimes	sleepy	
football	somewhere	slowly	
girlfriend	sunflower	spider	
goldfish	sunshine	sticker	
grandfather	tiptoe	subtract	
grandmother	toenail	table	
haircut	toothbrush	teacher	
highway	toothpick	uncle	
hilltop	washcloth	unkind	
homemade	waterfall	water	
inside	weekend	worker	

Flexing Words

Objective

Students will flex syllables within multisyllabic words in order to read them correctly.

Implement Activity

When students need practice reading multisyllabic words that contain syllables in which the letters do not make their expected sounds. Students should have been introduced to multisyllabic words and have read multisyllabic words before attempting this activity.

Materials

- Large whiteboard or chart paper
- Dry-erase marker and eraser
- *Optional*: Multisyllable Strategy Poster (provided in the Appendix)

Procedures

1. Select four to five multisyllabic words that contain the schwa sound (see Table 1.12). Write them on a large whiteboard or on chart paper.
2. Explain to the students that in words with *more than one syllable*, letters sometimes don't make the sounds we expect them to make. This is especially true of vowels. Often vowels will make a sort of lazy sound like /u/ instead of their usual sounds (the sound of the schwa). Sometimes, when we sound out a long word with more than one syllable in it, we have to "play with" the vowels or try different vowel sounds until we make the word sound right. This is called "flexing" the word.
3. Model the procedure, provide guided practice, and then provide independent practice.
4. Observe students as they read text orally, and prompt and scaffold them as needed while they attempt to read the multisyllabic words.

Prompts

- "Flex the word."
- "Try another sound for this letter."
- "Play with this part and see if you can make it sound right."
- "Make it sound like a real word."

a	ə	<u>a</u>bout, <u>a</u>bove, <u>a</u>fraid, <u>a</u>go, <u>a</u>live, <u>a</u>like, <u>a</u>lone, <u>a</u>round, <u>a</u>way, b<u>a</u>nan<u>a</u>, breakf<u>a</u>st, chin<u>a</u>, comm<u>a</u>, equ<u>a</u>l, hospit<u>a</u>l, ide<u>a</u>, magaz<u>a</u>ne, ped<u>a</u>l, princip<u>a</u>l, sever<u>a</u>l, thous<u>a</u>nd, tot<u>a</u>l, ov<u>a</u>l, usu<u>a</u>l
e	ə	abs<u>e</u>nt, ang<u>e</u>l, child<u>e</u>n, cal<u>e</u>ndar, canc<u>e</u>l, diff<u>e</u>rent, di<u>e</u>t, ev<u>e</u>n, fu<u>e</u>l, giv<u>e</u>n, happ<u>e</u>n, it<u>e</u>m, lev<u>e</u>l, nick<u>e</u>l, oft<u>e</u>n, probl<u>e</u>m, qui<u>e</u>t, tow<u>e</u>l, tunn<u>e</u>l, trav<u>e</u>l
i	ə	foss<u>i</u>l, penc<u>i</u>l, pup<u>i</u>l
o	ə	butt<u>o</u>n, cany<u>o</u>n, carr<u>o</u>t, diam<u>o</u>nd, hon<u>o</u>r, may<u>o</u>r, <u>o</u>bserve, parr<u>o</u>t, peri<u>o</u>d, ri<u>o</u>t

TABLE 1.12

Schwa Words

Flexing Words

"Let's look at some words that we might need to flex. Here's the first word." [*away*] "This is a word we already know, but let's just pretend we don't know the word. If we sound out the first part, we would say /ā/. Then if we read the second part it would be *way*. When we put those parts together, we get *a-way* [pronounce the first syllable with a long a sound] "That doesn't sound quite right. I'm going to play with the first part of the word a little and try the /u/ (schwa) sound, *away*. Now that sounds right. The dog ran away.

"Let's look at another word" [*pupil*] "Help me sound out the first part: *puuu*" [long u sound] "Now sound out the second part, *piiiillll*. Put the parts together, *pu-pil*." [pronounce the second syllable with a short i sound] "That doesn't sound quite right. Can you try playing with the vowel to make it sound like a real word? Terrance, you are exactly right. The word is *pupil*. A pupil is another word for a student. You are a pupil in this school.

"Let's try another one together . . ."

Notes

❑ The schwa (ə) occurs in an unaccented syllable. It sounds similar to a short *u*, although sometimes it sounds more like a short *i*.

❑ As you select words for the activity, try to choose words that your students will recognize. The flexing strategy is difficult to apply unless the word that is finally produced is in the student's speaking vocabulary. A student who doesn't recognize the word when it sounds right will not know when to stop trying different sounds. Take care not to frustrate students. Simply tell them words when necessary, and explain what the words mean. Try to use these words in your speaking vocabulary so that the students will learn to recognize them.

• Give the student a sound to try in place of the one that doesn't sound right. Say, "Try the /_/ sound here."

SCAFFOLDING

Writing Multisyllabic Words

Objective
Students will segment the syllables of a multisyllabic word in order to write the word.

Implement Activity
When students need practice spelling multisyllabic words.

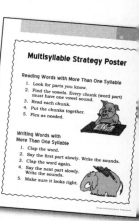

> **STRATEGY FOR WRITING MULTISYLLABIC WORDS**
> 1. Clap the word.
> 2. Say the first part slowly. Write the sounds.
> 3. Clap the word again.
> 4. Say the next part slowly. Write the sounds.
> 5. Make sure it looks right.

Materials
- Small whiteboards or chart paper
- Dry-erase markers and erasers
- Multisyllable Strategy Poster (provided in the Appendix)

Procedures
1. Select three to five multisyllable words (see Table 1.11, page 25). Explain to the students that they will practice writing multisyllabic words. First, they will clap the syllables in the word. Then they will say the first syllable slowly and write the sounds they hear (listen and spell strategy). Then they will clap the word again. Next they will write the sounds they hear. They must also check the parts to see whether they look right.
2. Refer to the Multisyllable Strategy Poster as you model the process.
3. Provide guided and independent practice.

Writing
Multisyllabic Words

"Today we are going to write multisyllabic words. Listen to the first word, *dinner*. Say the word. Good. Let's clap the word *dinner*. Good. There are two chunks in the word *dinner*. I am going to write the first chunk saying the sounds slowly as I write *diiinnnn*, *din*. Then I will sound out the next chunk, *ner*, and write it. Now I will read the word *dinner* and check it to be sure it looks right. It is your turn to write a multisyllabic word. The next word is *paper*. Say the word *paper*. Good. Now clap the word *paper*. Say the first chunk slowly, *paaa*, and say the sounds as you write. Say the next chunk, *per*, and say the sounds as you write. Good. Now read the word quickly and check it."

- Break the task into small steps using the strategy. Model each step of the strategy as needed.

Print Concepts and Fluency

The **PRINT CONCEPTS AND FLUENCY** component of Responsive
Reading Instruction (RRI) focuses on methods to increase
oral reading fluency. In Phase 1 of this part of the lesson,
the purpose is to teach basic concepts about print (see
Table 2.1). Young children who have not yet learned to
read may not know that print progresses from left to
right or know the meanings of the terms *word*, *letter*, and
sentence. In the earliest stages of RRI, the teacher should
assess student knowledge and implement activities to
teach the print concepts students do not know.

TABLE 2.1

Responsive Reading Instruction Activities: Print Concepts and Fluency

	Phase 1	Phase 2	Phase 3
Print Concepts and Fluency	• Teaching Left-Right Directionality • Teaching Print-Related Vocabulary • Teaching 1:1 Correspondence	• Repeated Reading With a Model • Partner Reading • Reading Phrases	• Repeated Reading With a Model • Partner Reading • Reading Phrases

Student understanding of print knowledge can be assessed informally by reading a book to the student and asking the student to point to a word, letter, or sentence or to the place on the page where the student should start reading and which direction he or she should go. This can be done as a group, having students take turns pointing to items in a big book (i.e., enlarged text) as you record their responses on your Anecdotal Record Form.

Once students understand basic print concepts, the purpose of **PRINT CONCEPTS AND FLUENCY** shifts to the development of oral reading fluency, as students progress to Phases 2 and 3 of instruction. Fluent reading is accurate, quick, and smooth. Phrases are grouped together, punctuation is observed, and reading has appropriate expression. When reading is highly fluent, it sounds effortless.

What Does Research Say?

Students who understand basic print concepts are ready to learn simple words and letter-sounds and to begin reading connected text (Snow et al., 1998). At first, reading is normally slow as students focus on trying to recognize or decode each word as a single unit. A primary goal of RRI is to support students as they develop fluent and accurate oral reading skills.

Why Is Fluency Important?

Quite simply, when students focus on one word at a time, they have very little attention left to actually tune in to the meaning of the text. Growth in fluency not only increases the ease with which the student reads, but it also has a direct influence on comprehension (National Reading Panel, 2000). The labored reading of students who are not fluent interferes with comprehension. When reading occurs in such a manner, readers must struggle to reconstruct meaning *after* decoding because they cannot pay attention to decoding and comprehension at the same time. A fluent reader moves through text without stops or pauses and recognizes words automatically, freeing up attention for comprehension. Students become fluent when they can recognize many words "on sight," just as adults do, and can decode unknown words quickly and efficiently. The fewer recognizable or known words readers have to draw upon, the more they will have to pay attention to decoding.

Teachers can obtain valuable information about their students' progress in fluent reading by regularly assessing oral reading fluency using brief passages at the same level of difficulty. One useful and valid tool for monitoring student growth in fluency is the *Dynamic Indicators of Basic Early Literacy Skills* (DIBELS) (Good & Kaminski, 2003).

How Can Teachers Help Students Develop Oral Reading Fluency?

Chard, Vaughn, and Tyler (2002) surveyed research about instruction that supports fluency and concluded that the most effective strategies were (1) providing students with a model of fluent reading, (2) having students practice by reading text repeatedly, and (3) providing feedback to students. These three techniques are the core of RRI fluency instruction. Teachers *model* by reading brief portions of text to the students. Students *practice* repeatedly by reading familiar books with the teacher and by participating in partner reading. And teachers *provide positive feedback* (specific praise), prompts, and *scaffolding* to encourage students to read smoothly, accurately, and quickly.

Planning the Print Concepts and Fluency Part of the RRI Lesson

During Phase 1 of RRI you will teach print concepts during this part of the lesson (See Table 2.1). *The print concepts activities can be done with the entire group of students* rather than just the Star Reader, since students may not yet know the Partner Reading routine or be ready to read without teacher support. Plan to implement only one of the print concepts activities in a lesson, and select the activity based on the needs you observe in your students. You can conduct informal assessments of print concepts by asking students to perform tasks such as pointing to the first word on a page, pointing to the first or second letter in a word, demonstrating understanding of other print-related vocabulary, or pointing to text while you read it (to demonstrate left-right directionality and 1:1 correspondence). You may also record observations in your Anecdotal Records that indicate that students may need instruction in particular print concepts.

RRI lessons in Phases 2 and 3 will include fluency instruction (See Table 2.1). *In nearly every Phase 2 and 3 lesson you will implement Repeated Reading with a Model with the Star Reader while the other students engage in Partner Reading.* You may add Reading Phrases for the Star Reader when that student has a habit of reading word-by-word and you want to teach the student to group words into phrases. Note that there are several strategies described during Repeated Reading with a Model. It may be helpful at first to note the specific strategies you plan to implement in your lesson plans. Part of planning for fluency instruction is selecting the one or two familiar books the Star Reader will read. Remember that this should be text on the Star Reader's independent or instructional level that he or she has read in previous lessons, but it should not be memorized. When you organize your materials for the fluency work, be sure that you have a group of two to four familiar books for students to read in Partner Reading.

Print Concepts and Fluency

Phase 1

Teaching Left-Right Directionality

Objective

Students will read and write with left-to-right directionality, with return sweep.

Implement Activity

When students are in the earliest stage of reading development and there is a possibility they do not understand that English print is written and read from left to right on the page.

Materials

- Big book or photocopy of enlarged text
- Standard books

Procedures

1. Model reading from a big book or enlarged text. Explain that you always go in the same direction and that you are pointing to each word as you read.
2. Provide guided practice. Have students take turns pointing to the big book (with your help) as the group reads chorally with the teacher.
3. Transfer this activity to standard books, but be prepared to model and support the students' practice.

SCAFFOLDING

- When you first transfer the activity from enlarged text or big books to standard text, it is helpful to use text that is made up of one-syllable words, with rather large print and plenty of space between the words. Be prepared to model again if students become confused.

Teaching Print-Related Vocabulary

Objective

Students will understand and use vocabulary related to print concepts.

Implement Activity

When students are in the earliest stage of reading development, particularly when they may not have a clear understanding of the words and concepts taught in the activity. Assess the students by asking them to point to items in a book (such as the first word on the page, a particular letter, etc.).

Materials

- Magnetic letters
- Magnetic whiteboard or metal tray (cookie sheet)
- Burner covers (one per child)
- Sentence strips
- Scissors
- Big books
- Standard books

Procedures

1. With magnetic letters, make a CVC word like *sun* on a whiteboard or metal tray. Another option is to make student names (such as *Bob*).
2. Pull the letters far apart and tell the students that these are *letters*. Make the sound of each letter in isolation as you point to it. Push the letters together and tell the students the letters are now a *word*.
3. Students practice the same process with magnetic letters on burner covers. Have them pull the letters apart, and then ask them to make the letters into a word.
4. Later, apply the concept to text and point out the spaces between the words. Extensions to this activity include the following:
   - Make a word with magnetic letters and model by pointing to the first and last letters of the word. Provide opportunities for guided and independent practice.
   - Introduce the concept of a sentence by writing a sentence on a sentence strip and cutting the words apart or by making a short sentence with magnetic letters. Model and provide practice in identifying words and putting words together to make a sentence.
   - Point out the capital letter at the beginning of the sentence and the punctuation at the end. Then model how to locate a sentence in a big book and in a standard book.

5. Ask students to point to a word, letter, or sentence in a book they have read.

6. Use terms such as *word*, *letter*, and *sentence* often as students read. Check for understanding periodically, and review and reteach if necessary.

7. Model and teach the following concepts and provide guided practice both with magnetic letters and in the text:
   - Beginning and ending of a sentence
   - First and last word in a sentence
   - Capital letter, period, question mark
   - First and last letter in a word
   - Beginning and ending of a book
   - First and last page in a book
   - Beginning of the page (or top of the page)
   - Locating specific page numbers in the book

RRI teachers have learned not to take it for granted that students already know the meanings of terms such as *word*, *letter*, and *sentence* unless we have checked for understanding by asking students to demonstrate the concepts with print (for example, pointing to the first word of a sentence). We have found that a surprising number of RRI students at the beginning of first grade do not know what a word or a sentence is.

The procedures described here must be implemented and practiced over several days. Students will become overloaded if you try to teach too much too quickly. Check for understanding frequently, and provide ample review and practice.

Teaching One-to-One Correspondence

Objective

Students will read while pointing to the text with a one-to-one correspondence between the printed and spoken word.

Implement Activity

When students are in the earliest stage of reading development and they may not understand that there is a match between the written and spoken word when reading.

Materials

- Magnetic letters
- Magnetic metal tray
- Simple sentence composed by teacher (written in lesson plan)
- Big book or enlarged copy of a text
- Large whiteboard, dry-erase marker, and eraser
- Sentences from a leveled book enlarged on a photocopier

Procedures

1. Before the lesson, think of a simple sentence. Be sure that your sentence is composed only of one-syllable words at first. Example: "The cat ran up the big tree." This is only an auditory exercise at first. Students will be listening to you. Do not display the written sentence in front of them.
2. Show the students how to clap (or pat the table or their knees) one time for each word in a brief sentence. Have students practice clapping words in several sentences.
3. You may need to repeat modeling and guided practice for several days.
4. When students seem to be able to separate words that they hear in a sentence, review the concept of *word* and how to find a word in text. Choose one of the following:
   - Use a big book or an enlarged copy of text to help students find words.
   - Write a sentence on a large whiteboard. It may be helpful to underline the spaces between words with a colored marker or point out the spaces to the students.
   - Photocopy two pages of text to show students the spaces between the words. If you are using an enlarged copy, underline the spaces with a colored marker.

Prompts

- "Read with your finger."
- "Make it match."

- If some students have trouble clapping the sentence, guide their hands when they clap.
- Guide students' fingers to make the print they are reading match the words they are saying.

SCAFFOLDING

Notes

- ❏ Don't draw vertical lines between the words (i.e., *Bob | sat | up.*) because the students will tend to notice the line instead of focusing on the spaces.
- ❏ **Sentences with one-syllable words only**:
  - The cat ran up the big tree.
  - A man was in the house.
  - The girl sat in a chair.
  - A boy ran down the street.
  - The kids had fun at school.
  - A dog ran to the boy.
  - He clapped his hands.
  - She got a new toy.
- ❏ **Sentences with mostly one-syllable words and including some two-syllable words**:
  - My mother went to town.
  - Jason [or substitute a two-syllable name of a student in the group, if possible] ran down the street.
  - I like to eat pizza.
  - The puppy is cute.
  - My sister is big.

Phases 2, 3

Repeated Reading With a Model

Objective

Students will read connected text fluently, accurately, and with appropriate expression.

Implement Activity

When students need practice reading smoothly with speed, accuracy, and expression.

Materials

- Familar text
- Fluency Prompt Card (provided in the Appendix)
- *Optional*: Note card
- *Optional*: Watch or kitchen timer
- *Optional*: Unfamiliar text

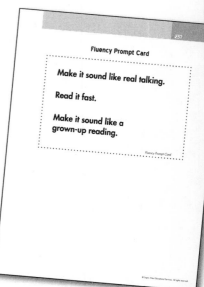

Fluency Prompt Card

Make it sound like real talking.

Read it fast.

Make it sound like a grown-up reading.

Procedures

1. The Star Reader rereads one to two familiar books aloud. These books should not have been memorized. It is very important for the student to actually read the text orally.

2. To support the development of fluent reading, implement any of the following strategies:
   - Provide a model: Sit slightly behind the student, and very softly read along with him or her, setting a pace that is slightly challenging but not so fast that the student cannot keep up. Be sure the student points to the words he or she is reading, so that the student does not simply imitate what you are saying without engaging with the text (Heckelman, 1969).
   - Read along with the student on alternate pages, or model by reading one page yourself and having the student read the next one.
   - Prompt students to read more fluently, and remember to give specific praise when students are successful. Using the Fluency Prompt Card (provided in the Appendix) can help a teacher use consistent language and keep "teacher talk" to a minimum.
   - Discuss and demonstrate the role of punctuation in phrased reading. Tell students that they should pause after each period in the text. Model how to read by pausing after periods. Demonstrate how the voice usually goes up at the end of a question. Demonstrate a brief pause at a comma, and read with emphasis or excitement at an exclamation point. Later, discuss the meaning

of quotation marks. (Remember to introduce only one of these elements at a time and to provide lots of practice before going to another one.)

- Have the students mask phrases with their fingers and read complete phrases rather than word by word. (See the Reading Phrases activity on page 106.)

Repeated Reading With a Model

The Star Reader is reading from a book, and the teacher is sitting slightly behind, reading along softly. The teacher says, "Let's read that page in the book together."

They read together. "Oh no! A big hermit crab is inside" (Randell, 1996c).

The teacher says, "You did a good job of making that sound like real talking. Now you try reading the next page by yourself."

The student reads. "Here comes a fish, a big hungry fish" (Randell, 1996c)

The teacher continues to model and read alternate pages with the student, as needed.

- Some students develop habits of focusing on only one word at a time and do not read very fluently as a result. It may help to smoothly move a small note card over the text as the student reads in order to keep him or her looking ahead (Clay, 1993). Tell the students that you are "pushing their eyes" to read faster. Be sure to go at a rate that slightly challenges the reader but is not so fast that he or she cannot keep up. Stop and go back if the student falls behind. Do not make this frustrating, but keep it somewhat challenging. It is best to do this for only a short period at a time. Then ask the student to try to continue reading in phrases for the rest of the book.
- Have the Star Reader read an unfamiliar text, or section of text, on his or her level, while you time the student using a watch or kitchen timer. Then have the student practice reading the same text one or two times while you model as needed. The student then reads the text again, as you time it. The object is to beat the original time. It is important for the students to compete only with their own previous times and not with each other (Samuels, 1994).

Prompts
- "Make it sound like real talking."
- "Read it fast."
- "Make it sound like a grown-up reading."

- Read along with the student at points of difficulty.

Partner Reading

Objective

Students will read connected text with fluency, accuracy, and expression.

Implement Activity

When students understand print concepts and are ready for fluency activities. This activity is for the two students who are not the Star Reader for the day, during the time the teacher works one on one with the Star Reader. Teach and model this routine several times so students will understand what is expected of them.

Materials

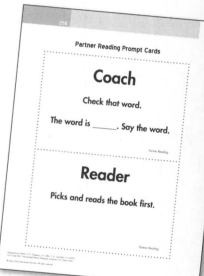

- Three or four books students are familiar with from previous lessons
- Partner Reading Prompt Cards (Coach and Reader) (provided in the Appendix)
- *Optional*: Baskets for books

Procedures

1. Before students arrive, select a set of two to three books for the students to use when partner reading. The books should be familiar from previous lessons but not memorized. They should be on the Instructional or Independent level of *each* student who will be reading them.

2. Students sit side by side so that they can share a book, holding it between them. The partner readers should sit apart from the teaching table, but the teacher should be able to see and monitor them easily.

3. One student is assigned the role of Coach and one the role of Reader. Give a Coach card to the student Coach. There should be no argument about who gets which card. That is the teacher's decision as part of the routine.

4. The Reader selects one of the books to read. As the Reader reads through the book, the Coach follows along. If the Reader gets stuck on a word or reads a word incorrectly, the Coach prompts the reader to try again or supplies the correct word. Model a kind and polite way to do this, and encourage the students to support one another. Promote partner reading as a team effort.

5. The students exchange roles and repeat the process. The Reader may choose any book from the set. Students may reread the same book during this period.

6. Variations: The students may take turns reading every other page or paragraph in the book.

Prompts

- If the Reader reads a word incorrectly, the Coach may say, "Check that word" before supplying the word.
- The Coach may say, "That word is ____. Say the word." Have the Reader repeat the word before reading on.

Partner Reading

The Coach and Reader are sitting side by side with the same book. The Reader reads the book while the Coach follows along. The Reader reads, "Here is lizard. He is sleeping [asleep] in the sand" (Randell, 1996g). The Reader has read the word *asleep* incorrectly. The Coach nicely stops the Reader at the end of the sentence. The Coach says, "Check that word" and points to the word *asleep*. The Reader tries to sound out the word. If the Reader is unsuccessful, the Coach says, "That word is *asleep*. Say the word." Then the Reader continues to read the rest of the book while the Coach follows along. Finally, the Reader and Coach switch roles.

Note

❏ While two of the students in the group are partner reading, you will work with one student (the Star Reader) on fluency. When finished, that student will switch places with one of the partners. You will then work with one of the original partners on assessment, and the two new partners will partner read. If you are working with a group of four students, one student will read independently during this time.

It is *very important* to take time the first week to practice the partner reading routines so that no bad habits are formed. See a snapshot illustrating the process of teaching this routine on pages 214–215 in PUTTING IT ALL TOGETHER. After the students become familiar with the routines, continue to monitor student behavior. If necessary, reteach the routines. Establishing routines early will help children respond well to partner reading.

Sometimes students spend a lot of time sorting and picking out books to read. This wastes too much time and can become a behavior management issue. It helps to keep a maximum of four familiar books in a basket from which the students may choose.

Some students with attention issues have great difficulty staying on task while working with a partner. Although partner reading is more beneficial and should be implemented whenever possible, there are times when students may need to read independently instead of with a partner. Be sure that these students are reading *orally*, not looking at pictures or trying to read silently, as repeated oral reading increases fluency.

The partner-reading format is adapted from Mathes, P., Torgesen, J. K., Allen, S. H., & Allor, J. H. (2001). First Grade PALS (Peer-Assisted Literary Strategies). Longmont, CO: Sopris West.

Reading Phrases

Objective

Students will read phrases smoothly and rapidly to increase reading fluency.

Implement Activity

When students are reading words accurately but tend to read in a choppy, word-by-word way.

Materials

- Note cards
- Leveled text

Procedures

1. Before the lesson, consult Table 2.2 and select three to four phrases. Write the phrases on note cards.
2. Explain to students that they will be reading the phrases quickly and smoothly. Model: Show the students how to read the phrases just like they talk (Dolch, 1955).
3. Pull the activity into text by using your fingers or a note card to mask off phrases in a book. Have students practice reading a phrase as a unit. Model and provide as much guided practice as necessary.

Prompts

- "Read it fast."
- "Make it sound like real talking."
- After you have taught the meaning of the word *phrase*: "Read the phrase."

- Have students "frame" the phrases in a book with their hands (lay fingers around the phrases) instead of pointing to each word so that they will focus on more than one word.

TABLE 2.2

Fluency Phrases

a big dog	if you can
a little dog	in the box
a new book	in the car
all about her	in my bag
all about him	in the hole
after you go	in the house
all the people	in the rain
around the block	in the sea
away they ran	inside the house
by his bed	is gone
by the car	is going
down the street	just right
far away	long ago
for my birthday	many times
for the dog	my friend
from school	off the wall
go to town	on the cake
has to go	on the table
he says	out the door
her dog	over the hill
her mom	play outside
his dad	ran around
the first time	ran away
the last time	said Dad
the little dog	said Mom
the little kitten	so much
the little boy	take it away
the next day	the first one
the old woman	the first time
then he said	the last time
then she said	the little dog
they went	up the steps
through the grass	up there
to school	was eating
too late	went away
too little	went down
took it away	went to sleep

Assessment

The purpose of the **ASSESSMENT** component of a Responsive Reading Instruction (RRI) lesson is twofold: (1) to observe individual students in order to plan instruction that addresses students' strengths and needs, and (2) to monitor students' progress over time.

What Does Research Say?

Four types of assessments are used in effective early reading programs: screening measures, diagnostic assessments, progress-monitoring assessments, and outcome measures (Kame'enui et al., 2002).

Screening Measures

Screening measures are normally administered at the beginning of a school year to identify students who have reading difficulties that may require supplemental intervention, such as RRI. These assessments are brief and focus on the reading skills that research says are vital to reading development. Researchers have found that children's letter knowledge and phonological awareness are good predictors of future reading progress (see Scarborough, 1998). Screening measures can be administered to all first-graders in a school to identify those students who would benefit from intervention. Schools that implement RRI as a first grade intervention must screen their first grade students to identify the children who are at risk for reading difficulties. Several high-quality screening assessments are available, including the Dynamic Indicators of Basic Early Literacy Skills (Good & Kaminski, 2003) and the Texas Primary Reading Inventory (see Foorman, Fletcher, & Francis, 2004).

Diagnostic Assessments

Diagnostic assessments are used mainly to identify students' strengths and weaknesses. The information derived from these assessments can guide instructional decisions. Researchers have demonstrated repeatedly that teachers who assess student performance directly and use that information to plan instruction have better educational outcomes (Ysseldyke, 2001). Quite simply, teachers who know what their students know and do not know, and what their students can and cannot do, know what to teach!

Effective teachers of struggling readers provide targeted instruction designed specifically to both build on students' strengths and to address students' areas of need. Teachers cannot possibly respond to student needs without some form of assessment, and diagnostic assessments are a key component of RRI.

Progress-Monitoring Assessments

It is especially powerful to assess student growth in specific reading skills at regular intervals over an extended period of time (Fuchs & Fuchs, 1986). This is called progress monitoring. Monitoring students' progress in important skills through repeated assessment gives teachers concrete evidence of student growth. When students do not make adequate progress, teachers can examine their own teaching and make changes or adjustments that may accelerate students' progress (Fuchs, Fuchs, & Stecker, 1989).

Teachers of beginning readers can monitor progress in skills such as reading high-frequency words and knowing the sounds of letters and combinations of letters. Teachers can monitor their students' progress in reading connected text by assessing the students' ability to read accurately and fluently. Brief (one- to two-minute) Oral Reading Fluency Assessments are sensitive and reliable for monitoring growth in fluency (Baker & Good, 1995; Deno, Mirkin, & Chiang, 1982).

RRI teachers monitor their students' progress in letter name and sound knowledge, high-frequency-word reading, the accurate reading of text of increasing difficulty, and oral reading fluency.

Outcome Measures

Outcome measures can identify the students who meet educational goals at the end of the school year (such as reading on grade level) and those who do not. It is important for teachers of struggling readers to know whether their students can meet the benchmarks established for all first graders. Benchmark Book Assessments and Oral Reading Fluency Assessments provide RRI teachers with information about the year-end reading abilities of their students.

Planning the Assessment Part of the RRI Lesson

In the assessment component of RRI, the teacher administers an individual assessment every day to *one* student in the group. This student is always the Star Reader from the *previous* lesson. Determine which assessment you will administer *before* each lesson so you can copy and organize forms and materials in advance. Table 3.1 shows you the types of assessments used in the three different phases of RRI.

Choosing the assessment to administer is an important part of planning the RRI lesson. Your choice will depend on the kind of information you need

	Phase 1	Phase 2	Phase 3
Assessment	• Anecdotal Records • Assessment of Reading Accuracy • Benchmark Book Assessment • Letter-Name Assessment • Letter-Sound Assessment • High-Frequency-Word Assessment	• Anecdotal Records • Assessment of Reading Accuracy • Benchmark Book Assessment • Letter-Name Assessment • Letter-Sound Assessment • High-Frequency-Word Assessment • Oral Reading Fluency Assessment	• Anecdotal Records • Assessment of Reading Accuracy • Benchmark Book Assessment • Letter-Sound Assessment • High-Frequency-Word Assessment • Oral Reading Fluency Assessment

TABLE 3.1

Responsive Reading Instruction Activities: Assessment

to plan instruction for each student. In the early lessons, you may assess students' knowledge of letter names. Throughout the program, you should periodically assess students' learning of letter-sounds and high-frequency words. These assessments are usually administered to each student about every three to four weeks. As students gain proficiency in reading connected text, you will monitor their growth in oral reading fluency at least once a month by administering the Oral Reading Fluency Assessment. In all other lessons, you should administer an Assessment of Reading Accuracy. Periodically, you will assess student accuracy on one of the leveled Benchmark Books listed on page 122 to determine whether students are ready to be instructed at a more advanced text level.

Assessment

Anecdotal Records

Objective

Students will successfully apply skills and strategies in reading and writing.

Administer This Assessment

In every lesson.

Materials

- Anecdotal Record Form (provided in the Appendix)
- Clipboard

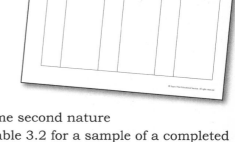

Procedures

1. Keep the Anecdotal Record Form on a clipboard in front of you.
2. As you observe the students, write down quick notes on the form to capture what the students are doing well and to note their needs for more instruction and practice. Anecdotal Records are very important in RRI. Making a conscious effort to take notes daily will help note-taking become second nature to you as an RRI teacher. See Table 3.2 for a sample of a completed Anecdotal Record Form.
3. Try to make your note-taking as unobtrusive as possible. Students should not worry about the information you are writing down. Explain that you are taking notes to help you remember what the group did in the lesson. Students should quickly grow accustomed to the note-taking and ignore it.
4. The Anecdotal Record Form can be used for an entire week of notes. You can use more than one form per week, if needed. Remember: You are taking quick notes. The format of your notes is not important as long as you can read the notes! Sometimes circling a particular word may help you remember that a student keeps repeating a mistake and that you need to address the confusion the next day.

Anecdotal Records (3 students)		
Name: **Drew**	Name: **Casey**	Name: **Beatrice**
Date 11/5–11/9 Book Level E	Date 11/5–11/9 Book Level E	Date 11/5–11/9 Book Level E
error <u>went</u> <u>says</u> want said work on ea words eat (said) Benchmark tomorrow/ level F was able to sound out <u>shopping</u>	needs to work on phrasing (they) needs –ing corrected errors in writing! 11/5 book—*I Saw a Dino* forgot book 11/6	confuses d & b practice sh sound work on "Say it slowly" ignored errors in reading— needs self-monitoring

TABLE 3.2

Illustration of Completed Anecdotal Record Form

Using the Information

Notes from Anecdotal Records help pinpoint the specific instructional needs of each individual student. Anecdotal Records will guide your instruction in:

- Letters or sounds
- High-frequency words
- Patterns in words (phonograms and letter combinations)
- Decoding and spelling using the RRI strategies
- Self-monitoring during reading and writing

Anecdotal Records will also provide information about:

- Certain types of prompting and scaffolding the student needs
- Which activities worked well for a student
- Which activities did not work well
- Which strategies (good or bad habits) the student applied to read and spell words

The Anecdotal Record Form is also a good place to note which book or books the student takes home each day (see page 18). These forms are used daily along with many other sources of information. After a school week is over, place the Anecdotal Record Forms in a three-ring binder with other records to keep as a reference for future planning.

Assessment of Reading Accuracy

Objective

The student will read connected text accurately.

Administer This Assessment

When there is a need to know:

- The highest level of text difficulty a student can read at the Instructional level
- Whether a student is making progress in text of increasing difficulty
- Whether a particular text is at a student's Instructional level
- What elements (e.g., letter-sounds, words) are causing difficulty for the student
- Whether the student is applying skills effectively while reading connected text
- Whether the student is self-correcting errors while reading

Materials

- Assessment of Reading Accuracy Form (provided in the Appendix)
- Clipboard
- A book that was read during the supported reading part of the previous RRI lesson
- Calculator

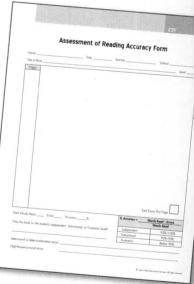

Procedures

1. (Before the lesson) You will be assessing the *previous lesson's* Star Reader. Complete the identifying information at the top of the Assessment of Reading Accuracy Form for this student (see Table 3.3).
2. Sit next to the student you will assess (side by side at the table). Use a clipboard so the student does not focus on what you are writing. As you administer the assessment, the other two children continue to partner read.
3. Have ready a book (or part of a book) the student read on the previous day during the **SUPPORTED READING** part of the lesson. Read the title of the book to the student before the student starts to read. *Do not teach or review anything else before the reading.*
4. As you listen, quickly record the student's errors (words substituted, inserted, or omitted) and self-corrections, as well as words told to the

TABLE 3.3

Completed Assessment of Reading Accuracy Form

Assessment of Reading Accuracy Form

Name _Cindy_   Date _11-6_   Teacher _M. Smith_   School _Pinedale_

Title of Book _My Home_   Level _B (Benchmark)_

Pages	
2	s- T ――――― said
3	house sc dog ――――― ――― home bird
4	house sc ―――――― home
5	✓
6	✓
7	✓
8	fl- float ――――― fly

Example of Text Read for an Assessment of Reading Accuracy

The text of the Level B Benchmark Book _My Home_ is:
- "I like my home," said the spider.   p. 2
- "I like my home," said the bird.   p. 3
- "I like my home," said the rabbit.   p. 4
- "I like my home," said the dog.   p. 5
- "I like my home," said the man.   p. 6
- "I like my home," said the spacegirl.   p. 7
- "My home can fly."   p. 8

From Cowley, J. (1996). _My home_. Bothell, WA: Wright Group. Used with permission.

Total Errors This Page | 3 |

Total Words Read _46_   Errors _3_   Accuracy _93_ %

% Accuracy = Words Read – Errors	
Words Read	
Independent	95%–100%
Instructional	90%–94%
Frustration	Below 90%

Was the book on the student's _Independent, Instructional,_ or _Frustration_ level? _____Instructional_____

Letter-sound or letter-combination errors _final y in a 1-syllable word (fly)_

High-frequency word errors _said_

student. Record the errors on the Assessment of Reading Accuracy Form using the procedures listed in the next section, Recording Errors in an Assessment of Reading Accuracy.

5. *Do not prompt or teach the student during the assessment.* The *only* allowable statement you can make as the tester is "Try it" if the student stops or appeals to you for help.

Recording Errors in an Assessment of Reading Accuracy

Remember: What the *student* says always goes on top of the line, and what the *book* says always goes below the line. Always put the student on top! See Table 3.4 for guidance.

1. On the Assessment of Reading Accuracy Form, write the page number for each page the student reads.

2. If the student reads all of the words on a page correctly (with no self-corrections), simply write one check mark next to the page number.

3. If the student substitutes an incorrect word for the one in the book, quickly write down the word the student said and draw a line under it. Then write the correct word (from the text) under the line. If the student is reading too quickly for you to record the correct word under the line during the assessment, write at least the first two letters of the word from the text, and then go back to the book after the assessment, find the word the student misread, and write the correct word under the line (under the word the student said).

4. If the student adds an extra word (insertion) that is not in the book, write down what the student said and draw a line under it. Put a dash under the line to show that the word was not in the book.

5. If the student skips a word in the text (omission), record a dash and draw a line under it. Write the word the student skipped under the line. (If the student skips a whole line, point to the correct place and ask the student to begin there. Do *not* count this as an error.) Do not tell students words unless they stop for more than five seconds or ask for help.

6. If the student stops on a word for more than five seconds or asks for help with a word, you may choose to tell the word. If you tell the student a word, write the word, draw a line over it, and put a *T* next to it. (*T* is for told.) Before you tell the student the word, you may say, "Try it."

7. If the student self-corrects an error, write the word the student said by mistake, draw a line under it, write the word from the text under the line, and write *SC* next to the student's response. (*SC* stands for self-corrected.)

Correctly Read Line of Text	✓	
Incorrect Words = 1 error per word	things	(student said)
	thinking	(book said)
Inserted Words = 1 error per word	went	
	—	
Omissions = 1 error per word	—	
	animal	
Teacher Tells Word = 1 error	— T	
	riddle	
Self-corrections (Don't count as errors.)	went SC	
	which	

TABLE 3.4

Recording Errors in an Assessment of Reading Accuracy

Scoring

1. Count the errors the student made on each page of the Assessment of Reading Accuracy Form and record the numbers in the box at the bottom of each page. Total these numbers for the entire book (or selection). Self-corrections do not count as errors.
2. Write down the total number of words the student read and the total number of errors.
3. Using a calculator, determine the percent accuracy by using the formula on the Assessment of Reading Accuracy Form. Move the decimal point two places to the left. Round results ending in 0.5 or more *up* to the nearest whole number. Round results ending in decimals smaller that 0.5 *down* to the nearest whole number.
4. Determine whether the percent accuracy is at an *Independent*, *Instructional*, or *Frustration* level using the guidelines on the form.
5. Complete the section of the form that relates to the kinds of errors the student made. Write down high-frequency words missed, letter-sounds or combinations (*ai, sh, ou,* etc.), and any other patterns that indicate that the student needs instruction and practice in particular skills, in applying the decoding strategy, or in self-monitoring.

Using the Information

If a student scores below 90 percent accuracy on a daily Assessment of Reading Accuracy, continue instruction at the same text level. If the student scores below 90 percent accuracy on several assessments at this level *and* is clearly frustrated, you may need to move the student to the next lower text level for a time. (See the book selection section under Planning the Lesson in SUPPORTED READING.)

Look at the kinds of errors the student is making:

1. What letter-sounds or letter combinations is the student missing?
2. What high-frequency words is the student missing?
3. What strategy does the student use when he or she comes to a hard word?
   - Does she try to sound out words but have trouble doing it?
   - Does he read the first part of a word and guess the rest?
   - Does she leave endings off of words?
   - Is he waiting for you to tell him difficult words?
   - Is the student self-correcting errors?

IN OUR CLASSROOM

Sometimes it is hard to keep from offering hints or prompts as a student is reading during the Assessment of Reading Accuracy. It can be frustrating when the student appears to have forgotten what was learned on the previous day. Sometimes we tend to take it personally when a student is not successful. It helps if we mentally "change hats," taking off our "teacher hat" and putting on our "tester hat" when we administer assessments, to remind ourselves that our roles are different in the two situations. *Remember that the purpose of assessment is to gain valuable information, not to prove that you taught the student a particular skill.*

The Assessment of Reading Accuracy is one of the most important tools we have to guide us as we plan instruction. It is most helpful when we look very carefully at the types of errors a student is making. Look for any patterns that occur in the student's errors. It also helps to lay three or four assessments down on a table and look at whether there is a change in the patterns of errors. This gives us information about the student's strengths and weaknesses and tells us what to emphasize in future lessons.

Phases 1, 2, 3

Benchmark Book Assessment

Objective

The student will read connected text accurately.

Administer This Assessment

When there is a need to know the appropriate text level for RRI instruction.

General Guidelines

Benchmark Books are a particular set of leveled books used to monitor student progress using text of increasing difficulty. To assess where instruction should begin, you should administer an Assessment of Reading Accuracy (page 116) using Benchmark Books (or you may substitute the Developmental Reading Assessment [Beaver, 1997]). Specifically, administer the Benchmark Book Assessment for a particular text level whenever a student consistently demonstrates the ability to read that level of text independently during RRI lessons. If the student is able to read the Benchmark Book for that level with at least 90 percent accuracy, *with no previous practice and no help from the teacher*, the student may be ready to move to the next text level. *Note:* In some cases it may be appropriate to move a student to a higher level for RRI instruction even though the student is not able to pass a Benchmark Book Assessment on his or her current level. Do not keep a student on one text level for a long period of time based only on the Benchmark Book Assessment.

Materials

- Suggested Benchmark Books (page 122)
- Assessment of Reading Accuracy Form (provided in the Appendix) or Developmental Reading Assessment (Beaver, 1997)
- Clipboard
- Pen or pencil

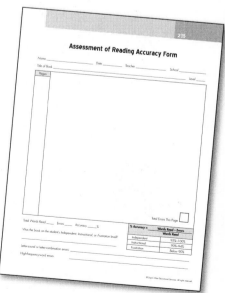

Procedures

1. Before the lesson: You will be assessing the *previous lesson's* Star Reader. Complete the identifying information at the top of the Assessment of Reading Accuracy Form for this student. Select a Benchmark Book (see page 122); the book you use to assess the student should be new to the student; it should *not* be a book previously taught.

2. Sit next to the student you will assess (side by side at the table). Use a clipboard so that the student does not focus on what you are writing.

3. Read the brief introduction that accompanies the Benchmark Book you are using (see Table 3.5).

4. Have the student read the text in the Benchmark Book as you administer an Assessment of Reading Accuracy. Make sure that the other two children continue to partner read. Take care that they do not listen to the reading, as they may be assessed with the same text later.

5. If a student is struggling and clearly will not pass the Benchmark Book Assessment at 90 percent accuracy, you may stop the reading and retest the student at a later date.

Using the Information

If the student is unable to pass the Benchmark Book Assessment at 90 percent accuracy, continue to instruct the student using text on the current level (rather than moving to more difficult text). Retest on the same Benchmark Book at a later date. See the *Note* under General Guidlines on page 121.

SUGGESTED BENCHMARK BOOKS

Here is a list of suggested Benchmark Books. Other books on the same levels may be substituted for these books as long as you use them consistently. However, there is a wide range of difficulty of books within a single level. For benchmarking, select books that are more difficult rather than less difficult. Remember: Do not use the Benchmark Books in your regular lessons. Save them for the assessment part of the RRI lesson. Please see the list of Children's Literature Cited on pages 337-338.

Level A	*My Family*	Level H	*Great Big Enormous Turnip*
Level B	*My Home*	Level I	*Baby Monkey*
Level C	*Hot Dogs*	Level J	*Mouse Soup*
Level D	*Along Comes Jake*	Level K	*Frog and Toad Are Friends*
Level E	*The Red Rose*	Level L	*Hill of Fire*
Level F	*Gingerbread Boy*	Level M	*Red and Blue Mittens*
Level G	*Friends*		

Benchmark Book Assessment

Daniel is consistently reading at Level A independently.

"Daniel, I want you to read a book called *My Family*." Have the book closed in front of him. "Now, please listen to me, Daniel. The title of this book is *My Family*. A little girl shows us pictures of her family. Read to find out about her family. I'll read the first page and you read the rest."

Point and read on page 2. Read "This" on page 3, and say, "You read the rest." Daniel reads the rest of the book while you administer an Assessment of Reading Accuracy.

From Cutting, J. (1996). *My Family*. Bothell, WA: Wright Group.

TABLE 3.5

Benchmark Book Introductions

Level	Title	Word Count	Introduction to Benchmark Books
A	My Family	**23** Pass: 2 E	A little girl shows us the pictures of her family. Read to find out about her family. I'll read the first page and then you read the rest. [Point and read on page 2. Read the word "This" on page 3, and say, "You read the rest."]
B	My Home	**46** Pass: 4 E	A lot of animals said, "I like my home." [Show the picture on page 7.] Read to find out why the space girl likes her home.
C	Hot Dogs	**84** Pass: 8 E	Tom and Dad are hungry. See what happens when they cook hot dogs.
D	Along Comes Jake	**86** Pass: 9 E	Everyone in the family helps around the house. Read to find out what happens when Jake comes along. Read *Along Comes Jake*.
E	The Red Rose	**127** Pass: 13 E	There is a red rose growing in Mr. Singh's garden. Read to find out what happens to the rose.
F	Gingerbread Boy	**137** Pass: 14 E	A woman and a man made a gingerbread boy. Read to find out what happens to the gingerbread boy.
G	Friends	**64** Pass: 6 E	There are many different kinds of friends. Read to find out about all kinds of friends and about things that friends can do. [Child reads pp. 2–16 only.]
H	Great Big Enormous Turnip	**163** Pass: 17 E	Once an old man planted a turnip. It grew and grew until it was enormous. That means it was really big. Read to find out what happened next. [Child reads pp. 2–15 only.]
I	Baby Monkey	**206** Pass: 21 E	Baby Monkey wanted to find out what he looked like. Read to find out what happened next. [Child reads pp. 2–11 only.]
J	Mouse Soup	**236** Pass: 24 E	A nest of bees landed on top of a mouse's head! Read to find out what happened. [Child reads pp. 12–19 only.]
K	Frog and Toad Are Friends	**192** Pass: 20 E	Toad is sad because he never gets any mail. Read to find out how Frog makes him feel better. [Child reads pp. 53–57 only.]
L	Hill of Fire	**290** Pass: 30 E	A farmer is unhappy because nothing ever happens in the village where he lives. Read about the farmer and his son, Pablo. [Child reads pp. 5–16 only.]
M	Red and Blue Mittens	**244** Pass: 25 E	Helen wants to go to Gail's house to play in the snow. But Helen lost one of her mittens. See what happens to the girls that day. [Child reads pp. 2–10 only.]

| Assessment | Phases 1, 2 |

Letter-Name Assessment

Objective
Students will provide the letter names of letters presented in both uppercase and lowercase formats.

Administer This Assessment
When there is a need to know which letter names students know and do not know.

Materials
- Letter-Name Assessment Form (provided in the Appendix)
- Letter-Name Assessment List (provided in the Appendix)
- Masking sheet (if needed)
- Clipboard

Procedures
1. Before the lesson: Complete the identifying information at the top of the Letter-Name Assessment Form. Place the form on a clipboard so the student does not focus on what you are writing.
2. Place the Letter-Name Assessment List in front of the student.
3. Point to the first set of letters on the list. Ask the student to identify each letter name, one at a time. Use a sheet to mask letters if the student has difficulty focusing on only one set of letters at a time.
4. On the Letter-Name Assessment Form, put a check in the Response column if the student gives the correct answer.
5. If the response is incorrect, write the incorrect response in the space provided.
6. Mark a dot in the Response column if the student does not attempt to respond.

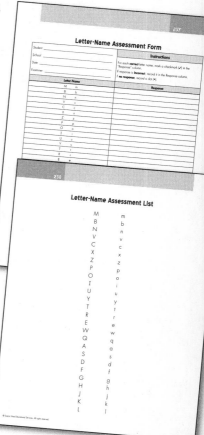

Scoring
1. Tally all correct letters for a total number of correct responses.

2. Record the errors at the bottom of the page by writing the student's response above the correct response as you would on an Assessment of Reading Accuracy Form. Then record the letters the student did not attempt.

Using the Information
- Examine the errors and the letters not attempted. The errors represent letters that are confusing the student. Focus instruction on these elements.
- Test students periodically during Phase 1 and the first part of Phase 2 on their letter-name knowledge.

Note
- ❏ It is more important for students to learn letter-sound associations than letter names. Most of your instruction should be focused on teaching students the most common sounds of each letter.
- ❏ You may show the student both the uppercase and lowercase letter at the same time, or you may choose to cover one column with a masking sheet and test knowledge of uppercase and lowercase letters separately.

Letter-Sound Assessment

Objective

Students will provide the most common sounds of letters and letter combinations.

Administer This Assessment

When there is a need to know which letter-sound associations students know and do not know in order to plan instruction.

Materials

- Letter-Sound Assessment Form— List 1 or Lists 2 and 3 (provided in the Appendix)
- Letter-Sound Assessment—List 1, 2, or 3 (provided in the Appendix)
- Masking sheet (if needed)
- Sound Pronunciation Guide (provided in the Appendix)
- Clipboard

Procedures

1. Before the lesson: Select the Letter-Sound Assessment—List 1, 2, or 3 (provided in the Appendix and reproduced in Table 3.6). Complete the identifying information at the top of the corresponding Letter-Sound Assessment Form. Place the form on a clipboard.
2. Place the list you are using in front of the student. Point to the first item on the list.
3. Ask the student to identify each letter-sound, one at a time. Use a sheet to mask letters if the student has difficulty focusing on only one letter at a time.
4. When you administer List 2, you will ask students to give you sounds for the letter combinations. Give credit if the students make either of the acceptable sounds for oo (pronounced as in the word *spoon* or in the word *look*). When the *oo* appears again later in the list, the student should supply its *other* sound.

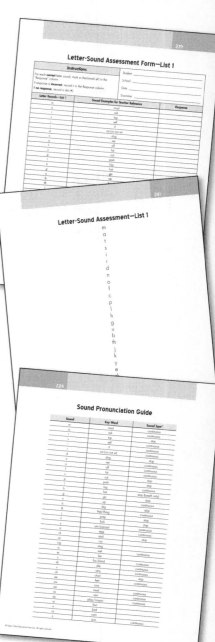

5. The Letter Sound Assessment Form for List 1 includes a list of words illustrating the most common sound of each letter or letter combination. These are for your reference and are *not* to be supplied by the students.

6. When you administer List 3, you will ask students to read *words* that contain certain letter combinations. The target sound for each word is listed in the Teacher Reference column. Students are not expected to give these sounds in isolation because their sounds often depend on their positions within words.

7. On the Letter-Sound Assessment Form, put a check in the Response column if the student gives the correct answer. *The correct answer is the most common sound of the letter.* This includes short vowel

Letter-Sounds List 1	Letter-Sounds List 2	Letter-Sounds List 3
m	ch	blew
a	ee	boil
t	ow	soy
s	oa	watch
i	ai	bottle
r	ay	head
d	ur	judge
n	ir	gentle
o	or	giant
f	z	cent
c	oo	circle
p	qu	try
l	oo	silly
h	a_e	above
g	ee	sank
u	e_e	write
b	ea	knot
th	ue	caught
j	u_e	fought
k	ou	phone
y	ow	lamb
e	i_e	picture
ck	oe	action
ar	o_e	mission
ing	igh	partial
w	au	special
er	aw	precious
x	al	cautious
sh	all	billion
v		

TABLE 3.6

Illustration of Letter-Sound Assessments Lists 1–3

sounds instead of long vowel sounds. The Sound Examples provided on Lists 1 and 2 of the Letter-Sound Assessment Form illustrate the most common sounds for each letter or letter combination. (You may also refer to the Sound Pronunciation Guide in the Appendix.) If the student provides an acceptable sound for a letter, but not the letter's most common sound (such as the long vowel sound rather than the short vowel sound or the sound /j/ for the letter *g*), ask, "Do you know another sound that letter makes?"

8. Write incorrect responses in the space provided.

9. Mark a dot in the Response column if the student does not attempt to respond.

Scoring

- Record the total number of correct responses.
- Record the errors at the bottom of the page by writing the student's response above the correct response, as in Table 3.4, page 119. Then record the letters or sounds the student did not attempt.

Using the Information

- Decide which sounds need to be taught and which need to be firmed up. Address the letter confusions in the **WORD WORK** part of the RRI lesson.
- Test students periodically throughout the school year on their letter-sound knowledge.

Notes

❑ Remember: It is more important for students to learn letter-sound associations than letter names. Focus your assessment and instruction primarily on letter-sounds.

❑ Keep in mind that a student may know the letter-sound associations when they are presented separately from words but may not be able to use them in the context of sounding out words. Provide practice and scaffolding in applying letter-sounds to sound out words.

❑ An Assessment of Reading Accuracy (page 116) can provide you with information about the student's ability to apply letter-sound correspondence to read unknown words. Your daily Anecdotal Records collected during the **SUPPORTED READING** component of RRI will also demonstrate the student's application of skills while reading unfamiliar text.

Phases 1, 2, 3

High-Frequency-Word Assessment

Objective
Students will identify high-frequency words with automaticity.

Administer This Assessment
When there is a need to know which high-frequency words are known and unknown by students in order to plan instruction and monitor their progress.

Materials
- High-Frequency-Word Assessment Form (provided in the Appendix)
- High-Frequency Words—Lists 1, 2, 3, or 4 (provided in the Appendix)
- Clipboard

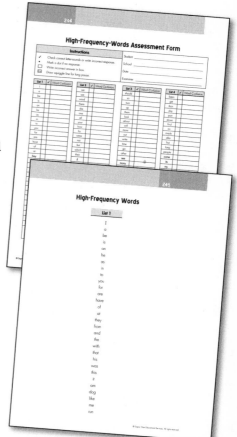

Procedures
1. Before the lesson: Complete the identifying information at the top of the High-Frequency Word Assessment Form and place it on a clipboard.
2. Select which High-Frequency Words list or lists you will administer (consult Table 3.7). Test only one or two lists of words at a time.
3. Place a list of words in front of student.
4. Ask the student to read the words on the list or lists you have selected. Mask words with a sheet if the student has difficulty focusing on only one line at a time.
5. Tell the student to skip a word if he or she does not know it. The goal is for students to recognize these words quickly and automatically.
6. Record information on the High-Frequency-Word Assessment Form (see Table 3.8 for guidance).

Scoring
At the bottom of each list on the High-Frequency-Word Assessment Form, write the total number of words correct (out of a possible 30 words correct per list).

Using the Information
- Refer to this assessment for planning the **Word Work** part of the RRI lesson. You will find a section containing reading and writing activities that provide practice on high-frequency words in the **Word Work** chapter (see page 76).

- High-frequency-word recognition continues to develop throughout first grade (and afterward). Keep in mind that the goal is instant, automatic recognition of these very common words. Students should read each set of words with increasing mastery. As students become proficient with one set, they are ready to progress to a new set. However, it is important to give them continuing opportunities for practice to keep their skills sharp and to periodically reassess sets of words on which students have previously demonstrated mastery to make sure they are maintaining their skills.

TABLE 3.7

High-Frequency Words

List 1	List 2	List 3	List 4
I	we	should	been
a	use	so	get
be	word	two	than
is	there	up	day
on	she	them	part
he	one	look	down
as	all	about	find
in	your	will	no
to	how	more	made
you	by	out	after
for	were	write	first
are	not	time	long
have	but	go	people
of	which	other	come
at	their	see	its
they	if	many	my
from	do	has	now
and	what	make	could
the	had	him	away
with	when	then	did
that	each	her	may
his	an	would	who
was	said	into	call
this	or	these	way
it	can	some	number
am	big	blue	eat
dog	have	jump	little
like	play	going	under
me	here	our	went
run	ran	saw	must

Student Response	What to Record on Assessment Form
Student reads word correctly.	Place a *checkmark* in the small box beside the word, in the column labeled ☑.
Student does not attempt word.	Mark a *dot* instead of a checkmark in the small box beside the word, in the column labeled ☑.
Student's answer is incorrect.	Write the incorrect answer in the large box beside the word, in the column labeled "Word Confusion."
Student pauses more than two seconds while trying to remember a word.	Draw a *squiggly line* instead of a checkmark in the small box beside the word, in the column labeled ☑.

TABLE 3.8

High-Frequency Word Assessment: Administrative Procedures

Oral Reading Fluency Assessment

Objective

Student will read from a book for one minute while the teacher determines the rate and accuracy of the reading.

Administer This Assessment

When there is a need to monitor student growth in oral reading fluency. In Phases 2 and 3 of RRI, each child should be given an Oral Reading Fluency Assessment at least once every month.

Materials

- Digital kitchen timer
- Oral Reading Fluency Assessment Form (provided in the Appendix)
- A leveled book that is one level *below* the current Instructional level and that the student has *not* previously read.
- Clipboard

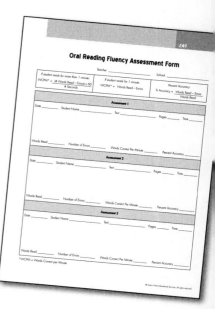

Procedures

1. Before the lesson: Select a book that is one level below the level at which the student is currently being instructed in RRI. Select the portion of the book the student will read for the assessment. Follow the general guidelines provided here on the approximate length of text needed to conduct one-minute fluency assessments for students at different text levels. It is important to note that students who read more fluently will need longer text passages than those described in these guidelines.
   - Levels A and B: do not monitor fluency
   - Levels C–E: at least 30 words
   - Levels F and G: at least 40 words
   - Levels H and I: at least 60 words
   - Levels J and above: at least 100 words
2. Before the lesson: Complete the identifying information at the top of the Oral Reading Fluency Assessment Form provided in the Appendix. Note that there is space on the form to record *three* oral reading fluency assessments. Place the form on a clipboard.
3. Set the timer for one minute.
4. Read the title of the book to the student.

5. Point to the first word in the section you want the student to read. Ask the student to start on this word and to read until the timer goes off. As the student reads the first word, start the timer.

6. As the student reads:
   - Record the student's errors by writing his or her response over the text word, as you would in an Assessment of Reading Accuracy (see Table 3.4 on page 119).
   - Errors are *substituted words, omitted words, and words told to the student. Because of the nature of this particular assessment, extra words inserted by the student are not counted as errors.*
   - Note self-corrections as you would in an Assessment of Reading Accuracy. Self-corrections do *not* count as errors.

7. If the student hesitates for five seconds, tell the student the word and record it as an error.

8. Record the point in the text at which the student was reading at the end of the one-minute period.

Scoring

- Count the number of words the student read during the one-minute period, including the error words. Write this number on the blank line after Words Read on the Oral Reading Fluency Assessment Form.
- Count the number of words on which the student made errors. Remember that self-corrections and extra words inserted by the student are *not* counted as errors. Subtract the number of errors from the number of total words the student read in the one-minute period to calculate the words correct per minute (WCPM).
- WCPM = words read – errors. Record these numbers on the Oral Reading Fluency Assessment Form.
- Transfer this information to the Oral Reading Fluency Assessment Summary Form.
- Use the percent accuracy formula to calculate the accuracy of the timed reading. Percent accuracy = words read – errors divided by total words read. Change the decimal to a percentage by moving the decimal point two places to the left.

Using the Information

- As a general rule, students should read grade-level material (approximately Level G) with at least 90 percent accuracy and at a rate of 27 WCPM by January of first grade. The goal for the end of first grade is for students to be able to read grade-level text (approximately Level I) with at least 90 percent accuracy and at a rate of 54 WCPM. According to the DIBELS assessment (Good & Kaminski, 2003), students with the end-of-first-grade oral reading fluency levels of 40 WCPM have "low risk." However, the average rate at this point is about 54 WCPM (Good, Wallin, Simmons, Kame'enui, & Kaminski, 2002).

- After the timed reading, think about the following questions: Is the student able to read the text with at least 90 percent accuracy? Is the student correctly identifying words? Is the reading phrased, or is the student reading one word at a time? Is the student reading smoothly with expression and attending to the punctuation?

- Look at the Oral Reading Fluency Assessment Summary Form (see page 136) to determine whether the student's fluency is improving from one assessment to the next. If there is not a pattern of improvement (reading more difficult text with increasing fluency), examine your lessons and other assessment data to determine what might need to be changed or adjusted to help the student make quicker progress.

- Use information about the student's fluency when planning the **PRINT CONCEPTS AND FLUENCY** component of the RRI lesson.

- Look at the types of errors the student made and use this information when planning the **WORD WORK** part of lesson. Students who lack fluency usually need practice in automatically recognizing high-frequency words and quickly decoding unknown words.

- If a student has problems with fluency, administer other assessments to find out whether there are other problems (remembering letter-sounds or high-frequency words, repeating too often while reading, etc.) that are affecting the student's fluency.

Monitoring Students' Progress in RRI

One of the most consistent findings of research in early reading instruction is the importance of monitoring student progress so you can change an instructional program when students are making inadequate progress. In RRI, teachers use four key forms to summarize students' progress over time. You will find copies of all four forms in the Appendix:

- Progress in Reading Levels Summary Form
- Benchmark Book Progress Summary Form
- Oral Reading Fluency Assessment Summary Form
- Assessment Results Summary Form

Progress in Reading Levels Summary Form

The Progress in Reading Levels Summary Form is used to track student progress in the Assessment of Reading Accuracy (page 116). Use one form for each student.

Each time you administer an Assessment of Reading Accuracy during an RRI lesson:

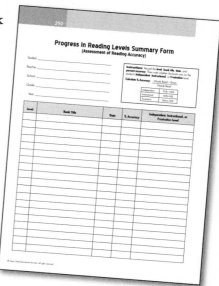

- Record the book level, title, and assessment date.
- Record the percent accuracy for the book.
- Determine whether the book was on the student's Independent, Instructional, or Frustration level and record in the appropriate column.
- Use the form to "get the big picture" of each student's progress through the book levels and level of accuracy on books read during RRI lessons.
- Keep the Progress in Reading Levels Summary Forms together in a binder with all of the student's assessment forms.

Benchmark Book Progress Summary Form

The Benchmark Book Progress Summary Form tracks each student's progress in Benchmark Book Assessments (page 121). Use it only to record student progress in Benchmark Book Assessments. After you administer a Benchmark Book Assessment, use the Progress in Reading Levels Summary Form described previously to record student progress in other text.

1. Record the title of the Benchmark Book you administered next to the appropriate book level. If you are using the Developmental Reading Assessment (Beaver, 1997), record the title of the appropriate book from that assessment.
2. Record the date of the assessment in the box provided at the top of the form.
3. Record the student's percent accuracy score next to the date.

4. If you readminister a Benchmark Book because a student does not pass a Benchmark Book with at least 90 percent accuracy on the first attempt, record the date and percent accuracy for the second time you administer the Benchmark assessment for that level on the same line under Second Try.

5. Keep the Benchmark Book Progress Summary Forms with all of the Benchmark assessments in a binder.

Oral Reading Fluency Assessment Summary Form

The purpose of the Oral Reading Fluency Assessment Summary Form is to track students' progress in oral reading fluency. Each time you administer an Oral Reading Fluency Assessment (page 132):

1. Record the name of the book and the date the fluency assessment was given.

2. Record the total number of words the student read, the number of errors, and the length of time the student read (usually one minute).

3. Calculate the words correct per minute and the percent accuracy using the formulas at the top of the form, and record in the appropriate columns.

4. Keep these summary forms in a binder with the student's Oral Reading Fluency Assessments.

Assessment Results Summary Form

After you administer the Letter-Name Assessment, Letter-Sound Assessment, High-Frequency-Word Assessment, and Assessment of Reading Accuracy at the beginning of the year, complete the Assessment Results Summary Form to get a picture of the overall results.

1. Circle the numbers of each list of letter-sounds or words that were administered.

2. Record any student errors in the appropriate column, placing the student's response over the correct response, as you would for an Assessment of Reading Accuracy.

3. Record any items (e.g., letters or words) the student has mastered.

4. Under Score, write the total number correct over the number of correct responses that are possible.

5. Under Benchmark Book Assessment at the bottom of the form, write the title and level of the highest level Benchmark Book read with 90 percent accuracy and the percent accuracy for that book.

6. This form can be shared with other teachers and with parents during a conference. It can be used periodically throughout the school year to track student progress.

Supported Reading

The purpose of **SUPPORTED READING** is to assist students as they develop accurate and fluent text reading and become strategic in their comprehension. **SUPPORTED READING** gives students the opportunity to apply the skills they have learned in the **WORD WORK** component of Responsive Reading Instruction (RRI) and to develop effective strategies for reading text, including the use of letter-sound relationships as the primary strategy for decoding and the use of both context and letter-sound relationships for self-monitoring and self-correction. The RRI teacher provides both scaffolding and instruction to assist students as they develop the skills needed to read text of increasing difficulty. The activities implemented during **SUPPORTED READING** in each phase of RRI are listed in Table 4.1.

What Does Research Say?

In a summary of research about early reading instruction, a panel of experts commissioned by the National Institutes of Health (Snow, Burns, & Griffin, 1998) concluded that the most successful teachers of reading in the primary grades teach phonics skills explicitly *and* provide many opportunities for students to practice reading engaging text. Studies of effective first grade classroom reading instruction (i.e., Foorman, Francis, Fletcher, Schatschneider, & Mehta, 1998) have demonstrated the value of providing phonics instruction in a *print-rich* environment. In the early stages of reading, this is best done in the context of oral reading. Reading orally provides students the opportunity to practice the reading skills they know and to receive instruction in specific reading skills that are necessary for the development of fluent reading.

When students receive scaffolding and feedback while reading, they are less likely to make repeated errors that can become habits over time. Students who receive scaffolding and feedback while reading connected text learn to read words more accurately and fluently (Reitsma, 1988). Perkins (1988) found that specific feedback that included modeling or directing students to sound out words when they made an error was more effective in promoting accurate phonemic decoding than more general feedback. The RRI teacher provides scaffolding to help students achieve success in reading and writing text but is always conscious that scaffolding is temporary support and that the student must learn to read and write without the teacher's help. For more research-supported information, see the Scaffolding and Feedback section on page 15 in the Introduction and Helping Students Become Independent Readers and Writers on page 216 in the last chapter, Putting It All Together.

TABLE 4.1

Responsive Reading Instruction Activities: Supported Reading

	Phase 1	Phase 2	Phase 3
Supported Reading	• Introducing a New Book • Reading a New Book • Modeling the Word-Identification Strategy • Teaching Students to Monitor Their Own Reading • "Does It Make Sense?" Game	• Introducing a New Book • Reading a New Book • Modeling the Word-Identification Strategy • Teaching Word Identification Using the Strategy • Teaching Students to Monitor Their Own Reading • "Does It Make Sense?" Game • Teaching Comprehension in Text Reading: Questioning • Teaching Comprehension in Text Reading: Story Structure	• Introducing a New Book • Reading a New Book • Teaching Word Identification Using the Strategy • Teaching Students to Monitor Their Own Reading • Teaching Comprehension in Text Reading: Questioning • Teaching Comprehension in Text Reading: Story Structure

Planning the Supported Reading Part of the RRI Lesson

Table 4.1 includes the activities that may be included in SUPPORTED READING in each phase of RRI. Note that Introducing a New Book and Reading a New Book will occur in *every* lesson. All lessons in Phases 2 and 3 will also include a comprehension focus.

Book Selection

Previously, RRI teachers used books leveled according to the Fountas and Pinnell (1999) system or the system accompanying the Developmental Reading Assessment (Beaver, 1997). However, students may read any text in RRI, as long as the text is on the students' Instructional reading levels. If decodable books or phonics readers are available, you may use these in RRI instruction, as long you can ensure that the text is on students' Instructional levels. It can be particularly useful to include books that contain many examples of a phonic element being taught (such as the /a/ sound or the *ai* vowel pattern). These books give students many opportunities to apply the skills they are learning while reading connected text. Using decodable books at the beginning of the program can be especially helpful in lessening children's tendency to guess words by looking at pictures in the books.

The most critical component of lesson planning for SUPPORTED READING is the selection of the book that will be read. The book is selected specifically for the Star Reader for that day. These are among factors to be considered in selecting a book:

- *Select a book of the appropriate level.* The book must be at an appropriate level of difficulty. Select a book on the student's *Instructional* level based on previous Benchmark Book Assessments and Assessments of Reading Accuracy conducted during the ASSESSMENT part of the RRI lesson. There is considerable variation in the difficulty of books within each book level. As you select a book, read through it and imagine what will be difficult and what will be easy for the student, based on your assessments and daily observation records.

- *Set students up for success.* The goal is to select a book that will challenge the student in some way, presenting opportunities for new learning and for the application of known skills. The book should be at a level of difficulty that the student will be able to read *successfully* with the support of the teacher. If students are asked to read text that is too difficult, they will be less likely to apply the decoding strategy effectively or to self-monitor and self-correct errors. Many students resort to a guessing strategy when asked to read Frustration-level text. This kind of ineffective strategy will become a habit if students are constantly asked to read very difficult text. If a book is too easy, a student will have nothing to learn from reading it. In general, though, it is better to err on the side of making the book more accessible to the student. Although it sounds contradictory, many teachers have found that keeping the text relatively easy helps students make more progress than does pushing them constantly with very challenging text. Experiences of success reduce anxiety and increase self-confidence, freeing the student to take risks and attempt to apply what they are learning. (See Three Levels of Text Difficulty below.)

- *Pick a book that supports what you want to teach.* Think about your key objectives for the Star Reader. For example, if a student needs to practice decoding CVC words in connected text, choose a book with many examples of this word type. If one of your objectives is that the student will read phrases rather than word by word, be sure the book supports this kind of reading.

- *Consider the student's background knowledge.* Think about whether the student is likely to have prior knowledge related to the subject of the book, allowing the student to make personal connections and inferences while reading. If this kind of background knowledge is lacking, you will need to supply it during the book introduction.

- *Choose a book the student will like.* The student should enjoy the experience of reading the book. Students are more likely to connect with and comprehend a book that they are motivated to read.

Three Levels of Text Difficulty. Many teachers are familiar with the terms *Independent-level*, *Instructional-level*, and *Frustration-level* text. For any student at any point in his or her development, a text will be at one of these levels of difficulty:

- *Independent level*—If the student can read the text on the first reading, without help, with at least 96 percent accuracy, it is on the student's Independent reading level.

- *Instructional level*—A book that a student can read independently with 90 percent accuracy or can read with the teacher's support without needing substantial scaffolding on more than three to four words is at the Instructional level. This is the ideal level of the new book selected daily for the Star Reader. Students can learn to read or improve their reading ability with teacher instruction and feedback using text at individual students' Instructional reading levels. In RRI, all books that are sent home should be books that the student has previously read and is able to read with at least 90 percent accuracy without help (as determined in an Assessment of Reading Accuracy performed during the **ASSESSMENT** part of the RRI lesson).

- *Frustration level*—Any text that the student cannot read with at least 90 percent accuracy without help is at the student's Frustration level. Asking a student to struggle through Frustration-level text actually interferes with reading progress. As mentioned previously, students tend to use ineffective strategies to compensate for the difficulty they are having, and these strategies can quickly turn into bad habits. For example, students may skip difficult words, guess at them, mumble something incoherent hoping that the teacher will let it pass, or constantly look at the teacher for help or confirmation.

When students read text that is at too high a level of difficulty, they become frustrated. They lose the most powerful incentive to keep working and improving—success! Responsive Reading Instruction works because it keeps students in appropriate text and provides scaffolding and instruction that ensures they are successful. When many students enter RRI, they already have a low self-image of their ability to learn to read. They may already think they are "dumb." RRI trades in those negative beliefs and images for feelings of success. Success frees a person to take risks and keep learning and improving. A person who feels like a failure shuts down. A person who feels successful marches on! RRI teachers must continually challenge their students to learn more and more, but they must always provide the students with a safe environment in which they can flourish. Frustration-level text is the enemy of growth!

Book Selection in Phase 1. In the earliest stages of learning to read, a student may recognize very few words and know few, if any, letter-sound associations. Often a student at this stage can only read his or her own name and the word *a.* It is important, even at this early stage, for students to be engaged in reading text. For this early stage, consult the set of Rebus Books in the Appendix. These books are made up of simple words and pictures. Several of the Rebus Books have blanks in which the teacher can write the student's name. RRI teachers may also make their own Rebus Books, combining recognizable pictures and words the students know. If you make your own Rebus Books, paste the pictures in line with the text rather than at the top of the page. Students should point to each picture as they read, with the understanding that the picture is taking the place of a word in the sentence.

Book Selection in Phase 2. For most of the student's program, select books that are leveled for difficulty in *Matching Books to Readers* (Fountas & Pinnell, 1999) or other text on students' Instructional reading levels. As described previously, you may also include decodable books or other text. Using decodable texts and semi-decodable texts can encourage students to use the phonics skills they are learning and help prevent the development of the habit of guessing words.

Book Selection in Phase 3. Students read more difficult books in Phase 3. The books tend to be much longer than those at the lower levels, and several are "chapter books." At this stage, have the Star Reader read only *part* of the new book during the **SUPPORTED READING** part of the lesson. Some options for the rest of the book include the teacher reading it to the students, having students continue to read part of the book chorally, or continuing the book on a different day. *Caution:* Remember that the new book is always selected at the Instructional level *of the Star Reader for the day.* Do not have different students continue reading the same book over several days (or have them read it in round-robin format, taking turns with pages) *unless* the book is on the Instructional or Independent level for *each* student in the group. It is better to return to a book three or four days later when the original student for whom it was selected is again the Star Reader than to have other children struggling to read a book that is too hard for them. Another option is to let the original Star Reader for the book take it home and continue to read it on his or her own, *if* the book is not too difficult for the student to read without your scaffolding.

Preparing a Book Introduction

The description of the activity Introducing a New Book (page 147) outlines considerations in the preparation of a book introduction. Write the introduction (or notes reminding you of key points) on the daily lesson plan.

Planning for Comprehension Instruction

Two activities in this chapter describe comprehension strategies that can be incorporated into the lesson. Comprehension instruction should be noted in the lesson plan. Write the key points that should be covered in each comprehension lesson on the daily plan.

Teaching Students to Read Words

Students in RRI are explicitly taught to use letter-sound association to read and spell unknown words. Students in RRI learn, practice, and apply one three-part strategy for reading unknown words (see Three-Step-Strategy Prompt Card provided in the Appendix):

Three-Step-Strategy Prompt Card

1. Look for parts you know.

2. Sound it out.

3. Check it!

1. *Look for a part you know.* Students are taught to look for letter combinations they recognize. This is important because some students attempt to sound out a word such as *this* with the sounds /t/ /h/ /i/ /s/ rather than recognizing the *th* combination as a unit. In addition, students in RRI learn to recognize larger word patterns such as the rime unit *-ing* in words such as *ring, sing,* and *bring.* The first part of the word-reading strategy encourages students to look for these word patterns and use them to help decode.

2. *Sound it out.* Students learn to say the sounds of the letters and letter combinations in a smooth, connected way and to blend the sounds together to form the word. It is important that students not develop the habit of stopping after each sound in a word (i.e., /c/ /a/ /p/) but connect the sounds as smoothly as possible (i.e., *caaap*). Saying the sounds in a smooth, connected fashion makes blending the sounds into a word much easier for the young reader.

3. *Check it.* (Decide whether it makes sense.) Students learn that after they sound out a word, they should go back to the beginning of the sentence in which the word occurred and read the sentence with the word they identified so that they can check whether the word makes sense in the sentence. Thus, they are taught to attend to the meaning of the text and to use context to self-monitor the accuracy of their decoding.

To teach this strategy for reading unknown words:

- *Model.* Show the student what you want him or her to do.
- *Provide guided practice.* This means going through the parts of the strategy with the student. (For example: Sound out a word with the student, leading the student along as necessary.)
- *Use prompting and praise during independent practice.* Prompt the student to execute the parts of the strategy independently, scaffolding as necessary. Praise successful and partially correct responses. Praise attempts to apply the strategy even if the attempts do not ultimately result in the correct word—but scaffold the student until the student arrives at the correct word. If the word is very difficult, sound it out for the student, or simply say the word.

Supported Reading

Phases 1, 2, 3

Introducing a New Book

Objective

The student will successfully read and comprehend a text not previously read.

Implement Activity

Each time you introduce a new book.

Materials

- New book selected with the Star Reader in mind
- *Optional:* Whiteboard, dry-erase marker, and eraser

Procedures

There are several options for introducing a new book, and they provide varying levels of support to the readers. Objectives addressed in the book introduction may include activating background knowledge to increase comprehension; setting a purpose for reading to increase comprehension; pre-teaching key vocabulary; pre-teaching the decoding of important words that might present difficulty; and teaching key comprehension skills and strategies.

In general, book introductions should be relatively brief. They should not provide more support than the students need to be successful, and *they should not* include a rehearsal or memorization of parts of the text. Options for procedures include the following:

1. *Briefly discuss the story line with the students and set a purpose for reading.* Ask questions that may help students relate the book to their own background knowledge or experience. You may use the book's pictures as you describe the story line, but *do not* provide more information than the students will need. You may only need to show the students two to three pictures. It is preferable to leave some lingering questions in order to provide a purpose for reading.

Brief Introduction for Narrative Text

"This is a book about a dog that always gets into trouble. Have you ever had a pet that got into trouble? Let's find out what happens to the dog in this book."

**Brief Introduction
for Expository Text**

"This book tells all about lions and tigers. Do you already know something about lions or tigers? How do you think they are different from each other? Let's read to learn more about lions and tigers."

2. *Make predictions about the book.* These may be based in part on the book's illustrations. Ask the students to tell what they think might happen in some parts of the book, and ask them to tell *why* they think that might happen. Make brief notes so that you will recall their predictions after the first reading of the book. It is normally best to make predictions based on the first part of the book unless there is a difficult concept later in the book that you would like to clarify by discussing the pictures related to it. If you refrain from discussing the pictures at the end of the book, you can establish a purpose for reading to find out whether the students' predictions were correct. After the first reading of the book, discuss their predictions and whether they were right.

3. *Pre-teach the meanings of challenging vocabulary words.* This will help the students comprehend the text with minimal interruption. Sometimes, however, it is helpful to stop during the reading to clarify the meanings of words in context. This often happens quite naturally as students ask questions about the book during the reading.

4. *Pre-teach important words that may be difficult to decode.* You may have the students locate a challenging word in the text, then write the word on a whiteboard and discuss it or practice sounding it out.

5. During most lessons, your book introduction will include a reference to one of the *comprehension strategies* described later in this section.

Prompts

- "What do you think will happen next?"
- "*Why* do you think that will happen?"

- Model the thought processes involved in the task (e.g., making predictions: "If I wanted to think about what might happen next in the story, I might look at this picture and think about how the bear is feeling, what he has already tried, and what he might try next.")

SCAFFOLDING

Remember that a book introduction should be brief. If you plan ahead what you will say and then write it in your lesson plan, it helps to keep the lesson moving on so the Star Reader has the majority of the time to orally read the book.

IN OUR CLASSROOMS

Phases 1, 2, 3

Reading a New Book

Objective

Students will apply reading skills and effective strategies while reading connected text with comprehension.

Implement Activity

In every lesson during **Supported Reading**.

Materials

- Anecdotal Record Form (provided in the Appendix)
- *Optional:* Three-Step-Strategy, Word-Identification, and Self-Monitoring Prompt Cards (provided in the Appendix)
- *Optional:* Three-Step-Strategy Poster (provided in the Appendix)
- *Optional:* Whiteboard, dry-erase marker, and eraser

Phase 1:

- Rebus Books (provided in the Appendix) or teacher-made books using student names, known words, and pictures of simple objects (one copy for each student in the group)

Phases 2 and 3:

- Leveled books (may include decodable texts or other text, one copy for each student in the group). The book selection is critical. Refer to Planning the **Supported Reading** Part of the RRI Lesson on page 141 for a description of the process for book selection.

Procedures

The new book (or with longer books, a portion of the new book) is read two to three times during each lesson.

First Reading:

1. Introduce the book using the procedures described in Introducing a New Book on page 147.

2. The Star Reader reads all (for very short books) or part of the book alone while the other two students listen and follow along in their own copies of the book.

3. As the Star Reader is reading, offer prompting, scaffolding, teaching, and praise.

4. When the student hesitates or attempts to decode a word but needs support, use the procedures described under one of these two activities: Modeling the Word-Identification Strategy (page 154) or Teaching Word Identification Using the Strategy (page 156).

5. When the student makes an error, use the procedures described in the activity Teaching Students to Monitor Their Own Reading (page 159).

6. When the student effectively applies reading skills and strategies that he or she has learned, or when the student corrects an error, offer specific praise.

Specific Praise

*"Good job at sounding out *th* in *this*. You figured out that hard word all by yourself!"*

"You made sure that word made sense in the sentence. That's what good readers do when they make a mistake."

7. Observe the Star Reader's successful, partially successful, and unsuccessful attempts to decode and self-correct, and make notes about the Star Reader's strengths and needs using the Anecdotal Record Form provided in the Appendix. See page 114 for a description of procedures for taking Anecdotal Records.

8. After the first reading of the book, provide two points of specific praise to the Star Reader and briefly teach the application of efficient strategies in one to two parts of the book where the student had difficulty. Do NOT try to teach more than two things at this point. Choose the one or two errors the student made that will provide the best opportunities to teach important skills, strategies, or concepts (Clay, 1993).

9. The other students in the group should be included in this discussion, but keep it brief.

10. You may also ask the students to find one to two specific words and practice reading them. It may be helpful to write the word on a whiteboard and teach how it can be read using the three-part word-identification strategy. Then have the students practice applying the strategy to the word as it appears in the book.

Changes Across the Phases:

- During Phase 1 and (possibly) during the early portion of Phase 2, prompt the students to point to each word as they read it. ("Point to the words.") Once the students have firmly established a 1:1 correspondence between the written and spoken word, encourage them to read without pointing. You may need to have a student resume pointing for a time if the student develops habits of skipping words or fails to attend to each word. For example, some students develop a habit of reading only the first portion of a word and guessing the rest of the word. A student with this habit should be asked to read somewhat more slowly and to point to each word while reading until the habit has been replaced with more efficient reading.

- During the last part of Phase 2 and all of Phase 3, students will be reading longer books. Because of limited time and student capacity for attention, the Star Reader should read only the first portion of the book alone. The rest may be read chorally, read by the teacher, or summarized by the teacher. (Be very careful in using round-robin reading. This should be used rarely, and *only* in situations in which there are very long stories that are *on an appropriate level for all students* in the group.)

Second Reading:

The teacher may select from several options for the second reading of the book:

1. The Star Reader and the two other students may reread the book or a portion of the book individually.

2. The three students may reread the book or a portion of the book chorally. (It is best if the teacher does NOT read along with them.)

3. Each student may read the book at his or her own pace in a quiet voice simultaneously. This option may be selected only if the book is at an appropriate level for *all* of the students.

- The initial scaffolding is appropriate book selection. If the book is clearly too difficult for the Star Reader, the teacher may opt to model reading aloud parts of the book or have the group read the book chorally with teacher support.

- The second level of scaffolding is a well-planned introduction. If the book selection was appropriate and the introduction was sufficiently supportive, the student should encounter few problems in the first reading.

- Scaffolding is critical during the reading of the new book. The level of support must be appropriate to enable the student to be successful, but it must not be too heavy. The goal is independent decoding and self-monitoring by the student. The level of support generally decreases as the student becomes more efficient at reading books at each successive level of difficulty.

SCAFFOLDING

Third Reading:

Have students read the book a third time if time allows. The purpose of this third reading is to encourage the students to read the text fluently. There are two options for this third reading:

1. The group may reread the book chorally for fluency.
2. Students may individually reread the book with prompting for fluency.

If the new book is clearly too difficult for the Star Reader to read, the teacher should read sections with or to the students or quickly select another book to teach that day. It may be helpful to have an alternate text ready to use in case this happens.

It may be helpful to have note cards with prompts written on them to help you remember what to say and to keep you from spending too much time talking while a student is reading. Prompt cards for this purpose are included in the Appendix (see Materials on page 150).

Note

❑ Refer to **PRINT CONCEPTS AND FLUENCY** for prompts, scaffolds, and activities that promote fluent reading.

Modeling the Word-Identification Strategy

Objective

Students will efficiently and automatically apply effective reading strategies to decode unknown words in order to read text fluently.

Implement Activity

When students are initially learning the word-identification strategy or when they have difficulty applying the strategy.

Materials

- Copies for each student in the group of an Instructional- or Independent-level book they have not previously read
- Whiteboard, dry-erase marker, and eraser
- Three-Step-Strategy Poster (provided in the Appendix)
- *Optional:* Magnetic letters

Procedures

As the Star Reader is reading and encounters an unknown word, demonstrate how you can apply the strategy to read the word. This is particularly important in Phase 1 and in the early stages of Phase 2, when many of the words in the book will not be decodable using the students' limited knowledge of letter-sound correspondences. Do *not* teach students to use the pictures to identify unknown words, as this develops a habit of guessing based on pictures and context. Display the Three-Step Strategy Poster on an easel or mount it on the board, and refer to it often as you model and teach the strategy.

When the Reader Encounters an Unknown Word:

1. Decide whether the word is conducive to modeling the strategy. If the word is irregular or presents any kind of difficulty that may confuse the student, simply tell the student the word. If the word can be used to model the strategy, go on to Step 2.
2. Say: "When I get to a word I don't know, I have a plan for reading it. First I look for a part in the word that I know."
3. Write the problem word on a whiteboard. If there are letters or letter combinations in the word that are known by any student in the group, ask the student to identify their sounds. Model the reading of letters, letter combinations, or word parts in the word.

4. Model saying the sounds of the word slowly in a smooth, connected way while running your finger smoothly under each letter in the word from left to right.

5. Blend the sounds and produce the word.

6. Locate the word in the text and repeat Steps 4 and 5 with the word as it appears in the book.

7. Model locating the beginning of the sentence and rereading it with the word you identified so that you can decide whether it makes sense in the sentence.

8. Have the student(s) proceed with reading the book.

9. As the students gain facility with sounding out words, have them do each part of the process after you.

Modeling may also be done by making the word with magnetic letters rather than writing it on a whiteboard. The teacher may also model the strategy only within the text. Providing variety in the format can help keep students interested and can be a memory aid.

The trick to teaching the RRI word-identification strategy is to be consistent. Each time the student encounters difficulty, you want him or her to apply the strategy (unless the word is irregular or very difficult). As students progress in learning to read, they will apply the strategy quickly and automatically. Also, they will be able to recognize more and more words "on sight," just as adult readers do, so there will be fewer words in the text that need to be decoded using the strategy.

IN OUR CLASSROOMS

Phases 2, 3

Teaching Word Identification Using the Strategy

Objective

Students will efficiently and automatically apply an effective strategy to decode unknown words in order to read text fluently.

Implement Activity

When students are initially learning the word identification strategy or when they have difficulty applying the strategy.

Materials

- Copies for each student in the group of an Instructional- or Independent-level book they have not previously read
- Three-Step-Strategy Poster (provided in the Appendix)
- Magnetic letters or whiteboard, dry-erase marker, and eraser
- Anecdotal Record Form (provided in the Appendix)
- *Optional:* Three-Step-Strategy Prompt Card (provided in the Appendix)
- *Optional:* Word-Identification Prompt Card (provided in the Appendix)

Procedures

As the Star Reader reads and encounters an unknown word, you may:

1. Prompt the student to apply the strategy.
2. Model all or part of the strategy and provide guided and independent practice. See the procedures in "Modeling the Word-Identification Strategy" on page 154. Refer to the Three-Step-Strategy Poster provided in the Appendix.
3. Write the word on a whiteboard, make it with magnetic letters, or mask the word within the text with your fingers. Next, prompt and scaffold the use of the

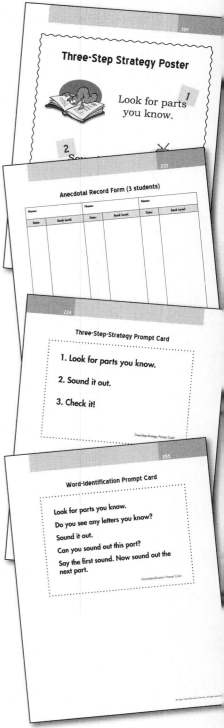

strategy. After the word has been decoded, have the Star Reader first read the word as it appears in the book, then reread the sentence in which it occurred to make sure it makes sense.

Prompts

Prompting has a critical role in supporting the application of the strategy. The following prompts can be used to scaffold the strategy's implementation:

- *"Look for a part you know."*
- "Do you see any parts you know?"
- "Do you see any letters you know?"
- "Is this like another word you know?"
- "What sound does this letter (part) make?"
- *"Sound it out."*
- "Say it slowly."
- "Can you sound out this part?"
- "Say the first sound. Now sound out the next part."
- "Try it."
- *"Check it."*
- "Go back and see if that makes sense."
- "Did that sound right?"
- Repeat the phrase or sentence exactly as the student read it (whether correct or incorrect) and ask, "Did that make sense?"

Praise

- Offer specific praise if the student uses the strategy, or part of the strategy, to correctly decode a word. Praise partially correct answers as well as correct answers, and use this partially correct response as a starting point to model, teach, prompt, scaffold, and praise so that the student may arrive at the correct response.

Students should not become frustrated as they struggle to read words. If a word is difficult for a student or if the student is having problems applying the strategy, provide scaffolding using one of the methods described previously, model the strategy for the student, or simply tell the student the word. After you tell a student a word, always have the student go back to the beginning of the sentence and read the word in context.

IN OUR CLASSROOMS

SCAFFOLDING

- Appropriate book selection is the initial scaffold for text reading.
- Scaffolding during **SUPPORTED READING** consists primarily of modeling and prompting, using the prompts listed previously.
- Write the difficult word on a whiteboard. Have the student identify known parts and sound out the word. Then return to the text and have the student sound out the word within the text and then reread the sentence to be sure it makes sense.
- Write the word in parts (either one letter at a time or one letter-combination or word part at a time) and have the student sound out increasingly longer parts of the word. For example, if the problem word is *stand*, the teacher would write the letter *s* on the whiteboard and ask the student to give the sound of the letter (/s/). Then the teacher would write the letter *t* after the *s* and ask the student to sound out both letters and blend just those two letters together (/st/). If the student knows the word part *and*, it can be written next as a unit and the student can read the entire word from the whiteboard (*st-and: stand*). If the student does not know the word part *and*, each individual letter can be written one at a time (*st-a-n-d*) and the student can read each letter and blend them to sound out the word. After the student reads the word in this way, return to the text and have him or her sound out the word within the text and then reread the sentence to be sure it makes sense (Clay, *1993*).
- Make the word with magnetic letters, separating the letter combinations or word parts the student knows. Show the student how to identify parts he or she knows in the word. Then have the student sound out the word. After the student reads the word in this way, return to the text and have the student sound out the word within the text and then reread the sentence to be sure it makes sense.
- Mask parts of the word in the book with your fingers to show the students the parts they know. Then have the students sound out the word.
- Write a word the student knows that has the same word part or parts as the problem word. For example, if the student is trying to read *play* and knows the word *day*:
  1. Write *day*, and write *play* directly under it. Underline the *ay* combination in each word.
  2. Ask the student to read *day*.
  3. Ask the student for the sound of the *ay* in *day*. (Teach the sound of *ay* if the student does not remember it.)
  4. Point to the *ay* in *day* and have the student read that word part, then read the whole word: *day*. Then point to the *ay* in *play*. Ask the student to read the underlined part, and then the new word.
  5. If this is still too difficult, have the student segment the word *day* into its two phonemes (/d/ /ay/) while you point to the letters. Then point to the letters in *play* and help the student sound out the word.
  6. Note the difficulty in your Anecdotal Record Form provided in the Appendix, and be sure to practice the *ay* pattern during **WORD WORK** in a future lesson.

Phases 1, 2, 3

Teaching Students to Monitor Their Own Reading

Objective

Students will use context and letter-sound associations to self-monitor and self-correct errors while reading.

Implement Activity

When students need to monitor and correct their own errors.

Materials

- Copies for each student in the group of an Instructional- or Independent-level book they have not previously read.
- *Optional:* Self-Monitoring Prompt Card (provided in the Appendix)

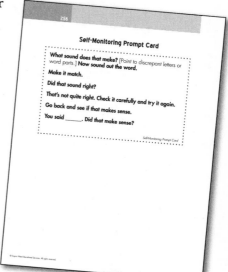

Procedures

1. When a student makes an error, allow the student a little time to realize that there was an error and to correct it independently.
2. If the student does not notice the error, prompt for self-correction.

Prompts

Prompting has a critical role in supporting the development of self-correction. The following prompts can be used to scaffold its implementation:

- "What sound does that make?" (Point to discrepant letters or word parts.) "Now sound out the word."
- "Check it."
- "Make it match."
- "That's not quite right. Check it carefully and try it again."
- "Go back and see if that makes sense."
- "Did that sound right?"
- Repeat the student's incorrectly read phrase or sentence and ask, "Did that make sense?"

Praise

- Offer specific praise for successful self-correction and for attempts at self-correction, even if they are unsuccessful.
- Praise the student when there is evidence that the student has noticed an error, even if there is no attempt to self-correct.

- Provide additional prompts if necessary to allow the student to be successful.
- Model the behavior you want to see. Read the sentence with the error word. Pause and talk about the fact that what you read sounded silly or didn't make sense. Then correct the word and read the sentence correctly.

SCAFFOLDING

IN OUR CLASSROOMS

It may be helpful to have a note card with a couple of prompts written on it to help you remember what to say and so that you won't spend too much time talking while a student is reading. See the Self-Monitoring Prompt Card in the Appendix for this purpose.

Limiting the amount of teacher talk is very important in this section of the lesson. This keeps the reading flowing along and allows the student to learn how to correct errors independently.

You may find that you are always saying the same things to the student. It is very easy to keep saying "Try that again" instead of using other prompts. Take time to look at the list of prompts to see if there is another prompt that will work, especially if the student is not correcting errors independently. And don't forget to praise students specifically for self-correcting their errors.

Phases 1, 2

The "Does It Make Sense?" Game

Objective

Students will monitor their own reading to be sure it makes sense.

Implement Activity

When students do not seem to understand the concept of text making sense or if they need practice in determining when a statement makes sense.

Materials

- A book or prepared statements.

Procedures

1. Tell the students you are going to play a game called "Does It Make Sense?" Tell them that when they read, it is very important that they listen to themselves and decide whether what they are reading makes sense. If it does not make sense, there is probably a mistake that needs to be corrected. Explain that when something makes sense, it sounds right. When something does not make sense, it sounds silly.

2. Demonstrate the concept by reading a statement that *does* make sense and one that *does not* make sense. Model the process you would use to find out whether a sentence makes sense. Talk about why the sentence did not make sense. Then model fixing up the statement that does not make sense so that it "sounds right."

3. Have students do a few examples as a group. Read some sentences that make sense and some that don't. Have the group decide whether each statement makes sense. Have them also discuss why some of the statements didn't make sense.

4. Have students try it individually. Scaffold as necessary.

5. Repeat this activity on subsequent days until it becomes easy for all students in the group.

6. Prompt the students to apply this strategy as they read during the lesson.

Introducing the "Does It Make Sense?" Game

"Today we are going to play a new game called 'Does It Make Sense?' Listen while I read a sentence: *Mom wanted to clean the room.* Does that make sense? Yes, because it sounds right. Have you seen your mom clean before? Now listen to another statement: *The school flew over the house.* Does that make sense? No, the sentence sounded silly. Can a school fly? No, it can't. When you are reading in a book and something doesn't make sense, you need to go back and reread and correct the mistake. Good. Now let's try another sentence together. *Here is a hot dog for did.* Does that make sense? No, it sounds funny. It should be, *Here is a hot dog for Dad.* Now I am going to give each of you a sentence. Make sure you listen to the sentence and decide 'Does that make sense?' Let's begin with Perry."

The teacher says a sentence for each student in the group to give each one an opportunity for independent practice. They discuss why some of the statements didn't make sense.

SCAFFOLDING

- Emphasize the part of a sentence that does not make sense.
- Ask questions that may lead the student to conclude that a statement does not make sense.

Scaffolding for the "Does It Make Sense?" Game

SNAPSHOT

For the sentence *The church ran up the tree*, ask, "Can a church run?" or "What is a church?"

Remember to give specific praise for correct responses.

IN OUR CLASSROOM

Read sentences from a book, keeping some of them intact so that they do make sense, and changing others so that they do not. You may want to write down some of each kind of sentence before the lesson so that you do not have to make sentences up "on the run." A few sentences are provided below to help you get started. For each word in the sentences that doesn't make sense, we have placed the correct word in parentheses. The incorrect words look similar to the correct words and are examples of the kinds of errors students may make as they read.

Sample Sentences That Don't Make Sense

- The boy ate a poor (pear).
- The man painted his horse (house).
- She put (played) with a red bucket.
- The boy came and took it always (away).
- Peggy spot (spilled) her water.
- The girl fell brown (down).
- We much (must) go home.
- Mom put on her sun hot (hat).
- Tell him to gave (give) it back!
- The little dog was green (greedy).

Phases 2, 3

Teaching Comprehension in Text Reading: Questioning

Objective

The student will demonstrate the comprehension of a text not previously read.

Implement Activity

When students need instruction in order to focus on comprehension as well as accurate reading.

Materials

- New book selected with the Star Reader in mind
- *Optional:* Chart tablet or whiteboard, dry-erase marker, and eraser

Procedures

In RRI, comprehension is taught in four steps:

1. *Before reading.* In the book introduction, focus on the aspect of comprehension you want to emphasize in this lesson. Model through a think-aloud, making logical predictions based on the pictures and on a brief introduction to the plot or subject matter. Ask students to make predictions relating to these aspects of comprehension. Guide them toward predictions that reflect the comprehension objective on which you are focusing. Since the students have not yet read the story, it is important to accept any reasonable answer. Be sure to ask students for reasons for their answers. You may decide to record the predictions on a chart tablet or whiteboard. You may choose to emphasize one or more of the following (no more than one to two in one book):
   - The events that happen in the story and the order in which they happen (sequence of events).
   - The reasons that things happen in the story or that characters act as they do (cause and effect).
   - Descriptions of the characters and their feelings.
   - What the story (or a particular page or part of the story) will be mostly about (the main idea).
   - In nonfiction text, what the students already know about the topic and what they think they will learn (interesting facts or processes that are described).
2. *During reading.* As students are reading, occasionally ask a question or make a specific comment that is related to the aspect of comprehension you have chosen to emphasize. Take care

not to interrupt the reading too often. Try to make questions or comments brief.

3. *After reading.* Revisit the questions and/or predictions that you discussed before reading or ask students to *briefly* summarize the text. Focus on the same aspect of comprehension as you did before and during reading.

4. *Written response.* During the **SUPPORTED WRITING** part of the RRI lesson, ask a question related to the aspect of comprehension that was your focus for that day. (See the Writing in Response to Text activity on page 189.)

Comprehension Instruction Focused on a Sequence of Events

Before reading. "This is a book about a witch who wants a funny haircut. I'm going to look at the pictures and tell you what I think the witch will do in the story. Listen: Hmmm. I see a picture of the witch going into a beauty shop or some place where people cut and fix hair. I think the first thing the witch will do is ask someone to cut her hair." Turning to the next page, the teacher says, "What do you think will happen next in the story? Why do you think that?"

During reading. "We were right when we said that the hairdresser would cut the witch's hair. What do you think will happen next?"

After reading. "Let's think about all the things that happened in this story. First, the witch went into the hairdresser's shop. What happened next? What happened after that?"

*Written response (during **SUPPORTED WRITING**).* "Think about the story we read about the witch who wanted a haircut. What happened at the end of the story?" (Wyvill, 1992)

Comprehension Instruction Focused on Characters' Feelings

Before reading. "This is a book about a witch who wants a funny haircut." After looking at a picture of the witch stomping her feet and looking angry, the teacher says: "Wow. I think the witch is feeling mad on this page! I wonder why she is acting so angry." After turning to the next page, the teacher says: "How do you think the witch is feeling on this page? Why do you think that? How do you think the hairdresser [point to picture] is feeling?"

During reading. After the student reads the words *The witch was mad*, the teacher asks, "Were we right about how the witch was feeling on this page? How do you know?"

After reading. "Let's think about how the characters were feeling in this story. When the hairdresser fixed the witch's hair the first time, how did the witch feel? How did the witch feel at the end of the story? Why do you think she felt like that?"

*Written response (during **SUPPORTED WRITING**).* "Think about the story we read about the witch who wanted a haircut. How did the witch feel at the end of the story?" (Wyvill, 1992)

Comprehension Instruction Focused for Nonfiction Text

Before reading. "This is a book about slugs and snails. What do you already know about slugs and snails?" The teacher asks the following question after looking at one or two pictures: "What do you think we might learn about slugs and snails?"

During reading. Turning to the next page, the teacher asks, "You thought we might learn about what slugs and snails eat. Were we right? What do they eat?"

After reading. "Let's look back at the things we thought we might learn from the book about slugs and snails. What did you learn from this book?"

*Written response (during **SUPPORTED WRITING**).* "Think about the book we read about slugs and snails. What was one interesting thing you learned about slugs or snails?" (Walker, 1993)

Phases 2, 3

Teaching Comprehension in Text Reading: Story Structure

Objective

The student will successfully identify story elements in a text not previously read.

Implement Activity

When students need to improve comprehension of narrative text.

Materials

- New book selected with the Star Reader in mind. (For this activity, the book must be a narrative or story. This activity will not work with nonfiction books.)
- *Optional:* Chart tablet or whiteboard, dry-erase marker, and eraser

Procedures

Use the same procedures as described in "Teaching Comprehension in Text Reading: Questioning" on page 163, but focus your instruction (before, during, and after reading) on the common elements found in narratives:

- *Setting:* Where and when the story takes place.
- *Characters:* The people or animals in the story. The main character is the person or animal who is in almost all of the story. (There may be more than one main character.)
- *Problem:* Something the main character wants or something that is going wrong.
- *Events:* The things that happen in the story as the characters try to solve the problem.
- *Outcome:* How the story ends; usually the way the problem is solved.

Introduce only *one* story element at a time, model it through a think-aloud, and have students practice identifying that element in various books over several days before introducing the next element. Remember that the RRI teacher teaches comprehension in four steps.

1. *Before reading.* First, focus your new-book introduction on a particular story element that you want the students to attend to. Be sure to explicitly teach what that story element means. For example, if you are going to focus on the problem in a story, begin by telling the students that in most stories the character or characters have a problem. Explain that this means that the characters want something or that there is something going wrong.
2. *During reading.* Ask a few questions during and after reading that focus on the *same* story element. Be sure that you do *not* interrupt

the reading too much or take too much time with questions or discussion during the reading.

3. *After reading.* Revisit the questions and/or predictions that you discussed before reading and summarize what students learned from the text. This is also a good time to review other story elements students have learned and apply them to this text as well. But remember to keep it brief!

4. *Written response.* Ask a question related to the same story element to elicit a sentence during supported writing.

Comprehension Instruction Focused on Story Characters

Before reading. "The characters in a story are the people or animals that are in the story. This is a book about a witch who wants a funny haircut. I'm going to look at the pictures to think about who will be the characters in this story. Well, one character is definitely the witch. She seems to be on nearly every page!"

After looking at the illustrations prior to reading, the teacher says, "What other characters do you think will be part of this story? Why do you think there will be a lady that gives haircuts in this book?"

During reading. "Were we right? Is one of the characters in the story a witch? What do we know about this character after reading this page?"

After reading. "Before we read the story we thought there would be two characters in it—a witch and a lady that gives haircuts, a hairdresser. Were we right? Were there any other characters in this story? Last week we talked about the *setting* of a story. What is the setting of this story?" The teacher scaffolds as necessary to review the concept of story setting.

*Written response (during **Supported Writing**).* "Think about the story we read about the witch that wanted a haircut. Who were the characters in the story?" (Wyvill, 1992)

Comprehension Instruction Focused on the Story Problem

Before reading. "Most stories have some kind of problem in them. That means that the character wants something or that there is something going wrong. When I see this picture, it looks like the witch is mad! I wonder what the problem could be. I'm going to guess that she is mad because she doesn't like the way the hairdresser fixed her hair. What do you think? Can you think of any other problems there might be in this story? Why do you think that?"

During reading. "Does the witch have a problem? What does she want?"

After reading. "We thought that the problem in this story would be that the witch was mad because she didn't like the way the hairdresser cut her hair. Were we right? Was this a problem for the hairdresser too? Why?"

*Written response (during **Supported Writing**).* "Think about the story we read about the witch who wanted a haircut. What was the problem in the story?" (Wyvill, 1992)

Supported Writing

The purpose of the **SUPPORTED WRITING** component of
the Responsive Reading Instruction (RRI) lesson is to
teach and provide practice in the following concepts
and abilities:

- Print conventions

- Phonological awareness

- Use of phonological analysis to spell words

- Ability to write complete sentences

- Ability to write in response to reading

- Basic editing skills

- A general facility with written expression

What Does Research Say?

Research has demonstrated a strong positive connection between students' development of reading skills and their development of writing skills, and several studies have demonstrated that emphasis on writing activities in early reading instruction positively affects reading development (see Adams, 1990).

Students apply a variety of skills during **SUPPORTED WRITING** instruction. First of all, they learn to compose a sentence orally and to record the words from the sentence, one by one, in writing. Through this early experience with writing, students' understanding of print concepts such as left-to-right directionality, the use of punctuation, or the need for spacing between words is reinforced. Through writing their own thoughts, students learn that print can be used to record speech and that reading is a process of turning that print back into speech. Adams (1990) describes the process of children developing understanding of print concepts through writing their own messages as creating "a natural bridge . . . from their oral language knowledge to their literacy challenge" (p. 371). Students recognize that their words can be written, that they can themselves read the words, and that other people can read them as well. Furthermore, they learn that text carries meaning and that reading is the re-creation of that meaning. As Adams observes, "Through writing, children learn that . . . text is . . . the human voice. . . . Through writing, children learn that the purpose of text is not to be read but to be understood" (p. 405).

As students say words slowly in order to record sounds while spelling words, they sharpen their awareness of individual phonemes in words and of the alphabetic principle. They also further their understanding of the nature and functions of print. These phonemic analysis skills are critical for reading and spelling development (National Reading Panel, 2000). See What Does Research Say? in the **WORD WORK** chapter of this book for a more detailed discussion of the roles of phonemic awareness and phonics instruction in learning to read.

A brief reflection about the nature of written English makes it clear that learning to spell words correctly depends on more than recognizing the sounds in words. For example, /$\bar{a}$/, the long a sound, can be represented in several ways, including *ai*, *ay*, *a* with silent *e*, and *eigh*. Beyond recognizing /$\bar{a}$/ in a spoken word such as *rain*, a student must know which option will make the word *rain* "look right." This is called *orthographic* knowledge. Because students in RRI are scaffolded to record letters through sound analysis and are also provided with parts of words that they cannot arrive at through this method, the final product is a correctly spelled word. The more students are exposed to the correct spelling of a word through reading and writing the word, the more likely they are to be able to produce the correct spelling on their own. When students write words, they attend to the letters within the words in detail. They focus not only on the sounds within words but also on the appearance of words, or their orthographic nature.

Besides learning about words, students learn how to compose and write sentences during **SUPPORTED WRITING**. They engage in the writing process (see Graves, 1983) on a beginning level. They learn how to plan their writing through their interaction with the teacher as they develop a response to the text they read that day. They compose the sentence in written form word by word. They edit what they have written, checking to be sure it makes sense, that words are written correctly, and that basic capitalization and punctuation rules have been applied. Finally, each sentence appears in its published form in the students' journals and can be read by others in the group and reread by the authors on subsequent days.

Planning the Supported Writing Part of the RRI Lesson

Supported Group Writing (Phase 1) *or* Supported Independent Writing (Phases 2 and 3) should be included in every lesson (see Table 5.1). As you plan for **SUPPORTED WRITING**, select a guiding question to help the Star Reader compose the sentence. If you are going to focus on a particular comprehension skill in **SUPPORTED READING**, such as a story structure component, design your question to target that skill (see pages 163-168). Be prepared to use Elkonin Sound Boxes whenever students need scaffolding to help them record the sounds in words. Include the direct teaching of self-monitoring and self-correction strategies from the beginning of the school year, and review as often as needed. Require that students edit their own sentences using these strategies.

	Phase 1	Phase 2	Phase 3
Supported Writing	• Supported Group Writing • Teaching Sound Analysis	• Supported Independent Writing • Teaching Sound Analysis • Teaching Students to Edit Their Writing • Writing in Response to Text	• Supported Independent Writing • Teaching Sound Analysis • Teaching Students to Edit Their Writing • Writing in Response to Text

TABLE 5.1

Responsive Reading Instruction Activities: Supported Writing

Supported Writing

Phases 1, 2, 3

Supported Group Writing

Objective
Students participate in the composition of complete sentences and in writing words and parts of words.

Implement Activity
When the students need to practice writing sentences in Phase 1. This activity is an opportunity for the group to work together on a sentence while the teacher gives support by modeling and scaffolding.

Materials
- Chart tablet and easel
- Standard colored markers
- Black marker
- 1" correction tape

Procedures
1. Ask the Star Reader to compose one complete sentence about a book read that day. Support the student and provide scaffolding as the sentence is developed. In the earliest lessons, elicit a sentence with the students' names in it, if possible.
2. Have the group repeat the sentence three times to help them remember it.
3. Distribute a different color of marker to each student in the group.
4. Take turns with the students as they write the sentence on a chart tablet. Ask the students to supply the parts of the sentence they can write. They may be able to contribute whole words or letters to represent sounds within words. Have each student write with a different color of marker to distinguish the contributions of each student to the sentence. Provide scaffolding, praise, and feedback. Be sure to include every student. Even if a student knows only how to write his or her name, or can only form one or two letters, be sure to provide opportunities for the student to make these contributions with your support.
5. Model and "think aloud" as you write with a black marker the words or parts of words that the students do not know.
6. Have the students read the sentence chorally. Then give them individual turns, or have one student point with the teacher while the group reads.

Supported Group Writing

With the help of the teacher and the rest of the group, the Star Reader composes the sentence *Jimmy and Maria and Damion like the birthday cake.* The students all repeat the sentence three times.

Each student has a different color of marker. The teacher asks Jimmy, "Can you write your name?" Jimmy steps up to the easel and prints his name on the chart tablet. The teacher points to the word and reads *Jimmy* then says, "Our sentence was *Jimmy and Maria and Damion like the birthday cake.* What word do we need to write next?" The teacher may provide scaffolding by starting the sentence again and pausing on the word *and.* The teacher asks, "What is the first sound you hear in *and*?"

Damion says /a/, so the teacher asks him whether he knows how to write that sound. Damion steps up to the chart and writes the letter *r.* The teacher says, "That is a good try, but we write the /a/ sound like this." The teacher covers up Damion's error with correction tape and writes the letter *a* on top of the tape. Then the teacher models saying the word *and* slowly, sound by sound, and recording each sound while saying it.

Again, the teacher repeats the sentence the students are trying to write and reads what has been written so far, pausing on the word *Maria.* The activity continues, as *Maria* writes her name with her marker.

The teacher scaffolds the students to help them remember that the word *and* follows the word *Maria* in the sentence and that it is the same as the word that was previously written. The teacher invites Damion to copy the word *and* after the word *Maria.* The teacher reads the word after Damion has written it, sound by sound in a smooth way, then blended together. "Yes," the teacher says, "this word is *and.* Damion, you did a good job of writing *and.*"

The activity continues, with students supplying any letters or words they know and the teacher providing a think-aloud as she supplies the rest of the sentence. For example, as the teacher writes the word *birthday,* the teacher says, "I hear /b/ at the beginning of *birthday.* I'll write /b/ like this [writing the letter *b*]. I'll write the rest of this long word myself." Rather than modeling all of the word *birthday,* which contains many letter combinations that the students have not yet been exposed to, the teacher simply says the word *birthday* and writes it.

At the end of the sentence, the teacher says, "I am going to put a period at the end of this sentence. It is kind of like a stop sign. It tells us when the sentence is complete."

Prompts

- Demonstrate thinking aloud as you write a word in a sentence by saying, for example, "When I come to a word I don't know how to spell, I sound it out." Demonstrate the process as you write.
- Ask, "What do you hear at the beginning of the word ____?" stressing the beginning sound.

- Vary the level of support to assist students in recording words and phonemes they know.
- Model and teach the use of phonemic analysis to spell words.
- Supply words or letters that are not accessible to the students.

Notes

❏ It is important for each student to get a different color of marker for this activity. Students benefit from seeing the evidence of their individual contributions.

❏ Use correction tape to cover up errors and ask the student to rewrite the word or word part correctly on top of the tape. Don't let errors go unnoticed; use the moments for quick teaching points. If the student has difficulty making the correction, supply the letter or letters for the student. Take care not to embarrass or frustrate students.

We use 1" correction tape to cover up student errors and emphasize for the students that everyone makes mistakes. That's why pencils have erasers!

Supported Independent Writing

Objective

Students write complete sentences as they apply their knowledge of spelling patterns, along with the strategies of phonemic analysis and analogy, to spell both known and unknown words.

Implement Activity

When the students need practice writing sentences independently. It is a daily part of the RRI lesson in Phases 2 and 3.

Materials

- Student journals (with either lined or unlined pages)
- Pencils or fine-point markers
- 1" correction tape
- Small sticky notes or sticky tabs
- Practice papers (blank sheets of paper with students' names and the date at the top, on which students will practice writing words and work out unfamiliar words)

Procedures

1. Pass out the students' journals and practice papers. Have them open the journals to the next blank page. This can be done efficiently if you use a sticky note or sticky tab to mark the page each day. Quickly write the date at the top of each student's page. Journals should be laid flat on the table in front of each student. The practice papers are blank sheets of paper on which the students will write words in Elkonin Sound Boxes (Elkonin, 1973). (See Teaching Sound Analysis, p. 180.) Students will also practice writing high-frequency words on the practice paper, try writing words they think they know but are unsure of, write known words that have patterns similar to the unknown words they are trying to spell, or try other similar strategies.

2. Ask the Star Reader a question related to the comprehension skill you emphasized in the new book during supported reading. The sentence should be in the student's own words. It should *not* be a memorized phrase from the book. Offer support as needed as the Star Reader composes a complete sentence to answer your question. *All students in the group will write the same sentence.*

3. Ask the students to recite the sentence three times—one time softly, one time louder, and one time fast (or in other ways, to add variety). The purpose of repeating the sentence is to help the students remember it as they record it word by word.

4. Have the students write the sentence in their journals. Monitor closely and use correction tape to hide errors. Use a new page in the journal each day. If you put the date at the top of each page you can use the writing samples to document student growth.

5. If students make errors, stop them immediately and take one of these actions:
   - Teach the word patterns.
   - Use Elkonin Sound Boxes to scaffold the students as they attempt to apply phonemic analysis to spell words. (See Teaching Sound Analysis, p. 180.)
   - Point out a word the students may already know that has a spelling pattern similar to the one they are trying to spell. For example, a student may not know how to write the word *around*. The student may be able to spell the first two letters but might not remember how to write /ou/ as in *out*. If the student knows how to write *out*, have the student write it on the practice paper, circle or underline the two letters that make the sound /ou/, and then try putting that sound into the word *around*.
   - Tell students any of the letters that they have not learned and words with irregular spellings. The goal is to ensure that the final representation is correct by having the students contribute as much as possible *without becoming frustrated*.

Scaffolding During Supported Independent Writing

A student is trying to write the word *chewing* and has written *chooing*. The teacher says, "Good job remembering that *oo* makes the sound /oo/. There is another way to write /oo/ like in *new*." The teacher shows the student how to write the sound /oo/ with *ew*. Then the teacher uses correction tape to cover the student's error and has the student correct the word *chewing*.

Prompting During Supported Independent Writing

A student wants to write the word *candy*. The teacher asks, "Do you know how to write *can*? Go ahead and write *can*. Great. Now say the word *candy* slowly. What's the next sound you hear? Yes, you hear /d/. Now, the last letter makes the sound /ē/ at the end of words. It is the letter *y*."

6. Ask students to read the sentence to themselves before reading it to you so that they learn to edit their writing. (See Teaching Students to Edit Their Writing on page 185.) Then ask each student to read his or her sentence to you fluently.

7. Some students may write a second sentence as time allows.

8. *Optional:* Ask students to read random words that they may have written either in the sentence or on the practice paper. Students may then read the sentence again fluently.

9. Each day, send the practice paper home with the student along with the books he or she has checked out. If you are providing large ziplock bags for the students to use to transport books to and from school, simply fold the practice papers and put them into the bags. You may suggest that students practice words on the practice paper at home, if appropriate.

Prompts

Prompt students to use what they know to spell unfamiliar words:
- "What letter makes that sound?"
- "What do you hear?
- "What do you hear next?"
- "Say it slowly and write the sounds."

Prompt students to self-monitor and self-correct errors:
- "Does that look right?"
- "Check it."
- "Read it with your finger and see if it's right."
- "There is a letter missing. Say it slowly and see if you can tell what is missing."

- Explicitly teach the process of writing words using phonemic analysis by modeling, leading the students through the process, and scaffolding them as they apply the strategy.

Note

❑ You can make student journals by simply stapling together or binding together pieces of paper. The pages may be lined or unlined. For students who are just learning to form their letters, it can be helpful to use paper with appropriate handwriting guide lines.

You can start off the year using pencils for writing and later change to fine-point markers (or use markers right away). The markers provide an incentive for students. Students need to practice good writing skills, and they use pencils for the majority of writing in the classroom, so markers are a novelty.

We usually make student journals using a binding machine with plastic binding combs. Journals can also be bound using metal rings like those used for keyrings, or you may keep each journal in a small 3-ring binder. When pages are stapled together they can be hard to fold flat to expose a new page.

Use correction tape, which is available at office supply stores, to cover errors when students write with markers. This also keeps students from erasing and making a mess or tearing the paper when they write with pencils. Correction tape will become an important tool for scaffolding students when they try to spell words.

You may opt to review or "test" words or letters learned during the **WORD WORK** portion of the lesson, or words that have been hard to remember or troublesome, before or after the sentence is written. If so, use the practice paper.

It can be helpful to have students progress though the sentence together, one word at a time (eg., everyone writes "The," then everyone writes "dog"), particularly in the earlier stages of RRI, and beyond for students who tend to be impulsive.

Teaching Sound Analysis

Objective

The students will use phonemic analysis to spell unfamiliar words.

Implement Activity

When students need instruction and scaffolding in order to apply phonemic analysis to spell unfamiliar words.

Materials

- Whiteboard, dry-erase marker, and eraser
- Student journals and practice papers
- Pencils or fine-point markers
- *Optional:* Plastic markers (disks, cubes, or other manipulatives)

Overview

Elkonin Sound Boxes (Elkonin, 1973) are used to provide a framework for scaffolding words the students are learning to spell. In the context of writing connected text, students will apply the skills in the **WORD WORK** activities Elkonin Sound Boxes Without Print, Elkonin Sound Boxes With Print, and Listen and Spell. Review the procedures for Elkonin Sound Boxes with Print and Listen and Spell (see pages 54 and 66, respectively). Students should have practiced those activities repeatedly during **WORD WORK** before they attempt them in supported writing.

Procedures

1. To implement sound analysis in **SUPPORTED WRITING**, begin by modeling the strategy with the whole group, using a whiteboard. Choose a word that contains four or fewer phonemes (sounds) and that contains letter-sounds the students know. On the whiteboard, draw a series of boxes, one box for each *sound* (*not* each letter) in the word.
2. Model by saying, "I am writing a sentence, and I want to write the word *frog*, but I don't know how to spell it. I'm going to use sound boxes to help me figure out the sounds in *frog*." Say the word *frog* slowly so that each phoneme can be heard. With your index finger, pull an imaginary plastic marker into each box as you say the sound that corresponds to it. Then say, "I hear the sound /f/ in this box [pointing to the first box]. So we need to write the letter *f* in the box to stand for /f/." If one of the students knows how to record the sound /f/, have the student come up to the whiteboard and write the letter in the first box. Proceed through the rest of the word in the same way. Then read the word and blend the sounds in the boxes to model

checking the word to be sure that it sounds right. Provide guided practice by drawing sound boxes on individual whiteboards and having the students "pull the sounds into the boxes" in words you choose. The easiest words are those with continuous sounds rather than stop sounds (see the Pronunciation Guide in the Appendix). Repeat this activity on several successive days to be sure that students are comfortable with the process.

3. Transfer the activity to the students' writing. For the first several days, continue to implement this as a group activity. As students are writing the sentence composed by the Star Reader in their journals, when they come to a word they don't know how to spell, draw sound boxes on your whiteboard to represent the number of sounds in the word. (*Note*: If the word is highly irregular, contains many sounds and sound combinations that the students do not know, or contains more than five phonemes, do not draw sound boxes for it. Simply write the word on your whiteboard to supply it to the students.) If the word is appropriate for sound boxes, have the students take turns coming up to the whiteboard, "pulling the sounds into the boxes," and recording the sounds they know. Scaffold as necessary, and supply any letters the students do not know.

4. Once students are comfortable with the process, transfer it to students' practice papers. When an individual student has difficulty recording the sounds in words, draw sound boxes for that word on the student's practice paper. Have the student "pull down" the sounds in the word using one index finger. It may be helpful to have him or her use real plastic markers at first, as described in the **WORD WORK** activity Elkonin Sound Boxes Without Print (page 37). Later, have the student pull imaginary markers into the boxes as the student says the word slowly. Scaffold the student's attempts to record each sound of the word in the correct box. Supply any unknown letters or letter combinations and any silent letters. Correct student errors so that the final product is the correctly spelled word. Often, a student records a sound using a "legal" way to spell that sound but not the proper spelling for the word the student is trying to write. For example, the student may spell the word *rain* as *r-a-n-e*. Say, "You are exactly right. That is one way to write /ā/. You are so smart to remember the silent *e* that can make the *a* say its name. But in the word *rain*, we spell /ā/ like this." Write the word correctly.

5. When recording a phoneme (sound) that is represented by more than one letter (such as *th-*, *sh-*, and *er*), write the full letter combination for that phoneme in *one* box (see Table 5.2). But be sure that each letter in a consonant blend (such as *bl-*, *sr-*, *tr-*, and so on) has its *own* sound box, since you can hear each sound in the blend individually.

TABLE 5.2

Use One Box for Each Sound in the Word

th	i	s

eigh	t

s	t	r	ee	t

6. When students are consistently successful in using sound boxes as a framework for recording the sounds they hear in words, take away the boxes and conduct the activity using the procedures in the activity Listen and Spell in **WORD WORK** (page 66). This activity describes a strategy in which students "stretch" words, saying them slowly, in order to hear and record the phonemes in the words. When students use the listen and spell strategy in supported writing, have them try out words on their practice papers before writing them in their journals.

TABLE 5.3

**Sound Boxes
for "Little"**

l	i	tt	le

Writing the
Sounds for "Little"

Students have trouble writing the word *little* in their journals. Stop all students and say, "Let's all say the word *little* slowly." Write four sound boxes on each student's practice paper (see Table 5.3). Say, "Say the sounds slowly and pull down the sounds. Write the sounds you hear. Good, you heard the sounds /l/, /i/, /t/, and /l/. Now let me show you how the /t/ sound looks in this word. There are two *t*'s in this word." If needed, tell students there is a silent *e* with the *l* to make *le* at the end of the word *little*.

Prompts

- When students use sound boxes, say, "Say the word slowly and pull down the sounds." Then say, "What sound did you hear in this box? Good. Write that sound."

- Say the word slowly along with the student, emphasizing the sounds the student is having difficulty hearing.
- Provide a model for letters the student does not know how to write.
- Teach letter formation as needed, and have the student practice on the practice paper.
- Sometimes it may be necessary for you to gently place your hand on top of the student's hand and assist the student in "pulling" each sound into the boxes.

In the early lessons, we tell the students that there are extra letters that they can't hear in a word but that those letters make the word "look right." For example, if the student has not yet learned the silent *e* rule and records the word *came* as *c-a-m*, we add the silent *e* at the end and tell the student that it makes the word look right. Later, when the student has learned about the silent *e* spelling of long vowel sounds, we prompt the student to apply the rule to correct his or her own spelling.

Use sound boxes and the listen and spell strategy whenever you can. They are powerful teaching tools that support the development of phonemic awareness, spelling, and decoding.

Don't forget to praise the students for specific things they do well when they are writing. Writing a sentence from beginning to end is hard work for many struggling readers.

Later on in the year, students will be able to write more than one sentence. Students always do the first sentence together, and if time allows they may each write an additional sentence that they compose.

Phases 2, 3

Teaching Students to Edit Their Writing

Objective

Students will employ a consistent editing strategy independently after they have completed a written product, independently identifying and correcting errors.

Implement Activity

Early in Phase 2 and whenever the self-monitoring and self-correction of writing errors needs to be reinforced.

Materials

- Whiteboard and two different colors of dry-erase markers
- Student journals
- Pencils or fine-point markers
- Chart tablet
- 1" correction tape
- Editing Countdown Poster (provided in the Appendix)

Procedures for Introducing the Editing Countdown Strategy

1. Tell students that you are going to teach them how to edit their writing after they complete a sentence. Explain that editing means checking their writing to be sure certain things are correct. Tell students that good writers edit their writing and correct their own mistakes.
2. Tell students that when they finish a sentence, they will always do the editing countdown, just like astronauts count down before the spaceship blasts off.
3. Write the numbers *5, 4, 3, 2, 1* on the whiteboard in one color. You will use a different color marker to write words next to each number as you introduce each step of the editing countdown strategy.
4. Tell students that each time they write a sentence in their journals, they will do the editing countdown to be sure that the sentence is ready to blast off. Remind them that it is important that they learn to check their own writing, just as good writers do.
5. Next to the number *5*, write the words *Capital Letters*. Read the words to the students. Tell students that the first thing they will do when they have finished writing a sentence is to check to be sure the first word and other important words in the sentence start with capital letters. Ask students whether they know what kinds of words might start with capital letters. Prompt them to recall (or tell them) that

names of people, pets, and cities start with capital letters. You may also discuss capitalizing the pronoun *I*, as well as the days of the week and/or months of the year. Also tell them to be sure that there are no capital letters where they do not belong.

6. Next to the number *4*, write the word *Punctuation*. Read the word to the students and tell them that the next part of the countdown is to check to be sure every sentence ends with the correct punctuation. If the word *punctuation* is unfamiliar to students, teach them that it means the periods, question marks, and other kinds of marks writers use. Remind them that most sentences end with a period and that questions end with question marks. If they have learned about the use of the exclamation mark to show excitement, it should be included in your explanation.

7. Next to the number *3*, write *Spaces*. Read the word to the students and ask them what they think they will check in this part of the countdown. Emphasize that it is important to be sure that there are spaces between the words they write so that others can read what they have written.

8. Next to the number *2*, write *Spelling*. Read the word to the students and tell them that it means to check the words they have written to be sure that they are spelled correctly.

9. Next to the number *1*, write *Sounds Right*. Read the phrase to the students and say that the last step in the Editing Countdown is to read the sentence to be sure that it sounds right. They should read each word they wrote and make sure they did not skip any words or put in any extra words. If they did, the sentence would sound funny. It wouldn't sound right.

10. *Under* the number *1*, write *Blast Off!* and say (pointing to each number as you review) that when they have checked the *Capital Letters*, *Punctuation*, *Spaces*, and *Spelling* in their sentences and have made sure the sentences *sound right*, then their sentences are ready to blast off like a rocket. Other people will be able to read the sentences and understand what the students wrote.

11. Show the students the Editing Countdown Poster and mount it in front of them. Orally compose a sentence that you will write on the chart tablet. Write the sentence, making some errors. Ask the students not to point out any of your errors yet. Tell the students that you are going to do the countdown.

12. Point to the number *5* on the poster and model checking the sentence you wrote for correct use of capital letters. Provide a think-aloud while you are checking to make sure that the first word of the sentence and any other important words, such as names, are written with capital letters. Correct any errors in the sentence.

13. Then point to the number *4* on the poster and tell students that you are going to check the punctuation. Provide a think-aloud while you are checking to make sure the sentence ends with the right

punctuation. Tell students you are checking to be sure there is a period at the end of the sentence. Correct any errors.

14. Next point to the number *3* and ask students what they think you will check next. As you think aloud, check to be sure that the sentence you wrote has enough spacing between words. Correct any errors.

15. Point to the number *2* on the poster and tell students that you are going to check the spelling. Provide a think-aloud while you are checking to make sure each word looks right. Correct any errors.

16. Ask the students what you should check next. Point to the number *1* and guide students to understand that you will check to be sure that the sentence sounds right. Reread the sentence while pointing to each word to be sure that you have not skipped a word or substituted an incorrect word.

Procedures for Practicing the Editing Countdown Strategy

1. Mount the Editing Countdown Poster permanently in a place where students can easily refer to it. (If you share your intervention space with other teachers, you may choose to copy the poster on stiff card stock and set it on an easel each day.)

2. The day after you introduce the strategy, have the students write a sentence in their journals, as usual. Guide them to apply the editing countdown to edit their writing. Go through the strategy step by step and provide plenty of support.

3. Repeat this for several days, until the students begin to apply the strategy more and more independently.

4. Monitor students each time they write during **SUPPORTED WRITING** to be sure they employ this strategy. Remind them to "do the countdown!" if they do not edit independently.

Scaffolding Students As They Apply the Editing Countdown Strategy

After a student has written a sentence that contains an error, the teacher watches to see whether the student will apply the editing strategy. The teacher will offer praise if the strategy is applied independently, especially if an error is corrected.

If there is an error that the student does not locate, the teacher will prompt the student, "You remembered to do the countdown and check your sentence, but you missed something. Check number 5 on the countdown poster. What do we check on number 5? Yes, number 5 reminds you to check for capital letters. Do you have a capital letter at the beginning of the sentence? Yes, you do. Are there any other words in the sentence that should begin with capital letters? Yes, the word *Sandy* is the dog's name. We know that a name should start with a capital letter. Good job of fixing up that word. Next time, remember to check all of the words in the sentence to see whether any of them might need capital letters."

Prompts

Prompting has a critical role in supporting the application of the strategy. The following prompts can be used to scaffold its implementation:

- Do the countdown!
- Your sentence is not quite ready to blast off.
- You need to recheck number *4, Punctuation.*
- Check number *1* in the countdown. What does number *1* remind us to do? Yes, there is something about your sentence that does not sound right. It doesn't make sense. See if you can find it.
- Touch each word as you read it and see if you can find the one that doesn't look quite right.
- There is a letter missing in this word. Say it slowly and see if you can tell what is missing.

- Model and reteach any part of the strategy as needed.

Note

❑ The first time you teach this editing countdown strategy, it will take the entire 10 minutes designated for **SUPPORTED WRITING**. The students will not write in their journals on that day. You may need to take time from **SUPPORTED WRITING** in other lessons to practice the strategy until the students are comfortable with it.

Students frequently develop habits of leaving off periods and capital letters and of rushing through the writing without checking their work. Teachers find themselves reminding the same students day after day, "What did you forget at the end of the sentence?" or using a similar prompt. This causes the students to depend on us as teachers rather than become independent writers. Teaching the editing countdown strategy is powerful for turning over the process to the students.

You may want to teach only one part of the strategy at a time and have students practice applying just that one strategy independently before you add the next one. For example, students could learn to check for capital letters and punctuation for a week or so before they learn to also check spacing.

This strategy can be turned into a game, with points for the students who remember to do the countdown by themselves without being reminded, or for those who find and correct errors independently.

Hold students accountable once you have taught the strategy. Emphasize that they are not "done" until they have checked their work. Cue them nonverbally by pointing to the poster. If they have problems locating errors, reteach the strategy, but don't fall into the trap of always checking the sentence for them.

Students will not recognize all of their spelling errors. If a student has problems locating a misspelled word, tell the student that there is one misspelled word and ask which word doesn't look right or point out the error word and ask if they can fix it.

If a student can't locate an error, don't allow the student to become frustrated. Point out the error and scaffold the student as he or she corrects the error.

Phases 2, 3

Writing in Response to Text

Objective

Students write a complete sentence about a topic related to a book they have read.

Implement Activity

To support reading comprehension following a **SUPPORTED READING** activity in which students were taught to apply specific comprehension skills.

Materials

- Student journals
- Pencils or fine-point markers
- Chart paper and standard markers
- New book

Procedures

1. Before the lesson, take a moment to look over the new book that will be introduced that day and to write a question that you will ask the Star Reader during **SUPPORTED WRITING**. The question should relate to the book introduced in **SUPPORTED READING**. If a certain comprehension skill was emphasized during **SUPPORTED READING**, the question should be related to the application of the same skill (see pages 163-168).

2. When this activity is introduced, and at other times as needed, show the students how to write a sentence that answers the comprehension question you ask. Model on chart paper. Use a think-aloud to model the process you use to arrive at the answer to the question. Demonstrate writing a complete thought that addresses the question.

3. Have students say the sentence three times as a group. Students repeat the sentence more than once by reading the sentence one time softly, one time louder, and one time fast.

4. Have each student write the same sentence in his or her own journal.

5. After the students become familiar with how to write in response to the text, follow the procedures in the Supported Independent Writing activity (page 176), and have the Star Reader compose the sentence in response to your question about the text.

6. Always praise students by pointing out some specific effective strategy or behavior they used when they wrote their sentence.

Writing in Response to Text

"Let's think about the book we just read, *My Wonderful Chair* (Cowley, 1994). The little girl in the story imagined the chair was a lot of different things. Can you think of different things the chair was in the story? Yes, once the chair was a throne, or a place where a queen or king might sit. Another time the chair was a stage for the girl to dance on. All of you have remembered many details from the story. Now think about the part of the story you liked and why you liked it."

The Star Reader composes a sentence: *I like the chair when it is a spaceship because it can fly.* Say, "You did a good job of making up a sentence that told the part of the story you liked and why you liked it. Everyone say the sentence one time softly." Students repeat sentence.

"Now say it one time louder." Students repeat sentence. "Now one time fast." Students repeat sentence.

"Now write the sentence." Monitor and scaffold students with the more difficult words.

7. Here are examples of comprehension questions to ask in early lessons:
   – What part of the story did you like and why?
   – What part of the story did you think was funny?
   – Tell me one thing you did or didn't like about the book.
   – What did [character from book] do in the story?
   – How do you think [character from book] felt at the end of the story? Why?

8. Here are examples of higher-level comprehension questions you can use later in later lessons:
   – What happened after the dog saved the women from the fire?
   – What happened after the dad found the world's most perfect picnic spot?
   – What happened before the boy found the bed he wanted to sleep in for the night?
   – Do you think the giant was sad, mad, afraid, happy, or grumpy? Why do you think the giant was so grumpy?
   – What did [character from book] want to do in this story?

9. If your focus during **Supported Reading** was on story structure elements, use questions that focus on them:
   - Who were the two most important characters in the book?
   - What was the setting at the beginning of the story?
   - What was Mark's problem in the story?
   - What did Mark do first to try to solve the problem?
   - What was the solution? How did the story end? Was the problem solved?

Prompt

- If a student reads a sentence to you with a word missing, say, "Something doesn't sound right. Go back and check your words," or "Go back and find out what is missing."

- You may give hints about the book, or students may take a quick look at the book to help them remember or check an answer. *Do not let students copy a sentence word by word from the book.*

When students come to words they don't know how to spell, they should be using the strategies taught to them to figure out the word. They should not copy from the book unless it is an unusual name or spelling.

Be sure that the Star Reader puts the sentence into his or her own words rather than reciting a line from the story. Be sure that it makes sense.

Putting It All Together

This chapter will help you understand how the pieces of
Responsive Reading Instruction (RRI) fit together. You
will learn in greater detail the steps involved in planning
the RRI lesson and will find examples of lesson plans for
different times of the school year. More information about
how to make RRI work is also provided, including:

- Setting students up for success
- Setting up the RRI room
- Staying organized
- Behavior management strategies
- Teaching students to follow routines
- Helping students become independent readers
  and writers
- Helping students who don't make
  adequate progress
- Reflecting on your own teaching

Planning the RRI Lesson

As mentioned in the Introduction, RRI is supported by research when it is implemented according to the procedures described in this book. If teachers depart from these procedures, the results may not be as strong as those reported in the research. However, most of the individual activities in this book can be incorporated into regular classroom reading lessons, providing support for struggling readers within the classroom setting.

As you have seen, *Responsive Reading Instruction* provides a "menu," or list, of activities for each part of the RRI lesson. To implement the intervention as it was implemented in the research described in the Introduction, you must select activities from these lists as you complete the Responsive Reading Instruction Lesson Plan (provided in the Appendix). The Introduction provides eight steps to follow in planning the RRI lesson. These steps are described in more detail here.

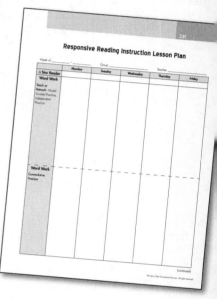

1. ***Study assessment data and Anecdotal Records from previous lessons to determine the reading level, strengths, and needs of the Star Reader for the lesson you are planning.*** As you plan, imagine the lesson activities from the Star Reader's point of view. What will be hard? What will be easy?

   Responsive Reading Instruction cannot be *responsive* without constant monitoring of what the students know and what they need to learn. The **ASSESSMENT** component is absolutely critical to the RRI program. Each daily lesson should be planned based on information you collect from Anecdotal Records and assessments in the previous lessons. Remember, each day, one of the students in each group will take a turn being the Star Reader, and the lesson plan is directed specifically toward the strengths and needs of this student. As you begin to examine your assessment records, look at the Star Reader's most recent assessments:

   – *Letter-Sound Assessment:* Look for letter-sounds that the Star Reader may be confusing or may be having trouble remembering. Reteach and review these as needed. You may also introduce one new letter-sound (or letter combination) during the lesson. Use the Sound Pronunciation Guide (provided in the Appendix) to help you determine a sequence for introducing letters (or follow the sequence in your core reading program). The Sound Pronunciation Guide separates sounds that may be confusing to students if they are taught too close together. You can also get information about letter-sounds the students need to either practice or learn from your Anecdotal Records and Assessments of Reading Accuracy. The following questions should guide your planning for letter-sound knowledge:

- Which letter-sounds (or letter combinations) do the students need to learn and practice?
- Which letter-sounds (or letter combinations) does the Star Reader need to learn and practice?
- Which of these elements will be the most useful for reading new words?

– *High-Frequency-Word Assessment:* Look for high-frequency words that the Star Reader may be confusing or may be having trouble remembering. Reteach and review these as needed. You may also introduce one new high-frequency word during the lesson. Provide practice in recognizing high-frequency words nearly every day. The goal is for students to recognize these words instantly when they see them. You can also get information about words the students need to either practice or learn from your Anecdotal Records and Assessments of Reading Accuracy. The following questions should guide your planning for high-frequency-word knowledge:

- Which high-frequency words do the students need to practice (in reading and in writing)?
- Which high-frequency words does the Star Reader need to practice (in reading and in writing)?
- Which of these high-frequency words will be the most useful for reading today's book?

– *Assessment of Reading Accuracy:* Examine the Star Reader's most recent Assessment of Reading Accuracy Form (or two to three of the student's most recent assessments). Examine the kinds of errors the student made, and look for knowledge and skills that need to be taught. The following questions should guide your planning based on the Assessments of Reading Accuracy:

- Was the book on the student's Instructional or Independent reading level? If not, what was hard?
- Was there some type of pattern in the kinds of errors the student made? Does the student leave off endings, miss words with certain letters or combinations of letters, or miss high-frequency "sight" words?

- What does the student do when words in the text are hard to read? Does the student: (1) successfully use the RRI decoding strategy? (2) use the strategy sometimes but not at other times? (3) try to sound out words but struggle to come up with the correct word because of incorrect letter-sound correspondences or because of a problem with blending the sounds together after saying the sound for each letter? (4) randomly guess at words, or start words with the correct letter-sounds and guess the rest? (5) skip words that are hard? (6) wait to be told words that are hard?
- What makes a book hard or easy for the Star Reader?
- What are one or two things that will be the most useful for the Star Reader to learn and practice?

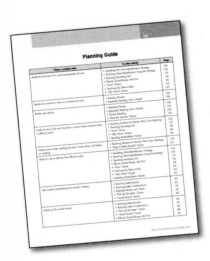

- *Oral Reading Fluency Assessment:* Examine the most recent assessment of oral reading fluency to find out whether the student needs to become more fluent and to try to pinpoint things that are slowing down the reading. The following questions should guide your planning based on the Oral Reading Fluency Assessments:
  - Does the Star Reader read one word at a time or group words into phrases?
  - Is the reading slow and labored or smooth and natural?
  - Are there words or phonic elements that seem to be slowing the student down?
- *Anecdotal Records:* Examine your Anecdotal Records for the past two or three lessons. What notes did you make about student successes and struggles?

2. *As you plan each part of the RRI lesson, use the answers to the questions presented in Step 1 to guide you as you choose from the activities in this book.* (It may be helpful to refer to Table I.1, page 8.) Choose those that are most appropriate for the Star Reader and for the group. Note that certain activities, such as those in **Supported Reading**, occur in some format during every lesson. Each activity has suggestions for when it should be implemented. See the Planning Guide on page 311 in the Appendix for more suggestions.

3. *Plan the* **Word Work** *component by first choosing the objectives for the lesson (what you want the students to learn) and then choosing from the list of activities that are likely to support the students in meeting the objectives.* Remember that the objectives for **Word Work** (such as learning the sound of the letter *m* or sounding out multisyllabic words) are based on two things: (1) the results of student assessments and Anecdotal Records and (2) your knowledge of which phonemic awareness activities, word reading or spelling skills, phonic elements, and/or high-frequency words are more useful at that point in the students' development. The **Word Work** chapter includes lists of phonological awareness activities, letter-sounds and letter combinations, and high-frequency words to

guide you. See, in particular, the Sound Pronunciation Guide (Table 1.1, page 25).

- *Plan for cumulative practice as well as new learning.* For struggling readers, a rough guide is that 80 percent of the **Word Work** time should be used to practice elements and skills the students have already been taught. Across time, your plans should show that something has been introduced in one lesson and then reinforced and practiced frequently in the following weeks.
- *Introduce no more than one to two new items of learning in a single lesson.* This may be one new letter-sound and one new high-frequency word or a new strategy (such as a phonemic awareness activity, sounding out words, or reading multisyllabic words).
- Try to include both reading and writing activities in each lesson.
- See **Word Work** for other hints about planning this important part of the RRI lesson.

4. *Select one to two books the Star Reader will read during the fluency component, and plan your focus for this part of the lesson (Phases 2 and 3).*

5. *Select the assessment you will administer to the Star Reader from the previous day.* Choose the assessment that will give you the most beneficial information as you plan future lessons for this student.

6. *Choose the new book for the Star Reader to read during* **Supported Reading.** Guidelines are provided in the **Supported Reading** chapter. Plan the book introduction and your comprehension focus.

7. *Plan the question you will ask the Star Reader in order to guide him or her in composing a sentence during* **Supported Writing.** Remember that this question should have the same focus as your book introduction and comprehension question during supported reading.

8. *Assemble and organize your materials and forms.* RRI teachers have consistently found that organization is the key to success! It is much easier to keep students engaged in learning when the lesson moves smoothly, at a brisk pace, from one activity to the next.

Completing the RRI Lesson Plan

Following is an example of an RRI lesson plan that shows activities for one RRI group for one week at a time. This will help to give you the big picture of how your instruction is progressing from day to day, but you should *plan only one to three days at a time* and base each daily plan on assessments and observations from the previous days. You cannot be responsive to students' instructional needs if you decide in advance what they will learn.

To complete the Responsive Reading Instruction Lesson Plan, see the form provided in the Appendix. (*Note:* This form can be copied front and back so that it will fit on one piece of paper.)

1. Complete the information at the top of the Responsive Reading Instruction Lesson Plan form, and fill in the name of the Star Reader for each day (see Table 6.1). Remember that a different student will be the Star Reader each day. Rotate the Star Reader designation continually through the group, in the same order. If a student is absent, go to the next student in the rotation. You may return to the student who was absent as soon as that student returns to school, or simply pick them up again when it is their next turn to be the Star Reader. (Note: RRI teachers find it best to complete plans in pencil so that changes can be made in case of absences or other unforeseen occurrences.)

TABLE 6.1

Top Part of Responsive Reading Instruction Lesson Plan

Week of _11–14_ – _11–18_		Group _9:00_		Teacher _M. Smith_	
	Monday	**Tuesday**	**Wednesday**	**Thursday**	**Friday**
☆ **Star Reader**	Victor	Lamont	Nicole	Victor	Lamont

2. *Plan* WORD WORK. Plan *three to five* activities for word work each day. Plan both new instruction and review of elements and skills you have already taught. Write the list of words you will use in the activities on your lesson plan form (see Table 6.2).

3. *Plan* PRINT CONCEPTS AND FLUENCY (10 minutes with ASSESSMENT). For print concepts lessons, provide enough detail so that you know exactly which words or letters you will need. For fluency lessons, select and write down the titles of one to two books the Star Reader will read (see Table 6.3).

4. *Plan the* ASSESSMENT (10 minutes with PRINT CONCEPTS AND FLUENCY). Remember that the assessment is administered to the student who was the Star Reader *the previous day*. Write this student's name on the Responsive Reading Instruction Lesson Plan form along with the assessment you will administer. If you are doing an Assessment of Reading Accuracy or Oral Reading Fluency Assessment, write down the name of the book you will be using. (Be sure that the forms and books you will need are on a clipboard and ready to go.)

5. *Plan* SUPPORTED READING. Write the title of the book the Star Reader will read. (Remember to select this book carefully. See the SUPPORTED READING chapter for more information.) Also, plan your comprehension focus (see pages 163–168). Write out your book introduction for the comprehension focus (see Table 6.4). (*Note:* As you gain experience as an RRI teacher, you may not need to write out the introduction each time. However, it is important to do this as you are learning to teach RRI. Your lesson will flow well, your pacing will

TABLE 6.2

Lesson Plan for Word Work

Week of ___11–14___ – ___11–18___   Group ___9:00___   Teacher ___M. Smith___

	Monday	Tuesday	Wednesday	Thursday	Friday
☆Star Reader	Victor	Lamont	Nicole	Victor	Lamont
Word Work Teach or Reteach: Model, Guided Practice, Independent Practice	**Teach:** Letter Combination: *ar* Elkonin Sound Boxes with Print: *tar, bar, jar, art, star, park, bark*	**Teach:** High-Frequency Word: *some* **Reteach:** Elkonin Sound Boxes with Print: *tar, bar, jar, park, star, dark*		**Teach:** Write High-Frequency Words: *what, some*	**Teach:** Letter Combination: *ow* (as in *cow*)
Word Work Cummulative Practice:	"Beat the Teacher" **Game:** Read high-frequency words List 2 (2 seconds) **Word Pattern Charts:** *sh* (cumulative practice/review)— *she, shop, ship, shin, shape, sheep, short, shake*	"Beat the Teacher" **Game:** Read high-frequency words List 2 + *some* (2 seconds) **Listen and Spell:** *part, dark, shark, shop, ship*	Word Linking: *car, tar, star, start, starting, part* "Beat the Teacher" **Game:** Read high-frequency words List 2 + *some* (2 seconds) **Silly Word Game:** *posk, sprim, zomp, glop* **Listen and Spell:** *art, park, dish, mash, marsh*	Word Linking: *far, farm, tar, tarp, target* Point Game: (review) *fish, shin, ship, shop, shark, sharp, flash, marsh, mark, marker* Letter Formation: *d*	Elkonin Sound Boxes with Print: *cow, now, pow, plow* **Write High-Frequency Words:** *what, some* Letter Formation: *d* "Beat the Teacher" **Game:** Read high-frequency words List 2 + *some* (2 seconds)

TABLE 6.3

Lesson Plan for Print Concepts/ Fluency

Week of ___11–14___ – ___11–18___   Group ___9:00___   Teacher ___M. Smith___

Print Concepts/ Fluency	Repeated Reading With a Model: *Baby's Birthday,* Level: D *Danny's Dollars,* Level: D	Reading Phrases: Phrase list and phrases on cards Frame phrases in the book: *What a Bad Dog!* Level: D	Repeated Reading With a Model: *Wake Up, Mom,* Level: D *What a Bad Dog!,* Level: D	Repeated Reading With a Model: *Danny's Dollars,* Level: D *The Hungry Kitten,* Level: D	Reading Phrases: Repeated Reading With a Model: *Danny's Dollars,* Level: D *Lizard Loses His Tail,* Level: D
Assessment	Letter-Sound	Letter-Sound	Reading Accuracy: *Lizard Loses His Tail,* Level: D	Reading Accuracy: *My Cat's Surprise,* Level: D	Reading Accuracy: *Father Bear Goes Fishing,* Level: D
Student:	Nicole	Victor	Lamont	Nicole	Victor

improve, and you will have a cohesive comprehension focus if you plan in advance.)

6. *Plan* SUPPORTED WRITING. The only planning you can do for this part of the lesson is to write out the question that you will use to focus the Star Reader's composition of a sentence. Remember that it should have the same comprehension focus as the book introduction in SUPPORTED READING (see Table 6.4). During the lesson, when the Star Reader composes the sentence, write it down on your lesson plan so that you will have a record of it.

TABLE 6.4

Lesson Plan for Supported Reading and Writing

Week of 11–14 – 11–18 Group 9:00 Teacher M. Smith				
Print Concepts/ Fluency	Repeated Reading With a Model: *Baby's Birthday,* Level: D *Danny's Dollars,* Level: D	Reading Phrases: Phrase list and phrases on cards **Frame phrases in the book:** *What a Bad Dog!* Level: D	Repeated Reading With a Model: *Wake Up, Mom,* Level: D *What a Bad Dog!,* Level: D	Repeated Reading With a Model: *Danny's Dollars,* Level: D *The Hungry Kitten,* Level: D	Reading Phrases: Repeated Reading With a Model: *Danny's Dollars,* Level: D *Lizard Loses His Tail,* Level: D
Assessment	Letter-Sound	Letter-Sound	Reading Accuracy: *Lizard Loses His Tail,* Level: D	Reading Accuracy: *My Cat's Surprise,* Level: D	Reading Accuracy: *Father Bear Goes Fishing,* Level: D
Student:	Nicole	Victor	Lamont	Nicole	Victor
Supported Reading Comprehension Focus and Introduction	In most stories, the characters have some kind of problem. There is something wrong or something they want. In this story, the little boy has a problem. Something happens to him when he helps his Mom. Let's read to find out what happens.	Yesterday we said that in most stories the characters have some kind of problem. Can you guess the problem in this story? I wonder whether anyone else in the story might have a problem.	The children in this story are looking for something. They have a problem because they can't find it.	"Does It Make Sense? Game There are three characters in this story. They are Mother Bear, Father Bear, and Baby Bear. Let's see what Mother Bear and Baby Bear do when Father Bear goes fishing.	These children are going to help a lot of animals. Let's see which animals they help first and which ones they help after that.
New Book	*Tom Is Brave,* Level: D	*Lizard Loses His Tail,* Level: D	*My Cat's Surprise,* Level: D	*Father Bear Goes Fishing,* Level: D	*Bread,* Level: D
Supported Writing Comprehension Question	What was the little boy's problem in this story? Write student sentence here.	What was Seagull's problem in this story? Write student sentence here.	What were the children looking for in our story? What did they find? Write student sentence here.	What did the characters do at the end of this story? Write student sentence here.	What animals did the children help first in this story? Write student sentence here.

The Responsive Reading Instruction Lesson Plan looks different at different times of the school year. Here are some examples of the three different lesson plans during the three phases of the year. There are sample lesson plans for the *beginning of the year* (Phase 1) (see Table 6.5), followed by a plan for the *middle of the year* (Phase 2) (see Table 6.6), and finally, there is a plan for the *end of the year* (Phase 3) (see Table 6.7).

TABLE 6.5

Lesson Plan for Phase 1 (Page 1)

Week of ___9-8___ – ___9-12___   Group ___8:10___   Teacher ___M. Smith___

	Monday	Tuesday	Wednesday	Thursday	Friday
☆ Star Reader	Preston	Bella	Alma	Preston	Bella
Word Work — Teach or Reteach: Model, Guided Practice, Independent Practice	**Teach:** Stretching Words: *am, eat, me, if* — Mystery Word Game: *me, be, day, and, fan* — Writing High-Frequency Words: *like*	**Teach:** Letter Formation: *d* — **Reteach:** Stretching Words: *am, eat, me, if* — Mystery Word Game: *me, be, day, and, fan*	**Teach:** Syllable Identification: (need pictures) — Letter-Sound: *s*; practice with *a, t, m*	**Teach:** Elkonin Sound Boxes Without Print: (2 sounds) *am, at, ate* — "Beat the Teacher" Game: List 1 words; practice only 5–6 words	**Teach:** Letter-sounds: *i*; practice with *a, t, m, s* — **Reteach:** Elkonin Sound Boxes Without Print: (2 sounds) *egg, he, if, is*
Word Work — Cummulative Practice:	Pick Up the Letter Game: *a, t, m*	Writing High-Frequency Words: *like* — Letter Sounds: *m, a, t*	Stretching Words: *no, see, day, she* — Letter Formation: *d* — Mystery Word Game: *me, be, day, and, fan* — Writing High-Frequency Words: *like*	Letter Formation: *d* — Mystery Word Game: *tea, face, egg* — Letter-Sounds: *m, a, t*	Stretching Words: *zoo, us, by, boo* — Syllable Identification: (need pictures) — "Beat the Teacher" Game: List 1 words — Letter Formation: *d*
Print Concepts/ Fluency	Teaching Print-Related Vocabulary: (practice concept of a word: *sun,* pull letters apart; point to the first and last letters)	Teaching Print-Related Vocabulary: (practice concept of a word: *man,* pull letters apart; point to the first and last letters)	Teaching Print-Related Vocabulary: (practice concept of a word: *sun,* pull letters apart; add letters to make *sunny*; point to the first, second, third, and last letters)	Teaching Print-Related Vocabulary: (review a letter, word, and point to words in a text; point out the spaces in a book; introduce a sentence by writing one on a sentence strip)	Teaching Print-Related Vocabulary: (review a letter, word, and point to words in a text; point out the spaces in a book; review concept of sentence)
Assessment	Letter-Sound List 1	Letter-Sound List 1	Letter-Sound List 1	High-Frequency-Words List 1	High-Frequency-Words List 1
Student:	Alma	Preston	Bella	Alma	Preston

(continued)

(continued)

TABLE 6.5

Lesson Plan for Phase 1

Week of	9-8	-	9-12	Group	8:10	Teacher	M. Smith

Supported Reading Comprehension Focus and Introduction	This book is called *I Can Go!* Let's look at the things that go. Here is a motorcycle. Do you know what this is? Good. A sailboat. Here is a spaceship [point to pictures]. Pre-teach word: *in*	This book is called *Me!* Let's look at what the girl is doing in this book. Here she is eating. Now she is laughing. Let's see what else she is doing.	This book is called *What Is Red?* Do you know of some things that are red? Let's take a look to see what is red in the story. On this page it says that stop signs are red. Let's look at the next pages. Here are some balloons. What else is red? Pre-teach word: *are*	This new book is called *My Pet.* Do you have a pet? There are many types of pets. Let's take a look at what kinds of pets there are. On this page there is a fish [point to picture]. Do you know what this pet is? And this is a lizard. [Point to picture on last page.]	This is one of my favorite books because it is about a birthday cake. There are many kinds of cake. Let's see what kind of birthday cake they will bake. A yellow cake! What color is this cake? Yes! A pink cake! Who is blowing out the candle?
New Book	*I Can Go!,* Level: Rebus Book	*Me,* Level: A	*What Is Red?,* Level: B	*My Pet,* Level: Rebus Book	*The Birthday Cake,* Level: A
Supported Writing Comprehension Question	Supported Group Writing What kinds of things can you go on? Write student sentence here.	Supported Group Writing The little girl in the story was doing a lot of things. What do you like to do? Write student sentence here.	Supported Group Writing What is something that is red? Write student sentence here.	Supported Group Writing What kind of pet do you like? Write student sentence here.	Supported Group Writing Who had a birthday in our story? Write student sentence here.

TABLE 6.6

Lesson Plan for Phase 2

Week of	1-7	-	1-11	Group	8:10	Teacher	M. Smith

	Monday	**Tuesday**	**Wednesday**	**Thursday**	**Friday**
☆ **Star Reader**	Preston	Bella	Alma	Preston	Bella
Word Work Teach or Reteach: Model, Guided Practice, Independent Practice	Reteach: Teaching Letter Combinations: *ee* (with cumulative review)	Teach: Teaching Letter Combinations: *ea* (with cumulative review)	Teach: Teaching High-Frequency Words: *would, about*	Teach: Teaching Letter Combinations: *ou, ow* (with cumulative review) **Reteach:** Teaching High-Frequency Words: *would, about*	Reteach: Teaching Letter Combinations: *ou* (with cumulative review)
Word Work Cummulative Practice:	Listen and Spell: tramp, shrimp, shin Writing High-Frequency Words: *could, more* The Point Game: b<u>ee</u>f, f<u>ee</u>t, d<u>ee</u>p, sl<u>ee</u>p, sh<u>ee</u>p, sw<u>ee</u>p, gl<u>ee</u>, thr<u>ee</u>, street	Elkonin Sound Boxes with Print: words with 4 sounds Listen and Spell: *tramp, shrimp, creep, speed* "Beat the Teacher" Game: High-Frequency-Word Cards, List 3	Point Game: wh<u>ea</u>t, t<u>ea</u>ch, tr<u>ea</u>t, m<u>ee</u>ting, w<u>ee</u>kend, sn<u>ea</u>ker, k<u>ee</u>ps Word Building: *eat, heat, cheat, cheating* Word Pattern Charts: <u>ea</u> Letter-Sounds: *ur, ir, ea, ee, ay, or, oo, a_e, z, ch, sh, v, er, ing, w, ou*	Word Linking: h<u>ea</u>t, h<u>ea</u>ted, ch<u>ea</u>ter, b<u>ea</u>ter, b<u>ea</u>ting, s<u>ea</u>ting Word Sorts: *ee, ea* (make word cards or use stickies) "Beat the Teacher" Game: High-Frequency-Word Cards, List 3	Point Game: sh<u>ee</u>t, pl<u>ea</u>se, tr<u>ea</u>t, p<u>ou</u>t, sh<u>ow</u>er, n<u>ee</u>ding, cr<u>ow</u>d, dr<u>ow</u>n, sh<u>ou</u>t, sw<u>ee</u>p, street Word Sorts: *ee, ea* Listen and Spell: *shrimp, cheat*

(continued)

(continued)

TABLE 6.6

Lesson Plan for Phase 2

Week of ___1-7___ – ___1-11___ Group ___8:10___ Teacher ___M. Smith___

Print Concepts/ Fluency	Repeated Reading with a Model: *Munching Mark,* Level: G *Clever Penguins,* Level: G	Repeated Reading with a Model: *Munching Mark,* Level: G *Clever Penguins,* Level: G	Repeated Reading with a Model: *Munching Mark,* Level: G *Ben's Tooth,* Level: H	Repeated Reading with a Model: *Too Many Bones,* Level: G *Clever Penguins,* Level: G	Repeated Reading with a Model: *Munching Mark,* Level: G *Pancakes for Supper,* Level: H
Assessment	High-Frequency Words List 3	Benchmark Book Level: H	Letter-Sound List 1	Reading Accuracy *Cow Up a Tree,* Level: H	Reading Accuracy *On Top of Spaghetti,* Level: G
Student:	Alma	Preston	Bella	Alma	Preston
Supported Reading Comprehension Focus and Introduction	Events are things that happen in a story. In this story the characters are looking for a bone. What is the first event? [Look at pictures.] Ben can't find his bone. What happens second? Jip looks in his basket. Let's read to find out what happens next.	Yesterday we looked at the events in a story called *Too Many Bones.* Today we look at the events in *Pancakes for Supper.* What is the first thing they do? Mix in the flour. What is the second thing? Let's read to find out what else the girls do.	Today we are going to read a story called *Cow Up a Tree.* The cow looks sad. It *sulks* [point to the word in the story]. This means the cow is sad. What are the characters trying to do on this page? They are trying to *bulldoze* [point to the word]. This is a bulldozer [point to picture].	This book is about a meatball on top of spaghetti. It's kind of a silly book. Let's take a look at where the meatball goes. Where does it go first? It rolled off the table. We will have to find out where the meatball goes next!	Today we are going to look at a nonfiction text. Nonfiction means the book is about something real. Looking at the book, what is this book about? Do you know anything about slugs and snails? What might we find out about slugs and snails?
New Book	*Too Many Bones,* Level: G	*Pancakes for Supper,* Level: H	*Cow Up a Tree,* Level: H	*On Top of Spaghetti,* Level: G	*Slugs and Snails,* Level: H
Supported Writing Comprehension Question	What happens at the end? Does Ben find his bone? Write student sentence here.	What is the last step to make the pancakes? Write student sentence here.	What do the characters do to get the cow down? Write student sentence here.	What happened after the meatball rolled under the bush? Write student sentence here.	What is one interesting fact you learned about slugs? Write student sentence here.

TABLE 6.7

Lesson Plan for Phase 3

Week of ___4-20___ – ___4-24___   Group ___8:10___   Teacher ___M. Smith___

	Monday	**Tuesday**	**Wednesday**	**Thursday**	**Friday**
☆ **Star Reader**	Bella	Alma	Preston	Bella	Alma
Word Work — Teach or Reteach: Model, Guided Practice, Independent Practice	**Teach:** Letter Combinations: *oy* (with cumulative practice) **Reading Multisyllabic Words:** *boyfriend, basketball, goldfish, handsome, cowboy*	**Reteach:** Reading Multisyllabic Words: *boyfriend, basketball, goldfish, handsome, cowboy*	**Teach:** Letter Combinations: *oi* (with cumulative practice)	**Teach:** Multisyllabic Writing (Introduce): *inside, lipstick, letter*	**Reteach:** Reading Multisyllabic Words: *goldfish, paper, cowboy*
Word Work — Cummulative Practice:	**Word Linking:** *boy, joy, joyful, enjoy* **"Beat the Teacher" Game:** (word cards set 4)	**Letter-Sounds and Combinations:** (cumulative practice including *oy*) **Point Game:** *trout, praying, turkey, hawk, screech, shout, dirty, taste, braid, afraid* **Listen and Spell:** *thank, shiver, cowboy* **Reading Multisyllabic Words:** *number, handsome, candy, royal*	**"Beat the Teacher" Game:** (word cards set 4) **Writing High-Frequency Words:** *who, what* **Listen and Spell:** *trick, black, crash, oil, spoil* **Reading Multisyllabic Words:** *sidewalk, enjoy, maybe, pancake, playmate, banana*	**The Point Game:** (*oy, ai, oi* words) *joyful, enjoy, spoil, broil, boyfriend, stain, plain, sprain, remain* **Letter-Sounds and Combinations:** (cumulative practice including *oi, oy*) **Silly Word Game:** CCCVCC words— *scramp, sprest, splam*	**Letter-Sounds and Combinations:** (cumulative practice including *oi, oy*) **Word Building:** *boil, boiling, broil, soil, spoil, spoiling, point, oink* **Word Sorts:** Words with *oi, oy*
Print Concepts/ Fluency	**Repeated Reading with a Model (timed):** *Tess and Paddy,* Level: J. Time student for 1 minute on a text. Student practices 1–2 times reading while you listen or model. Time student again.	**Repeated Reading with a Model (timed):** *Look Out for Your Tail.* Time student for 1 minute on a text. Student practices 1–2 times reading while you listen or model. Time student again.	**Repeated Reading with a Model (timed):** *The Ant and the Dove.* Time student for 1 minute on a text. Student practices 1–2 times reading while you listen or model. Time student again.	**Repeated Reading with a Model (timed):** *Look Out for Your Tail.* Time student for 1 minute on a text. Student practices 1–2 times reading while you listen or model. Time student again.	**Repeated Reading with a Model (timed):** *The Ant and the Dove.* Time student for 1 minute on a text. Student practices 1–2 times reading while you listen or model. Time student again.
Assessment	Oral Reading Fluency *The Ant and the Dove,* Level: I	Oral Reading Fluency *Just This Once,* Level: G	Reading Accuracy *Ant and the Dove,* Level: I	Benchmark Level: J	Reading Accuracy *My Sloppy Tiger Goes to School,* Level: J
Student:	Preston	Bella	Alma	Preston	Bella

(continued)

(continued)

TABLE 6.7

Lesson Plan for Phase 3

Week of ___4-20___ – ___4-24___   Group _____8:10_____   Teacher ___M. Smith___

Supported Reading Comprehension Focus and Introduction	Our new book is called *Look Out for Your Tail.* I wonder why the worm looks scared. I see some animals that are looking for something. What do you think will happen in the book? [prediction]	In this story there is an ant that looks like it is drowning. What is the hunter going to do in the story? Why do you think that? [prediction]	A lady named Mrs. Grindy is going shopping for shoes. I wonder what kind of shoes she will buy. Why do you think that? [prediction]	Do you know what it means to be sloppy? We are going to be reading about the events of the story called *My Sloppy Tiger Goes to School.* Look at this picture. What happens first? Let's read to find out what happens next.	In this story there is a problem with Chicken Licken. I wonder what might happen to the chicken and the duck as they try to solve the problem. [problem and solution]
New Book	*Look Out for Your Tail,* Level: J	*The Ant and the Dove,* Level: I	*Mrs. Grindy's Shoes,* Level: I	*My Sloppy Tiger Goes to School,* Level: J	*Chicken Licken,* Level: I
Supported Writing Comprehension Question	What did you think would happen in our book? Were you right? What really did happen? Write student sentence here.	What did you think would happen in our book? Were you right? What really did happen? Write student sentence here.	What kind of shoes did Mrs. Grindy choose? Why did she choose those shoes? Write student sentence here.	What was the first event in the story? What happened after that? Write student sentence here.	What was the problem with Chicken Licken? How was the problem solved? Write student sentence here.

Setting Students Up for Success

In RRI, students are set up for success and then given the support they need to be successful. This is one of the most critical aspects of RRI. RRI teachers select books that are not too hard and not too easy. The trick is to select books and plan instruction in which the students can be successful nearly all of the time—with the support of the teacher.

Some key ideas to remember:

- Always model and teach the procedures before practicing a skill.
- Provide guided practice in which you scaffold students as they learn.
- Give students a chance to be self-sufficient with independent practice.
- Once you have introduced something to the students, be sure to practice it again. Plan for cumulative practice in which you incorporate the new sounds or words with sounds or words they already know.
- Introduce only two new letter-sounds a week.
- Give students repeated practice by planning the activity several days in a row to strengthen the skill. Then review the skill during the following week.
- When a student seems confused, provide scaffolding and always reteach if necessary.
- When one activity doesn't seem to work for a student, try a new approach.

- Keep an eye on the time so that you do not spend too much time on one part of the instruction or any one activity. Remember that you always have tomorrow to practice the activity again.
- Have materials ready and prepared for a lesson. Always have a whiteboard and marker ready to help scaffold a student, if needed.
- Take Anecdotal Records throughout every lesson. Look at your records and assessments daily to find out what your students need.

Setting Up the RRI Room

The physical seating arrangement is critical to the success of RRI. Students must be seated at a table with the teacher, and all students must be within the teacher's reach. The teacher must be able to point out words in each student's book, mask parts of the words to scaffold word identification, and carefully monitor each student's writing, among other things. As mentioned, the Star Reader is always seated next to the teacher, side by side at the table.

RRI teachers have found that instruction is most efficient using rectangular or round tables that are just large enough to allow the students to write in their journals without crowding each other (see Tables 6.8 and 6.9). Horseshoe-shaped tables are normally less conducive to RRI because

TABLE 6.8

Physical Setup 1

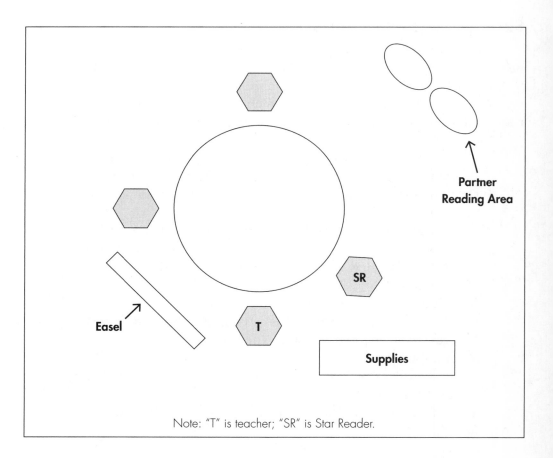

Note: "T" is teacher; "SR" is Star Reader.

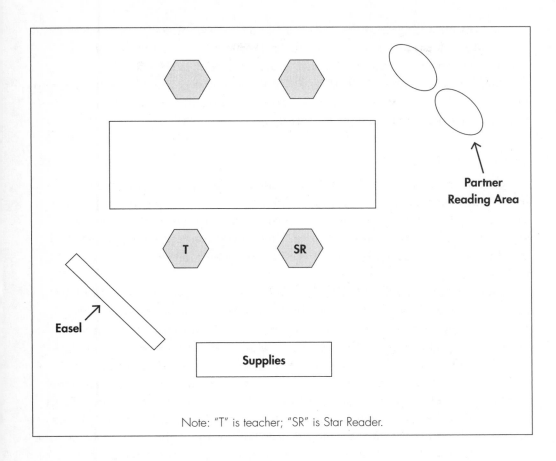

TABLE 6.9

**Physical
Setup 2**

Partner
Reading Area

T

SR

Easel

Supplies

Note: "T" is teacher; "SR" is Star Reader.

students tend to be spread too far beyond the teacher's reach, and it is awkward for the Star Reader to sit side by side with the teacher. Using student-sized tables and chairs helps students to stay on task. Students squirm less when they are comfortable and their feet can reach the floor. When they sit in chairs that are too big for them, they tend to swing their feet, and when the chairs are too small for the table (so that the table is at chest level), they tend to lay their heads on the table. Most RRI teachers are used to sitting in small chairs alongside the students and actually prefer this arrangement to having the students try to sit in chairs designed for adults or older students.

During the **Fluency** part of the RRI lesson, the students who engage in partner reading may move to an alternate space nearby if routines are established well enough for the students to stay on task (see Tables 6.8 and 6.9). It is a good idea for students to sit in chairs or on ottomans that will allow them to sit up straight rather than reclining on the floor or in beanbag chairs. Many students find it hard to keep their attention on reading if they sit on the floor or in beanbag chairs. The most important component of the **Fluency** part of the lesson is repeated oral reading practice, so keeping the students engaged in reading is the top priority. One RRI teacher in the research project described in the Introduction placed two small, cube-shaped ottomans against the wall next to a small bookshelf that was near the teaching table. This served as an activity center for partner reading.

A final reminder about the seating arrangement is that during the interactive writing activity in Phase 1 instruction, it is important for there to be ample space near the chart tablet so that students can stand alongside the tablet and contribute to the writing.

Staying Organized

One of the challenges faced by all teachers is organization. In RRI, teachers must organize books, materials, lesson plans, Anecdotal Records, and assessment forms for each group every day. Teachers have learned some tricks of the trade through experience that make it easier to stay organized, which has, in turn, allowed them to be more efficient and productive.

Use a large, loose-leaf binder for each group of students. Each binder can hold a section for weekly lesson plans and Anecdotal Records. This makes it easy to refer to the observation notes when planning future lessons. The binder should also contain a section for each student. In the student sections, collect all assessment forms and records of progress on reading accuracy and other assessments. There may also be a section documenting student attendance. As each lesson plan or assessment form (and all the other paperwork) is added to the notebook, it is simply placed on top of the ones that are already there. This puts all the records in reverse chronological order, so that it's easy to glance back at the most recent records to help plan future instruction.

It is also helpful to *have one or two clipboards for each group of students.* One clipboard holds the current lesson plan and a sheet for anecdotal observation notes. The other holds the form for the assessment that will be collected in the lesson. If this assessment is an Assessment of Reading Accuracy or Oral Reading Fluency Assessment, the book the student will read can be kept on the clipboard as well. Along with the clipboard, the teacher can *keep a separate basket of materials for each group.* The basket may contain the sets of books being used, magnetic letters and burner cover trays for preplanned lessons, word cards, and so on. It is very important to have these materials ready to go once the lesson starts so that the teacher will be able to teach the lesson at a brisk pace without the distraction of searching for materials. Keep the basket on a small student desk or table next to you. This will keep everything in easy reach and your teaching table uncluttered (see Tables 6.8 and 6.9).

This preparation and organization method also allows a teacher to work with several groups in sequence without a break. Later, during a planning period, the teacher can return to the clipboards and baskets to reorganize for the next lesson.

Behavior Management Strategies

Behavior management keeps the lesson going on the right path. At-risk students come with many needs. An RRI teacher's role is to maintain a positive environment with all of the students actively engaged in learning throughout every lesson. There are some simple things that can be done to facilitate positive behavior. This section includes a description of some simple behavior management strategies that teachers have found useful in supporting the positive, active participation of students in the RRI lesson. Start with having only three rules for your RRI room: Sit tall ("tummy to the table"), listen, and try hard. Reviewing these rules and referring to them during the lesson as needed should help students know what is expected of them.

As you will see in the activity called Reinforce Desired Behavior (page 210), it isn't just a matter of reiterating a rule when it is broken. It is even more important to praise students when they *do* follow the rules! Some behavior experts say that the ratio between praise and corrections, or between positive and negative remarks, should be three positives for every negative. Be conscious of the number of positive and negative things you say to the students throughout a lesson. It can be very enlightening to make an audiotape of one or two lessons and listen to it later. It can give you real insight into your ratio of "teacher talk" to active student involvement and your ratio of positive remarks to negative remarks.

RRI teachers consistently find that the greatest source of motivation in RRI is the success that students experience. First-graders generally know it is their job to learn to read, and they know when they are not successful. Many students in RRI have already experienced failure. RRI teachers have worked with students whose only opportunity for success during the day is during their RRI lesson. If you consistently apply the points made in Setting Students Up for Success (page 205), it will go a long way toward eliminating behavior concerns.

Another thing to keep in mind is that slow pacing invites boredom and behavior difficulties. Many of the students in RRI have problems keeping their attention on learning. That's why some of them didn't make adequate progress with classroom instruction alone. If you keep the lessons moving, seat these students up close to the table and near you, teach and reteach routines, keep teacher talk to a minimum, and plan your lessons with the students' learning and success in mind, these students will have a very good chance of learning to read. The strategy described next is one that has worked very well for RRI teachers.

Reinforce Desired Behavior

Objective

Students will increase appropriate behavior.

Implement Strategy

When students are engaging in inappropriate or disruptive behavior, such as talking out, bothering others, refusing to participate, or being uncooperative.

Materials

- Sticky notes
- Pencil or pen
- *Optional:* Stickers or other rewards

Procedures

1. First, decide whether you think the student is acting inappropriately because he or she is seeking attention either from you or from peers. Other causes of inappropriate behavior include a slow-paced lesson, not providing enough variety in lesson planning, choosing inappropriate activities or books, or teaching material that is too hard or too easy for the student.

2. If you think the student is seeking attention, try ignoring the negative behavior and reinforcing positive behavior whenever you notice it. It is very important that you use a pleasant, even voice tone and facial expressions as you do this. The key word is *positive*! Here are some simple ways to do this:
   - Provide specific praise to the student whenever the student acts appropriately.
   - Provide specific praise to other students whenever they act appropriately.
   - Allow students who act appropriately to have a simple privilege, such as writing with a colored marker during Supported Independent Writing (page 176).
   - Play a game in which you put a sticky note in front of each student on the table and award students with points each time you observe them acting appropriately. Be sure to award points to the student who has been having problems whenever he or she acts appropriately! Try to end the class in a positive way, with all of the students having plenty of points—the same amount, if you can manage it. Don't allow the students to gloat about having more points than others. It can be fun to have the student with the

most points stand up at the end of class and have the rest of the group—and the teacher—applaud for that student.

- Teacher Game: Another version of this game is something called the Teacher Game. In this version, one sticky note is placed in front of the teacher, with two columns drawn on the note. One column says "Teacher" and the other column says "Class." The class gets a point when the teacher catches any of the students behaving positively or following the rules. The teacher gets a point if a student does not act appropriately. Hopefully, the students will win at the end of the lesson and can be praised. It can be effective to have the teacher do something silly, such as walking around a chair three times or singing a silly song, to reward the students if they win. If you decide to go this way, be sure the students know about the prize all through the class. This will often be a strong motivator!

Prompts

- "Jennifer is sitting up in her chair ready to read. Nice job, Jennifer. You get a point!"
- "Roshawn, you are really working hard on writing your sentence. Great job of working hard."
- "Isabella, I can tell you are doing your best. That will really help you get better and better at reading!"

- If students are impulsive and tend to talk out without stopping to think first, it can help to provide scaffolding by talking with them individually outside of the lesson time and setting up some kind of nonverbal signal (like tapping gently on the table in front of them) to cue them to think before they speak or act.

SCAFFOLDING

IN OUR CLASSROOMS

The key to this technique is to keep it positive. Guard against making negative comments like, "If Jim would only behave, maybe he could get points, too." Try to find positive things that Jim is doing and immediately and consistently reward him. You might have heard the (rather strange) old saying, "You catch more flies with honey than vinegar." (Who really wants to catch flies anyway? I'd just use the flyswatter.) But, the saying has truth to it. Research has shown that reinforcing positive behavior works much better than punishing inappropriate behavior, and RRI teachers have found the same thing in their classrooms, too.

You are likely to get more of behavior that is rewarded. If a student is seeking attention in negative ways, you reinforce that negative behavior if you give the student attention by lecturing or punishing the student!

RRI teachers have sometimes given stickers at the end of the class to all students who have at least a certain number of points on their sticky notes. If you choose to do this, try to be sure that everyone in the group gets the sticker. Whatever you do, try not to set up a situation where the student with the behavior problem is the only one who doesn't get a sticker, especially if that student really tried to behave positively during the lesson but fell a little short of the other students. A warning about giving stickers or other physical rewards: Once you start, it's difficult to stop! Kids start to expect the reward and it loses its "punch"—it doesn't mean much if a student gets a sticker every single day. If you do choose to use tangible rewards like stickers, the most powerful way to use these rewards is to give them once in a while, rather than all the time. This is called "intermittent reinforcement," and it's the most powerful kind of reward (which is why some people put money in slot machines—they get rewarded *some* of the time . . . just enough to keep them going).

What Is Behind the Behavior?

If a student has behavior issues that might be keeping him or her from making progress in the RRI program, ask yourself what might be causing the behaviors you are seeing.

If you think the student might be bored, try these ideas:

- Plan the lessons carefully: Is the work too easy or too hard? Put variety in your lessons. Make it fun!
- Plan for active student involvement: Keep your pacing quick but not rushed. Be organized so there is very little wasted time.
- Use positive reinforcement: Remember that positive reinforcement means rewarding behaviors you want to see more of. There are many kinds of rewards, so this doesn't just mean passing out stickers.
- Keep a positive attitude: Show warmth and enthusiasm toward the students and the lessons.

If you think the student might be seeking attention, try these ideas:

- Use positive reinforcement: Try the Teacher Game described on page 211.
- Don't reward negative behavior: Remember—if a student is seeking attention in negative ways, you are rewarding that student when you give him or her attention, even if the attention is a lecture or reprimand.
- Look for ways to give the student attention for appropriate behavior.
- Use proximity: Position the student near you. Have this student sit next to you on the opposite side from the Star Reader.
- Try ignoring some behaviors: You might have to do this for a while before the student stops the behavior. And sometimes it will get a little worse before it gets better. Think of a young child throwing a tantrum. If you ignore it, the child will probably scream louder but eventually will get tired and stop.
- Keep a positive attitude, with warmth and enthusiasm.

If you think the student is acting out because he or she is afraid of failing or doesn't feel successful, think about these strategies:

- Share your assessment results that show the progress the student is making.
- Be sure to praise the student specifically and truthfully for the student's accomplishments, even small increments of progress.
- Plan carefully to set the student up for success—not too easy, not too hard. Be sure to provide scaffolding so that the student can be successful.
- Use positive reinforcement.
- Keep a positive attitude, with warmth and enthusiasm.

If you think the student is simply impulsive and has attention difficulties, try these strategies:

- Seat the student near you: Have the student sit next to you on the side opposite the Star Reader.

- Remember to insist on the "tummy to the table" rule.
- Keep the lesson pacing up: Keep teacher talk to a minimum and keep the students actively engaged. Try to reduce downtime.
- Teach routines, like the ones described in the next section.
- As described previously, consider talking with the student individually outside of the lesson time and setting up some kind of nonverbal signal (like tapping gently on the table in front of the student) to cue the student to think before he or she speaks or acts.

Teaching Students to Follow Routines

The RRI lesson follows the same format each day. This provides a framework for the teacher and students so that they know what to expect. Within this framework, there is variety, but the consistent routines resulting from the framework help make the lesson progress smoothly. This element of predictability provides security for the at-risk students in RRI. They don't have to worry about what they will be asked to do next. The routines they learn teach them what to do each day without being told. These routines provide a structure for the students and allow the RRI lesson to proceed with minimal interruption. They make transitions between activities go quickly, and they help assure that students will be on task and actively involved in learning throughout the lesson. Successful RRI teachers include routines for entering the room and preparing for the lesson, checking out books, partner reading, transitioning from one lesson component to the next, writing activities, and other activities.

Students Entering the Room and Lesson Transitions

Emma, Perry, and Denzel walk into the RRI teaching space with their take-home books in plastic bags. They look at the Star Reader chart. Emma says, "I'm the Star Reader today." Emma goes to the teaching table and sits next to the teacher's chair. The boys sit across the table. All three quickly remove their take-home books from the bags. (See the Home-School Connection on page 18.) The RRI teacher says, "Thank you. All of you brought back your books." The teacher puts a small selection of familiar books in front of each student. "Which book are you going to take home tonight?" All three pick a book on their reading levels and put it in their bags. They put the bags on the floor underneath their chairs. The **WORD WORK** portion of the lesson begins.

After 10 minutes of **WORD WORK**, the teacher says, "OK, it's time for partner reading and **FLUENCY**. Perry is the Coach today, and Denzel is the Reader." Perry and Denzel go to the partner reading area and begin to read. The teacher says, "Emma, please read your first familiar book to me." After Emma has read two familiar books while the teacher provides a model, the teacher says, "Emma, now I need to have Denzel come to the table so he can read his book from yesterday." Emma goes to the partner reading area and partner reads with Perry. Denzel comes to the table and is given an Assessment of Reading Accuracy. After the assessment, all students return to the table for **SUPPORTED READING**.

Notice that the students in the prior Snapshot knew what to do without reminders. Take time to explicitly teach each of the routines so that students can perform them independently or with minimal direction. The best way to teach these routines is to model what is expected and then allow students to practice the routine while you monitor it. Some routines will be more difficult for students to learn and may require several repetitions of the model and practice sessions on subsequent days.

In the early lessons, the timing of the lesson may be adjusted to accommodate teaching the routines. After a week or two, most routines will be in place. It is worth it to take the time for teaching routines because, when they are in place, the teacher and the students will be able to focus on the content of the lesson. As the year progresses, the routines of the lesson will become second nature. This allows the lesson to proceed at a brisk pace with minimal distractions and disruptions.

Teaching the Partner Reading Routine

Emma, Perry, and Denzel sit at the table at the beginning of one of the year's first lessons. "Today we will learn how to partner read. Emma will be my partner while Perry and Denzel watch. Then Perry and Denzel get a turn." Partner Reading Prompt Cards (provided in the Appendix) are on the table for modeling.

"Each day, the Star Reader will read with me at the teaching table. The other two of you will partner read. This helps you practice reading out loud so you will learn to read smoothly and quickly. The partners will move to those two chairs. Under one chair is a small basket with books we have already read in class. I have two cards. One says 'Coach,' the other 'Reader.'" The teacher shows students the cards. "In partner reading I'll give one card to each partner."

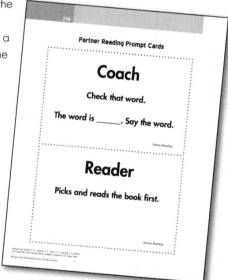

"Emma and I will now practice being the reading partners. Emma is the Reader. I am the Coach." The teacher hands Emma the Reader card. The teacher shows students the Coach card. "Emma, let's move quickly and quietly to the chairs in the corner. Good. Denzel, thank you for watching quietly. Emma, please pick up the basket of books from under your chair. Emma has the Reader card first, so she will pick a book to read from the basket. Emma did a good job of picking a book quickly and quietly. Watch how we sit side by side and hold the book between us so we can both see it. Emma reads the book first because she is the Reader. My job as Coach is to help Emma when she comes to a hard word, like a teacher helps you when you come to a word you may not know. On the Coach card there are two things the Coach might say to help the Reader: *Check that word*, and *The word is ____. Say the word.* If the Reader makes a mistake or comes to a word he or she can't read, I'll use one of these ways of helping. Perry, how do you think I will say the words?"

The teacher models, saying "Try that again" in a harsh voice and then in a quiet, friendly voice. "It's important for the Coach to use a friendly voice to help."

"Now watch how I help Emma when she comes to a hard word." Emma reads the book *Run*. She makes an error and says *leopard* in place of *lion*. The teacher gently interrupts. "I am the Coach, so I nicely stop Emma and say, 'Emma, check that word.' Emma will reread that part." The teacher points to prompts written on the Coach card.

(continued)

Teaching the Partner Reading Routine (continued)

"Another way to help her is to say, 'Emma, that word is *leopard*. Say *leopard*.' I would point to the word. Emma would need to reread the sentence again. Let's try it both ways." The teacher models both prompts. Emma continues to read the rest of the book. The teacher continues to model how the Coach would prompt Emma if she made more errors.

"When the book is finished, Emma and I trade cards. Now I am the Reader and she is the Coach. I pick a book to partner read. Now it is Perry and Denzel's turn to practice while Emma and I watch." The teacher gives the Reader and Coach cards to Perry and Denzel. "Perry, you are the Reader; Denzel is the Coach. Denzel, remember to be polite. I will be watching to help you. Nice job of moving to the chairs quietly and quickly. Perry found a book quickly. Good—you remembered to sit side by side with the book between you. Perry and Denzel, go ahead and partner read while we watch. Stop, please. Begin again because Denzel wasn't following along. Denzel, you can't help Perry unless you read along with him. Perry, make sure Denzel is on the same page as you before you begin. Good, Denzel. Now you are following along."

The teacher monitors as they read the rest of the book. "Denzel did a great job helping Perry with *said*. Please come back to the table."

The students will practice this routine for the next few days.

Teaching a routine this carefully may seem tedious, but doing so pays off. If students know what you expect them to do and they practice the routines, they will be able to carry them out without interrupting you. They will also be more actively involved in the activity. Be sure to regularly praise the students when you see them engaging in the routine correctly. Of course, you will have to reteach the routine from time to time. *It is advisable to reteach rather than correct or reprimand the students.*

Reteaching a Routine

"Denzel, you're the Star Reader today. Emma and Perry, you will partner read. Emma, you are the Coach; Perry, you are the Reader." The teacher hands them the cards. "You two are really doing a nice job of moving to the partner-reading area quickly and quietly."

Perry takes several minutes to flip through each book in the basket. Emma whispers that he should hurry up and he argues with her. The teacher stops working with Denzel and looks at Perry and Emma. "Emma and Perry, I think you have forgotten part of the partner-reading routine. Please come back to the table so we can practice. OK. Remember that the partners move quickly and quietly to the partner-reading chairs and sit side by side. The Reader quickly and quietly picks a book from the basket and the partners hold it between them so they can both read it. OK, Emma and Perry, please practice."

They move to the chairs and Perry picks a book right away. "Excellent, now you are remembering exactly what to do."

The partner-reading format is adapted from Mathes, P., Torgesen, J. K., Allen, S. H., & Allor, J. H. (2001). *First Grade PALS (Peer-Assisted Literary Strategies)*. Longmont, CO: Sopris West.

Helping Students Become Independent Readers and Writers

The ultimate goal for RRI is for the students to become independent readers and writers—even when the teacher is not around! Teachers want children to make a habit of using the strategies and tools provided by RRI. The RRI teacher must strive for a special form of balance throughout the instruction. RRI teachers don't want students to rely on the teacher to give them the answer every time they struggle with reading. Nevertheless, teachers want students to experience success through their scaffolding. The balance is between teacher control and student control and, as a rule, things should progress consistently in the direction of increased student control. When the student progresses to more complex text or learns a new skill, there may be a greater need for scaffolding. But always remember that the most important quality of scaffolding is that it is temporary.

If your students seem to rely on you too much to support them, reread Scaffolding and Feedback and Opportunities to Practice in the Introduction of this book. It also would be a good idea to study the continuum of control outlined in Tables 6.10–6.12. When teachers provide too much support, students often stop growing as independent readers and writers. Try to keep this continuum of control in mind throughout the school year.

Students sometimes develop habits such as looking at the teacher to find out whether a word was read correctly. RRI teachers have worked with some students who look at their teachers after nearly every word they read. Discourage this habit. Say to the student, "You don't need to look at me. You can do this yourself." Or "I'm right here and I'll help you if you need me, but I won't tell you if you are right when you look at me." You may have to say this several times. Be sure to keep a blank expression on your face if the student looks at you for confirmation. Do not smile or frown, and do not nod or shake your head. Or better yet, look down at your Anecdotal Record sheet and say in a pleasant voice, "Go on." RRI teachers have also found it helpful to move their chairs backward a bit if the Star Reader has a habit of looking at the teacher. (Use the clipboard to take Anecdotal Records.) If you are sitting somewhat behind the student, it's harder for the student to look at you. One RRI student had this habit so strongly ingrained that the teacher actually stood *behind* him as he read for a few days, just to show that he could do it without looking at the teacher!

TABLE 6.10

Continuum of Control: Stopping on a Difficult Word

	When the student stops on a difficult word:
Teacher Control (Greater Teacher Support)	• Tell the student the word or allow another student to tell the word.
	• Model the RRI strategy and sound out the word for the student.
	• Tell the student some letter sounds or letter combinations, then have the student decode the word.
	• Write the word on a white board one sound at a time, while the student supplies the sounds and decodes the word.
	• Mask the word to reveal letter sounds or combinations the student knows, then have the student sound out the word and check it.
	• Show the student another (known) word that has the same spelling pattern as the word the student is trying to read. (Higher scaffolding: Show the student what is the same about the two words, or remind the student of the known sounds.)
	• Ask: "Can you start the word?" or "Can you play the Point Game?" or "Can you sound it out?"
	• Prompt the student to use each part of the RRI strategy: "Look for parts you know. Sound it out. Check it."
	• Ask: "Do you know another word like this one?" (May scaffold by saying, "You know ____. That can help you read this word.")
	• Ask: "Do you see any parts you know?"
Student Control (Less Teacher Support)	• Say, "Try it!"
	Praise: "You worked that out all by yourself!"

Note

❑ The goal is to move *down* the chart to greater student control and less teacher control.

TABLE 6.11

Continuum of Control: Misreading a Word

	When the student misreads a word:
Teacher Control (Greater Teacher Support)	• Immediately correct the student by telling the correct word, or allow another student to tell the correct word.
	• Immediately stop the student and tell the student he or she made an error. Then model the correct word, sounding it out for the student.
	• Let the student read on to see whether he or she will self-correct, then tell or model the word if the student does not do this.
Student Control (Less Teacher Support)	• Let the student read on to see if the student will self-correct, then: – Say, "Try that word again and be sure to sound it out." – Say, "Go back and see if that makes sense." – Say, "Try that again." Or "Make it match." – Say, "You made a mistake in this part. Can you fix it?"
	Praise: "You fixed that all by yourself!"

Note

❏ The goal is to move *down* the chart to greater student control and less teacher control.

	When the student is trying to write a word he or she does not know how to spell:
Teacher Control (Greater Teacher Support)	• Tell the student how to spell the word, write it on a white board for the student to copy, or allow the student to copy the word from another student.
	• Tell the student how to write part(s) of the word.
	• Segment (stretch) the word for the student so that he or she can record the sounds. Emphasize specific sounds.
	• Supply Elkonin Sound Boxes and have the student "pull down the sounds" in the word while saying it slowly. Scaffold the process by helping the student recognize which box should contain each letter or letter combination. Tell any letters the student cannot hear and record.
	• Show the student another (known) word that has the same spelling pattern as the one the student is trying to write.
	• Say: "You know ____. That can help you write this word."
	• Have the student say the word slowly (segment it) and write it without boxes. Say, "Say it slowly and write what you hear."
Student Control (Less Teacher Support)	• Say "Try to remember what looks right in this word" (when the student must choose between different ways of spelling the same sound like *ai* and *ay* or *ou* and *ow*).
	• Say: "Try it. Write the word."
	Praise: "You worked that out all by yourself!"

TABLE 6.12

Continuum of Control: Trying to Write a Word Using Correct Spelling

Note

❑ The goal is to move *down* the chart to greater student control and less teacher control.

Helping Students Who Don't Make Adequate Progress

Using Information from Records

A big part of success in Responsive Reading Instruction is taking records and using the information from the records. From time to time, you may encounter a period of instruction in which a student isn't making enough progress. RRI includes many valuable tools that teachers can consult when students do not make adequate progress. This is the time to go back and look at your records. Then use the Planning Guide on page 311 in the Appendix to help you select activities.

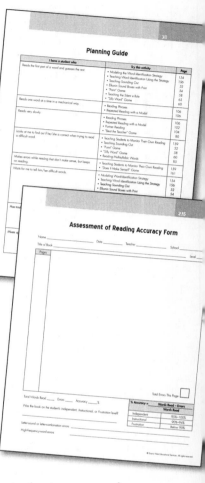

Assessment of Reading Accuracy

First look at the most current Assessment of Reading Accuracy Form. Look at the types of errors the student is making. Are the errors due to missing letter-sounds or high-frequency words? Is the student making too many errors and not self-monitoring? Is the student trying to apply the RRI strategy to read words?

Take a look at the Progress in Reading Levels Summary Form provided in the Appendix. The student may have been at a reading level too long and is still reading books at a Frustration level (below 90 percent accuracy). You may need to back the student down a level because the student may need more practice with easier text, or you may need to add more variety at the student's current level.

Anecdotal Records

What letters or words are you writing down on your Anecdotal Records? Anecdotal Records are capturing how the students are performing daily. When a student isn't making enough progress, certain difficulties may stand out in your Anecdotal Records. You may have introduced new sounds or words but may have forgotten to keep incorporating them in cumulative reviews.

Letter-Sound and High-Frequency-Word Assessments

Check the Letter-Sound and High-Frequency-Word Assessments to find out whether there are certain sounds or words the student is confusing or forgetting. You may need to readminister these assessments to get the most current information.

Reflecting on Your Own Teaching

As RRI teachers working with students who have serious difficulties learning to read, we continually reflect on our own teaching. If a student isn't making enough progress, we ask ourselves what changes we can make.

Here are some examples of questions to ask yourself as a self-reflective teacher:

Looking at your Anecdotal Records and assessments:
- What is hard for the students? What is easy?
- What kinds of mistakes did the students make?
- What did the students have success with?
- What did the students miss on the assessments?
- What does the student keep missing on the Assessments of Reading Accuracy?
- What did I observe and write down on my Anecdotal Records?
- Is the student ready to move up a level?
- When was the last time I took a Benchmark Book Assessment?

Thinking back over your lessons:
- When I tried a new activity, did it go well? If not, what could be the reason?
- Did I provide enough modeling and guided practice?
- Is there another way to approach that same strategy with magnetic letters or with a whiteboard?
- What other activity could I include in a lesson to teach or practice the objective?
- Was the new book too easy or hard?
- Am I trying to teach too much or too little?
- Am I spending too much time talking and decreasing the time the students have to actively participate instead of just sitting and listening to me?
- Am I introducing too many new things at once?
- Did I provide effective scaffolding?
- Did I provide enough positive feedback?
- What was hard for the students during Supported Writing?
- Am I taking time in my lesson to review concepts already taught?
- Am I spending too much time focusing on behavior?
- Am I keeping quick pacing in my lessons, spending 10 minutes on each component?
- Have I established routines to ensure that there is little off-task time?
- Are my materials, forms, and books organized well so that there is no wasted time during the lesson?

Conclusion

This book was written for students who find learning to read a challenge, and for their teachers. Responsive Reading Instruction is effective when implemented the way it is described in this book, as a small-group intervention. Strategies are presented for use in both your own classrooms and in reading intervention settings. Only those instructional strategies that are supported by well-conducted research are included.

While we hope that the material contained here will help you and your students to achieve success, we know it can be far from easy. No reading program provides 100 percent success. Programs don't teach children to read—teachers do! That is why the role of the teacher is so critical in RRI. The teacher is the only person who can administer assessments and use information from the assessments to select appropriate activities that respond to the needs of their students. Because of the central role of the teacher in planning instruction in RRI, teachers implementing RRI are encouraged to participate in quality professional development, both to learn to implement RRI effectively and to increase their knowledge of the nature of the English language and the processes involved in learning to read accurately, fluently, and with comprehension. One source of this kind of professional development is *Language Essentials for Teachers of Reading and Spelling* (LETRS), offered by Sopris West, the publisher of this book.

Although it's true that our students have many challenges, both at school and at home, we as RRI teachers have a "no-excuses" attitude. Yes, this student may live in a community of poverty. Yes, that student may have serious problems maintaining attention. But these are "our kids." This is the wonderful, sometimes frustrating, but always stimulating and rewarding job we have taken on. We know that what we do for these children can change the trajectory of their lives.

And so, we wish you the best as you teach students to read. You are changing the world—one kid at a time.

Appendix

Sound Pronunciation Guide

Sound	Key Word	Sound Type*
m	mad	continuous
a	ask	continuous
t	top	stop
s	sell	continuous
i	if	continuous
r	rat (*rrrr* not *er*)	continuous
d	dog	stop
n	net	continuous
o	off	continuous
f	fat	continuous
c	cat	stop
p	park	stop
l	log	continuous
h	hat	stop (breath only)
g	go	stop
u	up	continuous
b	big	stop
th	that/thing	continuous
j	jump	stop
k	kick	stop
y	yes (*yyyyyy*)	continuous
e	egg	continuous
ck	sock	stop
ar	car	
ing	sing	
w	wet	continuous
er	her	
x	fox (*kssss*)	continuous
sh	she	continuous
v	very	continuous
ch	chair	stop
ee	feet	continuous
ow	cow	
oa	toad	continuous
ai	rain	continuous
ay	play/crayon	continuous
ur	hurt	
ir	bird	
or	corn	
z	zoo	continuous

© Sopris West Educational Services. All rights reserved.

Sound	Key Word	Sound Type*
oo	boom	continuous
qu	quit (kw)	stop
oo	look	continuous
a_e	late	continuous
ee/e_e	tree; Pete	continuous
ea	seat	continuous
ue/u_e	blue/rude	continuous
ou	out	
ow	yellow	continuous
i_e	kite	continuous
oe/o_e	toe/bone	continuous
igh	night	continuous
au/aw	haul, saw	continuous
al/all	palm; fall	
ew	chew	continuous
oi/oy	boil, boy	
tch	watch	stop
le	able	continuous
ea	head	continuous
dge	judge	stop
ge/gi	gentle/giant	stop
ce/ci	century/circle	continuous
_y (1-syllable)	try	continuous
_y (2-syllable)	baby	continuous
a_	above/about	continuous
nk	sank	
wr	write	continuous
kn	knot	continuous
augh	caught	continuous
ough	fought	continuous
ph	phone	continuous
mb	lamb	continuous
ture	picture	
tion	action	
sion	mission	
tial	partial	
cial	special	
cious	precious	
tious	cautious	
ion	billion	

* Continuous sounds can be held for two seconds without distorting them. Stop sounds cannot be held without distorting them. They are pronounced very quickly. Some combination sounds do not fit clearly into the continuous/stop categories. These are left blank in the table.

Source: Adapted with permission from a Sound Pronunciation Guide developed by Jan Hasbrouck, Ph. D.

© Sopris West Educational Services. All rights reserved.

Phonograms

Use this list to select words to use in the activities entitled Word Linking, Word Pattern Charts, Word Sorts, and Word Building in the Word Work component of the Responsive Reading Instruction lesson. Start with many one-syllable examples first and then move on to the multisyllabic words.

Phonograms	One-Syllable Examples	Multisyllable Examples
-ab	cab, crab, gab, grab, jab, lab, tab, scab, stab	cabinet, fabulous
-ace	brace, face, grace, lace, mace, place, race, space, trace	embrace, fireplace, spaceship
-ack	back, black, clack, crack, hack, knack, lack, pack, rack, sack, shack, slack, smack, snack, stack, tack, track, whack	attack, hardback, haystack, paperback, racetrack, thumbtack
-ad	bad, clad, dad, fad, glad, had, lad, mad, pad, sad, tad	adding, maddening
-ade	bade, blade, grade, jade, made, shade, trade	handmade, homemade
-ag	bag, brag, drag, flag, gag, hag, lag, nag, rag, sag, snag, stag, swag, tag, wag	dishrag, flagpole, ragged, washrag
-age	age, cage, gage, page, rage, sage, stage, wage	enrage, encage, upstage
-ail	ail, bail, fail, frail, hail, jail, mail, pail, pails, quail, rail, sail, snail, tail, trail, wail	fingernail, fishtail, jailhouse, ponytail, thumbnail, toenail
-ain	brain, chain, drain, grain, main, pain, plain, rain, slain, sprain, stain, train, vain	explain, maintain, remain
-air	air, fair, hair, lair, pair, stair	downstairs, repair, upstairs, wheelchair
-ake	bake, brake, cake, drake, fake, flake, lake, make, quake, rake, shake, snake, stake, take, wake	cupcake, pancake, remake, snowflake
-ale	bale, gale, hale, male, pale, sale, scale, shale, stale, tale, whale	resale, upscale, whalebone
-alk	chalk, stalk, talk, walk	crosswalk, sidewalk
-all	all, ball, call, fall, hall, mall, pall, small, squall, stall, tall, wall	baseball, eyeball, football, overalls, recall, snowball, waterfall
-am	am, clam, cram, gram, ham, jam, ram, scam, scram, sham, slam, swam, tram, yam	kilogram, milligram
-ame	came, blame, fame, flame, frame, game, lame, name, same, shame, tame	nickname, rename, sameness
-amp	camp, champ, cramp, damp, lamp, ramp, stamp	campfire, champion, stampede
-an	an, ban, bran, can, clan, fan, flan, man, pan, ran, scan, span, tan, than, van	began, fireman, mailman, policeman, postman, snowman, toucan
-and	and, band, bland, brand, gland, grand, hand, land, sand, stand, strand	candy, grandstand, handstand, handy
-ane	cane, crane, lane, mane, pane, plane, vane	airplane, windowpane
-ang	bang, clang, fang, gang, hang, rang, sprang, twang	gangster, hangman
-ank	bank, blank, crank, drank, flank, Hank, plank, prank, sank, shrank, spank, tank, thank, yank	spanking, thankful
-ap	cap, chap, clap, flap, gap, lap, map, nap, rap, sap, scrap, slap, snap, strap, tap, trap, wrap, yap	entrap, happen, happy

© Sopris West Educational Services. All rights reserved.

Phonograms	One-Syllable Examples	Multisyllable Examples
-ar	arch, arm, art, bar, car, char, far, jar, mar, march, par, scar, spar, star, tar	army, artist, argument, carpool, garden, party
-are (sounds like air)	bare, blare, care, dare, fare, flare, glare, hare, mare, pare, rare, scare, share, snare, spare, square, stare, ware	aware, barefoot, beware, careful, declare, nightmare, welfare
-ark	bark, dark, lark, mark, park, shark, spark	darkness, parkway, remark, sparkler
-ash	ash, bash, brash, cash, clash, crash, dash, flash, gash, hash, lash, mash, rash, sash, slash, smash, trash	dashboard, flashlight, trashcan
-at	at, bat, brat, cat, chat, fat, flat, gnat, hat, pat, rat, sat, that, vat	Batman, chit-chat, placemat, Saturday
-ate	ate, crate, date, fate, gate, grate, hate, late, mate, plate, rate, skate, state	classmate, grateful, participate
-ave	brave, cave, crave, Dave, gave, grave, pave, rave, save, shave, slave, wave	graveyard, pavement
-aw	caw, claw, crawl, draw, drawn, flaw, gnaw, jaw, law, lawn, paw, raw, saw, shawl, slaw, squaw, straw	awful, awkward, outlaw
-ay	bay, bray, clay, day, gay, gray, hay, jay, lay, may, pay, play, pray, ray, say, slay, spray, stay, stray, sway, tray, way	always, birthday, doorway, highway, maybe, payment, repay, Sunday
-e	be, he, me, she, we,	because, being, evil, maybe, zebra
-eak	beak, bleak, creak, freak, leak, peak, sneak, speak, squeak, streak, tweak, weak	squeaky, weakness
-eal	deal, heal, meal, seal, squeal, steal, zeal	healer, mealtime
-eam	beam, cream, dream, ream, seam, scream, steam, stream, team	daydream, downstream, sunbeam, upstream
-ear	dear, clear, fear, gear, hear, near, rear, smear, spear, tear, year	earring, endear, yearly
-eat	beat, bleat, cheat, cleat, feat, heat, meat, neat, peat, pleat, seat, treat, wheat	cheater, heated, neatness
-ed	bed, bled, fed, fled, red, shed, shred, sled, sped, wed	toolshed, wedding
-ee	bee, fee, free, glee, green, knee, see, sleep, street, tree, three	agree, degree, referee
-eed	bleed, breed, creed, deed, feed, freed, greed, heed, need, reed, seed, speed, steed, tweed, weed	indeed, reseed, speedway
-eep	beep, cheep, creep, deep, jeep, keep, peep, seep, sheep, sleep, steep, sweep, weep	asleep, deeper, peephole
-ell	bell, cell, dell, dwell, fell, jell, knell, sell, shell, smell, spell, swell, tell, well, yell	doorbell, fellow, smelly, spelling, yellow
-en	den, hen, men, pen, ten, then, when	mailmen, pencil, pigpen, splendid
-end	bend, blend, end, lend, mend, send, spend, tend, trend	backbend, ending, weekend
-ent	bent, cent, dent, gent, lent, rent, sent, scent, spent, tent, vent, went	dented, rented, renting
-est	best, blest, chest, crest, guest, jest, lest, nest, pest, quest, rest, test, vest, west, zest	biggest, contest, fastest, pretest, western
-et	bet, fret, get, jet, let, met, net, pet, set, wet, yet	better, hairnet, jetpack
-ew	blew, brew, chew, dew, drew, few, knew, new, pew, stew	anew, dewdrop, pewter

© Sopris West Educational Services. All rights reserved.

Phonograms	One-Syllable Examples	Multisyllable Examples
-ice	dice, ice, lice, mice, nice, price, rice, slice, spice, splice, twice, vice	entice, niceness
-ick	brick, chick, click, flick, kick, lick, pick, quick, sick, slick, stick, tick, thick, trick, wick	candlestick, flicker, homesick, kickball, lipstick
-id	bid, did, grid, hid, kid, lid, rid, skid, slid	kidding, middle
-ide	bide, bride, glide, hide, pride, ride, side, slide, stride, tide, wide,	beside, divide, inside
-ig	big, dig, fig, jig, pig, rig, sprig, swig, twig, wig	giggle, wiggle
-ight	blight, bright, flight, fright, knight, light, might, night, right, sight, slight, tight	delight, flashlight, frightful, midnight, mighty, slightly
-ill	bill, chill, dill, drill, fill, frill, gill, grill, hill, ill, kill, mill, pill, quill, sill, skill, spill, still, thrill, twill, will	chilly, downhill, thrilling, uphill, windowsill
-im	brim, dim, grim, him, prim, rim, slim, swim, trim	himself, impossible, impress
-ime	chime, crime, dime, grime, lime, mime, prime, slime, time	daytime, nighttime, pantomime, playtime, sometimes
-in	bin, chin, din, fin, grin, kin, pin, shin, sin, skin, spin, tin, thin, twin, win	begin, into, skinny, tailspin, tailfin
-ind	bind, blind, find, grind, hind, kind, mind, rind, wind	kindly, kindness, mastermind
-ine	brine, dine, fine, line, mine, nine, pine, shine, shrine, spine, swine, tine, vine, whine, wine	divine, goldmine, grapevine, shoeshine, sunshine
-ing	bring, cling, ding, fling, king, ring, sing, sling, spring, sting, string, swing, thing, wing, wring	kingdom, something, swinging, swingset, wingspan
-ink	blink, brink, chink, drink, kink, link, mink, pink, rink, sink, shrink, slink, stink, think, wink	stinkbug, winking
-int	hint, lint, mint, glint, print, splint, sprint, squint	newsprint, peppermint, spearmint
-ip	blip, chip, clip, dip, drip, flip, grip, hip, lip, nip, rip, sip, ship, skip, slip, snip, strip, tip, trip, whip, zip	clippers, daytrip, slipknot, unzip, whiplash, zipper
-ish	dish, fish, swish, wish	establish, dishes, finish, fisherman, wishes
-it	it, bit, fit, flit, hit, kit, knit, lit, pit, quit, sit, skit, slit, spit, split, twit, wit	outfit, splits
-ive	dive, drive, five, hive, jive, live, thrive	alive, lively
-ob	blob, cob, gob, glob, job, knob, mob, rob, slob, snob, sob	corncob, doorknob, gobble, robber
-ock	block, clock, crock, dock, flock, hock, knock, lock, mock, rock, sock, shock, stock	locksmith, rocky, shocking, sunblock
-od	cod, clod, nod, plod, pod, prod, rod, sod,	godfather, godmother, modern
-og	bog, cog, clog, dog, flog, fog, frog, hog, jog, log, smog	bulldog, bullfrog
-oil	boil, broil, coil, foil, soil, spoil	spoiling, turmoil
-oke	broke, choke, joke, poke, smoke, spoke, stoke, stroke, woke, yoke,	awoke, jokester, outspoken, smokestack, sunstroke
-old	bold, cold, fold, gold, hold, mold, old, scold, sold, told	resold, scolded, untold
-one	bone, clone, cone, crone, drone, hone, lone, phone, prone, shone, stone, tone, zone	alone, backbone, telephone, trombone

© Sopris West Educational Services. All rights reserved.

Phonograms	One-Syllable Examples	Multisyllable Examples
-ong	gong, long, song, prong, strong, wrong	longer, stronger, belong, along
-oo	boo, coo, too, woo, zoo	bamboo, igloo, kangaroo, shampoo, tattoo
-ook	book, brook, hook, cook, shook, took	cookbook, cookie, handbook, mistook, notebook, overlook, rookie
-oom	bloom, boom, broom, doom, gloom, groom, loom, room, zoom	bedroom, bathroom, gloomy
-op	bop, chop, cop, crop, drop, flop, hop, mop, plop, pop, shop, slop, sop, stop, top	popgun, shortstop, toyshop
-ope	cope, grope, hope, lope, mope, pope, rope, scope, slope	elope, microscope, telescope
-ore	bore, core, fore, gore, more, pore, score, shore, snore, sore, spore, store, swore, tore, wore,	before, encore, seashore
-orn	born, corn, horn, torn, worn, scorn, shorn, sworn, thorn	morning, corner, popcorn, thorny
-ot	blot, clot, cot, dot, got, hot, knot, jot, lot, not, plot, pot, rot, shot, slot, spot, trot	cannot, slingshot, sunspot
-ound	bound, found, hound, mound, pound, round, sound, wound	around, ground, astound, rebound, playground
-out	bout, clout, gout, grout, lout, pout, scout, shout, snout, spout, sprout, stout, tout, trout	about, lookout, knockout, outside, outer, outline, outfield,
-ow (long o)	blow, bow, crow, flow, glow, grow, know, low, mow, row, show, slow, snow, sow, stow, tow	arrow, borrow, marshmallow, pillow, rainbow, scarecrow, shadow, slowly, tomorrow, window
-ow	bow, brow, chow, cow, how, now, plow, prow, sow, vow	coward, eyebrow, power, shower, snowplow, somehow,
-own	brown, clown, crown, down, drown, frown, gown, town,	downtown, downward, nightgown
-own (long o)	blown, flown, grown, known, mown, shown, sown, thrown	grownup, unknown
-oy	boy, coy, joy, ploy, soy, toy	annoy, annoying, cowboy, enjoy, enjoyment, joyful, royal
-ub	cub, club, flub, grub, hub, pub, rub, scrub, shrub, snub, stub, sub, tub	bathtub, clubhouse, stubborn
-uck	buck, cluck, duck, luck, muck, pluck, shuck, stuck, struck, truck, tuck	lucky, unstuck
-udge	budge, drudge, fudge, grudge, judge, nudge, sludge, smudge, trudge	budget, judgment
-uff	buff, cuff, huff, puff, ruff, bluff, fluff, gruff, scuff, snuff, stuff	stuffing, fluffy, huffy, handcuff
-ug	bug, chug, drug, dug, hug, jug, mug, plug, pug, rug, shrug, slug, smug, snug, thug, tug	drugstore, slugger, tugboat, unplug
-um	bum, chum, drum, glum, gum, hum, plum, rum, scum, strum, sum	bubblegum, humdrum
-ump	bump, clump, dump, grump, hump, jump, lump, plump, pump, slump, stump, thump, trump	grumpy, jumping
-un	bun, fun, gun, hunt, nun, pun, run, shun, spun, stun, sun	funny, sunny, Sunday, uncle, under, unhappy, unless, hundred, until
-ung	clung, flung, hung, lung, rung, sprung, stung, strung, sung, swung	

© Sopris West Educational Services. All rights reserved.

Phonograms	One-Syllable Examples	Multisyllable Examples
-unk	chunk, bunk, dunk, hunk, junk, plunk, shrunk, skunk, slunk, spunk, stunk, sunk, trunk	chunky
-ur	bur, burn, cur, curb, fur, nurse, spur, slur, surf	hurry, murmur, occur, purple, surface, Thursday, turkey, turtle, urgent
-ush	blush, brush, crush, flush, gush, hush, lush, mush, plush, rush, slush, thrush	airbrush, hairbrush, toothbrush
-ust	bust, crust, dust, just, must, rust, trust	dusty, musty, unjust
-ut	but, cut, gut, hut, jut, nut, shut, strut	haircut, peanut
-y	by, cry, dry, fly, fry, my, ply, pry, shy, sky, sly, spy, spry, try, why	apply, defy, deny, July, lying, myself, python, reply

© Sopris West Educational Services. All rights reserved.

Responsive Reading Instruction Lesson Plan

Week of _____ – _____   Group _____   Teacher _____

	Monday	Tuesday	Wednesday	Thursday	Friday
☆ Star Reader					
Word Work **Teach or Reteach**: Model, Guided Practice, Independent Practice					
Word Work Cummulative Practice:					

(continued)

© Sopris West Educational Services. All rights reserved.

Responsive Reading Instruction Lesson Plan (continued)

Week of _____ – _____   Group _____   Teacher _____

☆ Star Reader					
Print Concepts/ Fluency					
Assessment					
Student:					
Supported Reading Comprehension Focus and Introduction					
New Book	Book: Level:	Book: Level:	Book: Level:	Book: Level:	Book: Level:
Supported Writing Comprehension Question					

© Sopris West Educational Services. All rights reserved.

Anecdotal Record Form (3 students)

Name:		Name:		Name:	
Date:	**Book Level:**	**Date:**	**Book Level:**	**Date:**	**Book Level:**

© Sopris West Educational Services. All rights reserved.

Anecdotal Record Form (4 students)

Name:		Name:		Name:		Name:	
Date:	Book Level:	Date:	Book Level:	Date:	Book Level:	Date:	Book Level:

© Sopris West Educational Services. All rights reserved.

Assessment of Reading Accuracy Form

Name _____ Date _____ Teacher _____ School _____

Title of Book _____ Level _____

Pages	

Total Errors This Page [ ]

Total Words Read _____ Errors _____ Accuracy _____%

Was the book on the student's *Independent*, *Instructional*, or *Frustration* level?

_____

% Accuracy =	Words Read – Errors
	Words Read
Independent	95%–100%
Instructional	90%–94%
Frustration	Below 90%

Letter-sound or letter-combination errors _____

High-frequency-word errors _____

© Sopris West Educational Services. All rights reserved.

Assessment of Reading Accuracy Form

Pages	

Total Errors This Page

© Sopris West Educational Services. All rights reserved.

Letter-Name Assessment Form

Student _____

School _____

Date _____

Examiner _____

Instructions

For each **correct** letter name, mark a checkmark (✔) in the "Response" column.

If response is **incorrect**, record it in the Response column.

If **no response**, record a dot (●).

Letter-Name	Response
M m	
B b	
N n	
V v	
C c	
X x	
Z z	
P p	
O o	
I i	
U u	
Y y	
T t	
R r	
E e	
W w	
Q q	
A a	
S s	
D d	
F f	
G g	
H h	
J j	
K k	
L l	

Errors:

Not Attempted:

© Sopris West Educational Services. All rights reserved.

Letter-Name Assessment List

M	m
B	b
N	n
V	v
C	c
X	x
Z	z
P	p
O	o
I	i
U	u
Y	y
T	t
R	r
E	e
W	w
Q	q
A	a
S	s
D	d
F	f
G	g
H	h
J	j
K	k
L	l

© Sopris West Educational Services. All rights reserved.

Letter-Sound Assessment Form—List 1

Instructions	Student

Instructions

For each **correct** letter sound, mark a checkmark (✓) in the "Response" column.

If response is **incorrect**, record it in the Response column.

If **no response**, record a dot (•).

Student _____

School _____

Date _____

Examiner _____

Letter-Sounds—List 1	Sound Examples for Teacher Reference	Response
m	mad	
a	ask	
t	top	
s	sell	
i	if	
r	rat (*rrr* not *er*)	
d	dog	
n	net	
o	off	
f	fat	
c	cat	
p	park	
l	log	
h	hat	
g	go	
u	up	
b	big	
th	that	
j	jump	
k	kick	
y	yes (*yyyyyy*)	
e	egg	
ck	sock	
ar	car	
ing	sing	
w	wet	
er	her	
x	fox (*kssss*)	
sh	she	
v	very	
a	ask	
g	go	

Errors:

Not Attempted:

Score _____

(number correct)

© Sopris West Educational Services. All rights reserved.

Letter-Sound Assessment Form—Lists 2 and 3

Instructions
For each **correct** letter-sound, mark a checkmark (✔) in the "Response" column.
If response is **incorrect**, record it in the Response column.
If **no response**, record a dot (•).

Student _____

School _____

Date _____

Examiner _____

Letter-Sounds—List 2		
Sound	**Teacher Reference**	**Response**
ch	chair	
ee	feet	
ow	cow	
oa	toad	
ai	rain	
ay	play / crayon	
ur	hurt	
ir	bird	
or	corn	
z	zoo	
oo	boom	
qu	quit (kw)	
oo	look	
a_e	late	
ee	tree	
e_e	Pete	
ea	seat	
ue	blue	
u_e	rude	
ou	out	
ow	yellow	
i_e	kite	
oe	toe	
o_e	bone	
igh	night	
au	haul	
aw	saw	
al	palm	
all	fall	

Errors:

Score _____
(number correct)

Not attempted:

Letter-Sounds—List 3		
Student	**Teacher Reference**	**Response**
blew	ew	
boil	oi	
soy	oy	
watch	tch	
bottle	le	
head	ea	
judge	dge	
gentle	ge	
giant	gi	
cent	ce	
circle	ci	
try	_ y (1 syllable)	
silly	_ _ y (2 syllables)	
above	a- (schwa)	
sank	nk	
write	wr	
knot	kn	
caught	augh	
fought	ough	
phone	ph	
lamb	mb	
picture	ture	
action	tion	
mission	sion	
partial	tial	
special	cial	
precious	cious	
cautious	tious	
billion	ion	

Errors:

Score _____
(number correct)

Not attempted:

© Sopris West Educational Services. All rights reserved.

Letter-Sound Assessment—List 1

m

a

t

s

i

r

d

n

o

f

c

p

l

h

g

u

b

th

j

k

y

e

ck

ar

ing

w

er

x

sh

v

a

g

© Sopris West Educational Services. All rights reserved.

Letter-Sound Assessment—List 2

ch

ee

ow

oa

ai

ay

ur

ir

or

z

oo

qu

oo

a_e

ee

e_e

ea

ue

u_e

ou

ow

i_e

oe

o_e

igh

au

aw

al

all

© Sopris West Educational Services. All rights reserved.

Letter-Sound Assessment—List 3

blew
boil
soy
watch
bottle
head
judge
gentle
giant
cent
circle
try
silly
above
sank
write
knot
caught
fought
phone
lamb
picture
action
mission
partial
special
precious
cautious
billion

© Sopris West Educational Services. All rights reserved.

High-Frequency-Words Assessment Form

Instructions		Student _____
✓	Check correct letter-sounds or write incorrect response.	School _____
•	Mark a dot if no response.	Date _____
☐	Write incorrect answer in box.	
⎰⎱	Draw squiggle line for long pause.	Examiner _____

List 1	✓	Word Confusion
I		
a		
be		
is		
on		
he		
as		
in		
to		
you		
for		
are		
have		
of		
at		
they		
from		
and		
the		
with		
that		
his		
was		
this		
it		
am		
dog		
like		
me		
run		

(No. correct of 30 items)
Score _____

List 2	✓	Word Confusion
we		
use		
word		
there		
she		
one		
all		
your		
how		
by		
were		
not		
but		
which		
their		
if		
do		
what		
had		
when		
each		
an		
said		
or		
can		
big		
have		
play		
here		
ran		

(No. correct of 30 items)
Score _____

List 3	✓	Word Confusion
should		
so		
two		
up		
them		
look		
about		
will		
more		
out		
write		
time		
go		
other		
see		
many		
has		
make		
him		
then		
her		
would		
into		
these		
some		
blue		
jump		
going		
our		
saw		

(No. correct of 30 items)
Score _____

List 4	✓	Word Confusion
been		
get		
than		
day		
part		
down		
find		
no		
made		
after		
first		
long		
people		
come		
its		
my		
now		
could		
away		
did		
may		
who		
call		
way		
number		
eat		
little		
under		
went		
must		

(No. correct of 30 items)
Score _____

TOTAL SCORE _____

© Sopris West Educational Services. All rights reserved.

High-Frequency Words

List 1

I
a
be
is
on
he
as
in
to
you
for
are
have
of
at
they
from
and
the
with
that
his
was
this
it
am
dog
like
me
run

© Sopris West Educational Services. All rights reserved.

High-Frequency Words

List 2

we

use

word

there

she

one

all

your

how

by

were

not

but

which

their

if

do

what

had

when

each

an

said

or

can

big

have

play

here

ran

© Sopris West Educational Services. All rights reserved.

High-Frequency Words

List 3

should

so

two

up

them

look

about

will

more

out

write

time

go

other

see

many

has

make

him

then

her

would

into

these

some

blue

jump

going

our

saw

© Sopris West Educational Services. All rights reserved.

High-Frequency Words

List 4

been

get

than

day

part

down

find

no

made

after

first

long

people

come

its

my

now

could

away

did

may

who

call

way

number

eat

little

under

went

must

© Sopris West Educational Services. All rights reserved.

Oral Reading Fluency Assessment Form

Teacher _____   School _____

If student reads for more than 1 minute:	If student reads for 1 minute:	Percent Accuracy:
WCPM* = $\dfrac{(\text{\# Words Read} - \text{Errors}) \times 60}{\text{\# Seconds}}$	WCPM* = Words Read − Errors	% Accuracy = $\dfrac{\text{Words Read} - \text{Errors}}{\text{Words Read}}$

Assessment 1

Date _____   Student Name _____   Text _____   Pages _____   Time _____

Words Read _____   Number of Errors _____   Words Correct Per Minute _____   Percent Accuracy _____

Assessment 2

Date _____   Student Name _____   Text _____   Pages _____   Time _____

Words Read _____   Number of Errors _____   Words Correct Per Minute _____   Percent Accuracy _____

Assessment 3

Date _____   Student Name _____   Text _____   Pages _____   Time _____

Words Read _____   Number of Errors _____   Words Correct Per Minute _____   Percent Accuracy _____

*WCPM = Words Correct per Minute

© Sopris West Educational Services. All rights reserved.

Progress in Reading Levels Summary Form
(Assessment of Reading Accuracy)

Student _____

Teacher _____

School _____

Grade _____

Year _____

Instructions: Record the **level**, **book title**, **date**, and **percent accuracy**. Then note whether the book was on the student's **Independent**, **Instructional**, or **Frustration** level.

Calculate % Accuracy: Words Read − Errors

Words Read

Independent	95%–100%
Instructional	90%–94%
Frustration	Below 90%

Level	Book Title	Date	% Accuracy	Independent, Instructional, or Frustration Level

© Sopris West Educational Services. All rights reserved.

Benchmark Book Progress Summary Form

Student _____

Teacher _____

School _____

Grade _____

Year _____

Instructions: Record the **date** and **book title**. Then record **percent accuracy** on same row. If student does not pass on first try, record information for second attempt on same row.

Calculate % Accuracy: $\dfrac{\text{Words Read} - \text{Errors}}{\text{Words Read}}$

Independent	95%–100%
Instructional	90%–94%
Frustration	Below 90%

Levels	BENCHMARK BOOKS Book Title	FIRST TRY Date	% Accuracy	SECOND TRY (if needed) Date	% Accuracy
A					
B					
C					
D					
E					
F					
G					
H					
I					
J					
K					
L					
M					

© Sopris West Educational Services. All rights reserved.

Oral Reading Fluency Assessment Summary Form

Name _____ Teacher _____ School _____

If student reads for more than 1 minute:	If student reads for 1 minute:	Percent Accuracy:
WCPM* = $\dfrac{(\text{\# Words Read} - \text{Errors}) \times 60}{\text{\# Seconds}}$	WCPM* = Words Read − Errors	% Accuracy = $\dfrac{\text{Words Read} - \text{Errors}}{\text{Words Read}}$

Name of Book and Level	Date	Total Words Read	Errors	Time	WCPM	% Accuracy

*WCPM = Words Correct per Minute

© Sopris West Educational Services. All rights reserved.

Assessment Results Summary Form

Circle lists used for each assessment.	Student Errors	Items Mastered	Score
Letter-Name Assessment 26 Letter Names			___/26
Letter-Sound Assessment List 1 (30 sounds) List 2 (29 sounds) List 3 (29 sounds)			___/30 ___/29 ___/29
High-Frequency Word Assessment List 1 (30 words) List 2 (30 words) List 3 (30 words) List 4 (30 words)			___/30 ___/30 ___/30 ___/30

Benchmark Book Assessment	Highest Benchmark Book Level read with 90% accuracy.
$\dfrac{\text{Words Read} - \text{Errors}}{\text{Words Read}}$ = % Accuracy _____	Title: _____ Level: _____

© Sopris West Educational Services. All rights reserved.

Three-Step-Strategy Prompt Card

1. Look for parts you know.

2. Sound it out.

3. Check it!

Three-Step-Strategy Prompt Card

© Sopris West Educational Services. All rights reserved.

Word-Identification Prompt Card

Look for parts you know.

Do you see any letters you know?

Sound it out.

Can you sound out this part?

Say the first sound. Now sound out the next part.

Word-Identification Prompt Card

Self-Monitoring Prompt Card

What sound does that make? [Point to discrepant letters or word parts.] **Now sound out the word.**

Make it match.

Did that sound right?

That's not quite right. Check it carefully and try it again.

Go back and see if that makes sense.

You said _____. Did that make sense?

Self-Monitoring Prompt Card

© Sopris West Educational Services. All rights reserved.

Fluency Prompt Card

Make it sound like real talking.

Read it fast.

Make it sound like a
grown-up reading.

Fluency Prompt Card

© Sopris West Educational Services. All rights reserved.

Partner Reading Prompt Cards

Coach

Check that word.

The word is _____. Say the word.

Partner Reading

Reader

Picks and reads the book first.

Partner Reading

Adapted from Mathes, P. G., Torgesen, J. K., Allen, S. H., and Allor, J. H. (2001).
First Grade PALS: Peer-Assisted Literacy Strategies. Longmont, CO: Sopris West.

© Sopris West Educational Services. All rights reserved.

Letter-Sound Cards

a	h	l
s	g	k
d	f	j

Suggestion: *Responsive Reading Instruction* includes blackline masters for *five* separate sets of letter and word cards for use in **WORD WORK**. To keep them organized, copy each set on a different color of card stock. Use **blue card stock** for these Letter-Sound Cards.

© Sopris West Educational Services. All rights reserved.

Letter-Sound Cards

e	w	q
y	t	r
o	i	u

© Sopris West Educational Services. All rights reserved.

Letter-Sound Cards

x	z	p
b	v	c
a	m	n

© Sopris West Educational Services. All rights reserved.

Letter-Sound Cards

B	M	g
C	V	N
<u>P</u>	Z	X

© Sopris West Educational Services. All rights reserved.

Letter-Sound Cards

U	I	O
R	T	Y
Q	W	E

© Sopris West Educational Services. All rights reserved.

Letter-Sound Cards

D	H	L
S	G	K
A	F	J

© Sopris West Educational Services. All rights reserved.

Letter-Combination Cards

ar	sh	ow
ck	er	ee
th	ing	ch

Suggestion: *Responsive Reading Instruction* includes blackline masters for *five* separate sets of letter and word cards for use in **WORD WORK**. To keep them organized, copy each set on a different color of card stock. Use **light green card stock** for these Letter-Combination Cards.

© Sopris West Educational Services. All rights reserved.

Letter-Combination Cards

ay	ai	oa
or	ir	ur
ee	a_e	oo

© Sopris West Educational Services. All rights reserved.

Letter-Combination Cards

u_e	ea	e_e
i_e	ow	ou
au	igh	o_e

© Sopris West Educational Services. All rights reserved.

Letter-Combination Cards

ew	al	aw
tch	oy	oi
wr	dge	le

© Sopris West Educational Services. All rights reserved.

Letter-Combination Cards

ough	ture	tial
augh	mb	sion
kn	ph	tion

© Sopris West Educational Services. All rights

Letter-Combination Cards

cial	cious	tious
all	−−y	−y

© Sopris West Educational Services. All rights reserved.

Silent *e* Word Cards

tap	hug	cap
tape	huge	cape

Suggestion: *Responsive Reading Instruction* includes blackline masters for *five* separate sets of letter and word cards for use in **WORD WORK**. To keep them organized, copy each set on a different color of card stock. Use **yellow card stock** for these Silent *e* Word Cards.

© Sopris West Educational Services. All rights reserved.

Silent e Word Cards

hat	pan	rat
hate	pane	rate

© Sopris West Educational Services. All rights reserved.

Silent e Word Cards

fin	man	win
fine	mane	wine

© Sopris West Educational Services. All rights reserved.

Silent e Word Cards

mat	at	bit
mate	ate	bite

© Sopris West Educational Services. All rights reserved.

Silent e Word Cards

kit	rid	hid
kite	ride	hide

© Sopris West Educational Services. All rights reserved.

Word Sorts Word Cards

bait	train	rain
make	same	date
payday	pray	away

© Sopris West Educational Services. All rights reserved.

Suggestion: *Responsive Reading Instruction* includes blackline masters for *five* separate sets of letter and word cards for use in **WORD WORK**. To keep them organized, copy each set on a different color of card stock. Use **purple card stock** for these Word Sorts Word Cards.

Word Sorts Word Cards

blade	nail	sway
today	say	plate
stayed	played	wanted

© Sopris West Educational Services. All rights reserved.

Word Sorts Word Cards

hinted	marched	looked
painted	hopped	jumped
smiled	frowned	trusted

© Sopris West Educational Services. All rights reserved.

Word Sorts Word Cards

shook	brook	cook
boom	tool	zoo
wool	wood	stood

© Sopris West Educational Services. All rights reserved.

Word Sorts Word Cards

boot	moo	book
stool	groom	broom
curb	hurt	fur

© Sopris West Educational Services. All rights reserved.

Word Sorts Word Cards

hurry	purse	purple
shiver	perky	dinner
shirt	stir	bird

© Sopris West Educational Services. All rights reserved.

Word Sorts Word Cards

girl	sir	first
birth	water	turn
river	runner	her

© Sopris West Educational Services. All rights reserved.

groan	oak	toast
joke	bone	smoke
slope	zone	hope

© Sopris West Educational Services. All rights reserved.

Word Sorts Word Cards

goat	spoke	float
foam	toad	boat
town	now	cow

© Sopris West Educational Services. All rights reserved.

Word Sorts Word Cards

found	out	mouse
cloud	loud	shout
power	found	around

© Sopris West Educational Services. All rights reserved.

Word Sorts Word Cards

clown	crown	down
shady	baby	lady
silly	funny	puppy

© Sopris West Educational Services. All rights reserved.

Word Sorts Word Cards

fry	sky	dry
jelly	candy	shy
fly	try	by

© Sopris West Educational Services. All rights reserved.

Word Sorts Word Cards

art	army	far
swarm	march	start
port	sort	corn

© Sopris West Educational Services. All rights reserved.

Word Sorts Word Cards

park	mark	jar
thorn	before	cord
born	torn	or

© Sopris West Educational Services. All rights reserved.

Word Sorts Word Cards

boy	joy	toy
soy	annoy	enjoy
point	spoil	oil

© Sopris West Educational Services. All rights reserved.

Word Sorts Word Cards

cowboy	coin	join
moist	oink	soil
meet	seed	tree

© Sopris West Educational Services. All rights reserved.

Word Sorts Word Cards

between	green	teeth
steam	seat	cream
free	creep	deep

© Sopris West Educational Services. All rights reserved.

Word Sorts Word Cards

team	treat	eat
easy	cheat	dream
grew	threw	chew

© Sopris West Educational Services. All rights reserved.

Word Sorts Word Cards

stew	blew	new
crawl	awning	raw
shawl	paw	straw

© Sopris West Educational Services. All rights reserved.

Word Sorts Word Cards

awful	saw	flew
bite	tire	fire
twice	hide	write

© Sopris West Educational Services. All rights reserved.

Word Sorts Word Cards

rice	mice	pride
delight	midnight	right
tight	fight	might

© Sopris West Educational Services. All rights reserved.

Word Sorts Word Cards

lightning

mighty

light

© Sopris West Educational Services. All rights reserved.

High-Frequency-Word Cards

be	a	I
he	on	is
to	in	as

© Sopris West Educational Services. All rights reserved.

Suggestion: *Responsive Reading Instruction* includes blackline masters for *five* separate sets of letter and word cards for use in **WORD WORK**. To keep them organized, copy each set on a different color of card stock. Use **orange card stock** for these High-Frequency-Word Cards.

High-Frequency-Word Cards

are	for	you
at	of	have
and	from	they

© Sopris West Educational Services. All rights reserved.

High-Frequency-Word Cards

that	with	the
this	was	his
dog	am	it

© Sopris West Educational Services. All rights reserved.

High-Frequency-Word Cards

run	me	like
word	use	we
one	she	there

© Sopris West Educational Services. All rights reserved.

how	your	all
not	were	by
their	which	but

© Sopris West Educational Services. All rights reserved.

High-Frequency-Word Cards

what	do	if
each	when	had
or	said	an

© Sopris West Educational Services. All rights reserved.

High-Frequency-Word Cards

have	big	can
ran	here	play
two	so	should

© Sopris West Educational Services. All rights reserved.

High-Frequency-Word Cards

look	them	up
more	will	about
time	write	out

© Sopris West Educational Services. All rights reserved.

High-Frequency-Word Cards

see	other	go
make	has	many
her	then	him

© Sopris West Educational Services. All rights reserved.

High-Frequency-Word Cards

these	into	would
jump	blue	some
saw	our	going

© Sopris West Educational Services. All rights reserved.

High-Frequency-Word Cards

than	get	been
down	part	day
made	no	find

© Sopris West Educational Services. All rights reserved.

High-Frequency-Word Cards

long	first	after
its	come	people
could	now	my

© Sopris West Educational Services. All rights reserved.

may	did	away
way	call	who
little	eat	number

© Sopris West Educational Services. All rights reserved.

Planning Guide

I have a student who	Try this activity	Page
Reads the first part of a word and guesses the rest.	• Modeling the Word Identification Strategy • Teaching Word Identification Using the Strategy • Teaching Sounding Out • Elkonin Sound Boxes with Print • "Point" Game • Teaching the Silent *e* Rule • "Silly Word" Game	154 156 52 54 58 63 60
Reads one word at a time in a mechanical way.	• Reading Phrases • Repeated Reading with a Model	106 102
Reads very slowly.	• Reading Phrases • Repeated Reading with a Model • Partner Reading • "Beat the Teacher" Game	106 102 104 80
Looks at me to find out if he/she is correct when trying to read a difficult word.	• Teaching Students to Monitor Their Own Reading • Teaching Sounding Out • "Point" Game • "Silly Word" Game • Reading Multisyllabic Words	159 52 58 60 85
Makes errors while reading that don't make sense, but keeps on reading.	• Teaching Students to Monitor Their Own Reading • "Does It Make Sense?" Game	159 161
Waits for me to tell him/her difficult words.	• Modeling Word-Identification Strategy • Teaching Word Identification Using the Strategy • Teaching Sounding Out • Elkonin Sound Boxes with Print • "Point" Game • Teaching the Silent *e* Rule • "Silly Word" Game • Reading Multisyllabic Words	154 156 52 54 58 63 60 85
Has trouble remembering the sounds of letters.	• Teaching Letter-Sounds • Teaching Letter Combinations • Alphabet Books and Charts • "Pick Up the Letter" Game • "Vowel Sound" Game	40 43 45 46 48
Mixes up the vowel sounds.	• Teaching Letter-Sounds • Teaching Letter Combinations • "Pick Up the Letter" Game • "Vowel Sound" Game • Elkonin Sound Boxes with Print	40 43 46 48 54

© Sopris West Educational Services. All rights reserved.

I have a student who	Try this activity	Page
Has trouble remembering what he/she has read.	• Reading a New Book • Teaching Comprehension in Text Reading • Writing in Response to Text	150 163 189
Writes words incorrectly and very quickly (without breaking them into their sounds).	• Elkonin Sound Boxes with Print • Listen and Spell • Word Sorts • Writing Multisyllabic Words • Word Pattern Charts • Word Linking • Teaching Sound Analysis • Teaching Students to Edit Their Writing	54 66 73 90 71 69 180 185
Has trouble remembering how to spell words.	• Listen and Spell • Teaching Letter-Sounds • Teaching Letter Combinations • Teaching the Silent e Rule • Elkonin Sound Boxes with Print • Word Sorts • Writing Multisyllabic Words • Word Pattern Charts • Word Linking • Teaching Sound Analysis	66 40 43 63 54 73 90 71 69 180
Can produce the sounds of letters when he/she tries to sound out a word but can't blend the sounds together to produce the correct word.	• Stretching Words • "Mystery Word" Game • Teaching Sounding Out	33 36 52
Tends to look at the pictures when he/she comes to a challenging word in a book.	• Modeling the Word Identification Strategy • Teaching Word Identification Using the Strategy • Teaching Sounding Out • "Point" Game • "Silly Word" Game • Elkonin Sound Boxes with Print	154 156 52 58 60 54
Reads short words well but is inaccurate when trying to read longer words.	• Reading Multisyllabic Words • Flexing Words • Writing Multisyllabic Words	85 88 90
Misses or confuses high-frequency words when reading text.	• Teaching High-Frequency Words • Writing High-Frequency Words • Word Building • "Beat the Teacher" Game	77 83 82 80
Has trouble thinking of a sentence to write in his/her journal.	• Supported Independent Writing • Teaching Comprehension in Text Reading • Writing in Response to Text	176 163 189

© Sopris West Educational Services. All rights reserved.

READ ALL ABOUT IT!
Reading Certificate

Week Ending: _____

I know the following letters: _____

I can write: _____

I can read these words: _____

These are the books I read this week: _____
_____

Teacher Comments:

READ ALL ABOUT IT!
Reading Certificate

Week Ending: _____

I know the following letters: _____

I can write: _____

I can read these words: _____

These are the books I read this week: _____
_____

Teacher Comments:

© Sopris West Educational Services. All rights reserved.

Implementation Guide

During the lesson:

First 10 minutes:

1. **WORD WORK**
   a. Do planned activities
   b. Remember: model, guided practice, independent practice
   c. Take anecdotal notes

Second 10 minutes:

2. **PRINT CONCEPTS AND FLUENCY**
   a. Star Reader reads familiar book and you prompt and model
   b. Take anecdotal notes
   c. Other students partner read

3. **ASSESSMENT**
   a. Assess yesterday's Star Reader
   b. Other students partner read

Third 10 minutes:

4. **SUPPORTED READING**
   a. Introduce new book (comprehension focus)
   b. First reading of all or part of the book by the Star Reader while other students follow along
      i. Model and prompt student to use the Word Identification Strategy
      ii. May write a problem word on a whiteboard
      iii. Scaffolding and praise
      iv. Comprehension questioning
   c. Second reading by all students
   d. Possible third reading for fluency
   e. Take anecdotal notes

Fourth 10 minutes:

5. **SUPPORTED WRITING**
   a. Ask the Star Reader a question about the new book (comprehension focus)
   b. Star Reader composes a complete sentence with your help
   c. All students repeat sentence
   d. All students write the same sentence in their journals
      i. Provide support and scaffolding
      ii. Use sound boxes
      iii. Teach students to check their work
      iv. Resulting sentence must be correct

© Sopris West Educational Services. All rights reserved.

Before the lesson:

1. Plan **WORD WORK** and assemble materials

2. Choose books for fluency work

3. Choose assessment and get copy of form and materials

4. Choose new book for Star Reader and plan/write introduction

5. Get copy of Anecdotal Record sheet and put all forms on clipboard

6. Plan the question you will ask the Star Reader for **SUPPORTED WRITING**

7. Be sure you have journals, pens, and correction tape for **SUPPORTED WRITING**

After the lesson:

1. Calculate the results of the assessment

2. Review your records to plan the next lesson

3. Think about what went well and what was difficult

Reflect on the lesson:

1. What was supposed to happen in the lesson?

2. What happened in the lesson?

3. What should stay the same?

4. What should I change?

© Sopris West Educational Services. All rights reserved.

Elkonin Sound Box Cards

© Sopris West Educational Services. All rights reserved.

Elkonin Sound Box Cards

Source: Adapted from Elkonin, D. B. (1973). "USSR." In Downing, John A. (Ed.), Comparative Reading: Cross-National Studies of Behavior and Processes in Reading and Writing. New York: Macmillan.

© Sopris West Educational Services. All rights reserved.

318

Where's _____ **?**

1

_____ is on a

3

FOLD

CUT HERE

_____ is on a

8

6

© Sopris West Educational Services. All rights reserved.

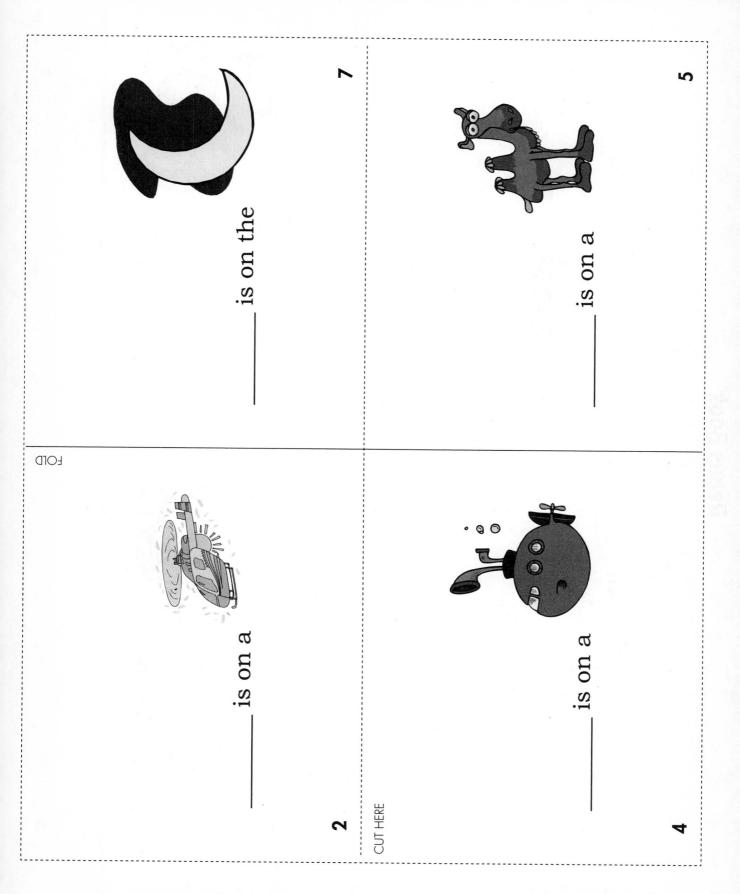

7

———— is on the

5

———— is on a

FOLD

———— is on a

2

CUT HERE

———— is on a

4

© Sopris West Educational Services. All rights reserved.

Rebus Book

FOLD

1

I can go!

3

_____ can go on a

8

CUT HERE

_____ can go on a

9

© Sopris West Educational Services. All rights reserved.

———— can go on a

7

———— can go on a

5

FOLD

———— can go on a

2

CUT HERE

———— can go on a

4

© Sopris West Educational Services. All rights reserved.

Rebus Book

My Pet

1

FOLD

My pet is a

3

My pet is a

6

8

CUT HERE

© Sopris West Educational Services. All rights reserved.

7

My pet is not a

5

My pet is a

FOLD

My pet is a

2

CUT HERE

My pet is a

4

© Sopris West Educational Services. All rights reserved.

Rebus Book

FOLD

I Can See

1

I can see a

3

I can see a

9

8

CUT HERE

© Sopris West Educational Services. All rights reserved.

7

I see the

5

I can see a

FOLD

I can see a

CUT HERE

I can see a

2

4

© Sopris West Educational Services. All rights reserved.

Rebus Book

FOLD

I Like to Eat

1

I like to eat

3

I like to eat

8

CUT HERE

6

© Sopris West Educational Services. All rights reserved.

7

I do not like to eat

5

I like to eat

I like to eat a

2

CUT HERE

I like to eat a

4

© Sopris West Educational Services. All rights reserved.

Star Reader

_____

_____

_____

© Sopris West Educational Services. All rights reserved.

Three-Step Strategy Poster

Look for parts you know.

1

2

Sound it out.

Check it.

3

Check it.

© Sopris West Educational Services. All rights reserved.

Editing Countdown Poster

⑤ Capital Letters

④ Punctuation

③ Spaces

② Spelling

① Sounds Right

Blast off!

© Sopris West Educational Services. All rights reserved.

Multisyllable Strategy Poster

Reading Words with More Than One Syllable

1. Look for parts you know.
2. Find the vowels. Every chunk (word part) must have one vowel sound.
3. Read each chunk.
4. Put the chunks together.
5. Flex as needed.

Writing Words with More Than One Syllable

1. Clap the word.
2. Say the first part slowly. Write the sounds.
3. Clap the word again.
4. Say the next part slowly. Write the sounds.
5. Make sure it looks right.

© Sopris West Educational Services. All rights reserved.

Responsive Reading Instruction Materials

- ❏ Small table (round or rectangular) and chairs
- ❏ Baskets or plastic boxes to organize materials for each group (1 per group)
- ❏ Writing journals for students
- ❏ Calculator
- ❏ Digital kitchen timer
- ❏ Scissors
- ❏ Poster board or paper and mounting tape
- ❏ Large whiteboard and easel
- ❏ Small whiteboards (4–5)
- ❏ Colored dry-erase markers (low odor) and erasers (4–5)
- ❏ Standard colored markers
- ❏ Fine-point colored markers
- ❏ Wet-erase markers
- ❏ Chart tablet
- ❏ Plastic markers (disks, squares, etc.)
- ❏ Pencils and pens
- ❏ Metal burner covers (at least 4–5)
- ❏ Magnetic letters (upper- and lowercase) (it can be helpful to have 2 sets of lowercase letters)
- ❏ Storage box for magnetic letters
- ❏ Cookie sheet or metal tray
- ❏ Sticky notes, small size

- ❏ Sticky tabs
- ❏ Small note cards
- ❏ Note cards
- ❏ Scotch tape
- ❏ Slinky Toys (4) (we prefer the metal ones)
- ❏ Set of books leveled according to the Fountas & Pinnell (1999) system, decodable books approximately leveled according to the same system, or other text on students' instructional reading levels
- ❏ Benchmark Books, or the Developmental Reading Assessment (Beaver, 1997), for tracking progress
- ❏ Big books (enlarged books designed to be read by a group of students) (1–2)
- ❏ Alphabet book or chart
- ❏ Three-ring binders for records (1 large per group or 1 medium per student)
- ❏ Clipboards (1–2) for each group you teach
- ❏ 1" correction tape
- ❏ Gallon-size ziplock bags for take-home books
- ❏ Small ziplock bags
- ❏ Sentence strips
- ❏ Cards with pictures of objects
- ❏ Stickers or other rewards (optional)

© Sopris West Educational Services. All rights reserved.

References

Adams, M. J. (1990). *Beginning to read: Thinking and learning about print*. Cambridge, MA: MIT Press.

Baker, S. K., & Good, R. (1995). Curriculum-based measurement of English reading with bilingual Hispanic students: A validation study with second-grade students. *School Psychology Review*, *24*, 561–578.

Bear, D. R., Invernizzi, M., Templeton, S., & Johnston, F. (1996). *Words their way: Word study for phonics, vocabulary, and spelling instruction*. Upper Saddle River, NY: Prentice-Hall.

Beaver, J. (1997). *Developmental reading assessment*. Parsippany, NJ: Celebration Press.

Chard, D. J., Vaughn, S., & Tyler, B. (2002). A synthesis of research on effective interventions for building reading fluency with elementary students with learning disabilities. *Journal of Learning Disabilities*, *35*(5), 386–406.

Clay, M. M. (1993). *Reading recovery: A guidebook for teachers in training*. Portsmouth, NH: Heinemann.

Deno, S. L., Mirkin, P. K., & Chiang, B. (1982). Identifying valid measures of reading. *Exceptional Children*, *49*, 36–45.

Denton, C. A., Vaughn, S., & Fletcher, J. M. (2003). Bringing research-based practice in reading intervention to scale. *Learning Disabilities Research and Practice, 18*, 201–203.

Dolch, E.W. (1955). *Methods in Reading.* Champaign, IL: Garrad Press.

Elkonin, D. B. (1973). USSR. In Downing, John A. (Ed.), *Comparative reading: Cross-national studies of behavior and processes in reading and writing* (pp. 551–579). New York: Macmillan.

Foorman, B. R. & Torgesen, J. (2001). Critical elements of classroom and small-group instruction promote reading success in all children. *Learning Disabilities Research & Practice, 16*(4), 203–212.

Foorman, B. R., Fletcher, J. M., & Francis, D. J. (2004). Early reading assessment. In W. Evans and H. J. Walberg (Eds.), *Student learning, evaluating teaching effectiveness* (pp. 81–125). Stanford: Hoover Press.

Foorman, B. R., Francis, D. J., Fletcher, J. M., Schatschneider, C., & Mehta, P. (1998). The role of instruction in learning to read: Preventing reading disabilities in at-risk children. *Journal of Educational Psychology, 90*, 37–55.

Fountas, I. C., & Pinnell, G. S. (1999). *Matching books to readers.* Portsmouth, NH: Heinemann.

Fuchs, L. S. & Fuchs, D. (1986). Effects of systematic formative evaluation: A meta-analysis. *Exceptional Children, 53*, 199–208.

Fuchs, L. S., Fuchs, D., & Stecker, P. M. (1989). Effects of curriculum-based measurement on teachers' instructional planning. *Journal of Learning Disabilities, 22*, 51–59.

Good, R. H., & Kaminski, R. (2003). *Dynamic indicators of basic early literacy skills* [DIBELS] (6th ed.). (Grades K–3.) Longmont, CO: Sopris West. www.soprweswest.com; http://dibels.uoregon.edu/.

Good, R. H., Wallin, J., Simmons, D. C., Kame'enui, E. J., & Kaminski, R. A. (2002). System-wide percentile ranks for DIBELS benchmark assessment (Technical Report 9). Eugene, OR: University of Oregon.

Graves, D. H. (1983). *Writing: Teachers and children at work.* Portsmouth, NH: Heinemann.

Graves, M. F., Graves, B. B., & Braaten, S. (1996). Scaffolded reading experiences for inclusive classes. *Educational Leadership, 53*(5), 14–16.

Heckelman, R. G. (1969). A neurological impress method of reading instruction. *Academic Therapy, 44*, 277–282.

Kame'enui, E. et al. (2002). *An analysis of reading assessment instruments for K-3: Final report.* Eugene, OR: University of Oregon, Institute for the Development of Educational Achievement. Retrieved on January 12, 2004, from http://idea.uoregon.edu/assessment/index.html.

Killoran, J., Templeman, T. P., Peters, J., & Udell, T. (2001). Identifying paraprofessional competencies for early intervention and early childhood special education. *Teaching Exceptional Children, 34*(1), 68–73.

Larkin, Martha J. (2001). Providing support for student independence through scaffolded instruction. *Teaching Exceptional Children, 34*, 30–34.

Lyon, G. R. (1995). Toward a definition of dyslexia. *Annals of Dyslexia, 45,* 3–27.

Mathes, P. G., & Denton, C. A. (2002). The prevention and identification of reading disability. *Seminars in Pediatric Neurology, 9*(3), 185–191.

Mathes, P. G., and Torgesen, J. K. (2004). *Early interventions in reading.* Columbus, OH: SRA.

Mathes, P. G., Denton, C. A., Fletcher, J. M., Anthony, J. L., Francis, D. J., & Schnatschneider, C. (2005). The effects of theoretically different instruction and student characteristics on the skills of struggling readers. *Reading Research Quarterly.*

Mathes, P., Torgesen, J. K., Allen, S. H., & Allor, J. H. (2001). *First Grade PALS (Peer-Assisted Literacy Strategies).* Longmont, CO: Sopris West.

National Reading Panel. (2000). *Teaching children to read.* Washington, DC: National Institutes of Health.

Perkins, V. L. (1988). Feedback effects on oral reading errors of children with learning disabilities. *Journal of Learning Disabilities, 21,* 244–248.

Rachotte, C. A., MacPhee, K., & Torgesen, J. K. (2001). Effectiveness of a group reading instruction program with poor readers in multiple grades. *Learning Disability Quarterly, 24,* 119–134.

Reitsma, P. (1988). Reading practice for beginners: Effects of guided reading, reading-while-listening, and independent reading with computer-based speech feedback. *Reading Research Quarterly, 23,* 219–235.

Samuels, S. J. (1994). Toward a theory of automatic information processing in reading, revisted. In R.B. Ruddell, M.R. Ruddell, & H. Singer (Eds.). *Theoretical models and processes of reading* (4th ed.) (pp. 816–861). Newark, DE: International Reading Association.

Scarborough, H. S. (1998). Early identification of children at risk for reading disabilities: Phonological awareness and some other promising predictors. In P. Accardo, A. Capute, & B. Shapiro (Eds.), *Specific reading disability: A view of the spectrum.* Timonium, MD: York Press.

Snow, C. E., Burns, S. M., & Griffin, P. (1998). *Preventing reading difficulties in young children.* Washington, DC: National Academy Press.

Torgesen, J. K., Wagner, R. K., & Rashotte, C. A. (1999). *The Test of Word Reading Efficiency.* Austin, TX: Pro-Ed.

Vaughn, S., Linan-Thompson, S., Kouzekanani, K., Bryant, D. P., Dickson, S., & Blozis, S. A. (2003). Reading instruction grouping for students with reading difficulties. *Remedial and Special Education, 24,* 301–315.

Wagner, R. K., Torgesen, J. K., & Rashotte, C. A. (1999). *Comprehensive Test of Phonological Processing.* Austin, TX: Pro-Ed.

Woodcock, R. W., McGrew, K. S., & Mather, N. (2001). *Woodcock-Johnson III Tests of Achievement.* Itasca, IL: Riverside.

Ysseldyke, J. (2001). Reflections on a research career: Generalizations from 25 years of research on assessment and instructional decision making. *Exceptional Children, 67,* 295–309.

Children's Literature Cited

Ant and the dove. (2000). Austin, TX: Steck-Vaughn.

Chicken licken. (1996). Bothell, WA: Wright Group.

Cowley, J. (1994). *My wonderful chair.* Bothell, WA: Wright Group.

Cowley, J. (1996a). *Along comes Jake.* Bothell, WA: Wright Group.

Cowley, J. (1996b). *The birthday cake.* Bothell, WA: Wright Group.

Cowley, J. (1996c). *Bread.* Bothell, WA: Wright Group.

Cowley, J. (1996d). *Cow up a tree.* Crystal Lake, IL: Rigby.

Cowley, J. (1996e). *Just this once.* Bothell, WA: Wright Group.

Cowley, J. (1996f). *Mrs. Grindy's shoes.* Bothell, WA: Wright Group.

Cowley, J. (1996g). *My home.* Bothell, WA: Wright Group.

Cowley, J. (1996h). *My sloppy tiger goes to school.* Bothell, WA: Wright Group.

Cowley, J. (1996i). *Tess and Paddy.* Bothell, WA: Wright Group.

Cowley, J. (1996j). *Wake up, Mom!* Bothell, WA: Wright Group.

Cowley, J. (1998k). *The red rose.* Bothell, WA: Wright Group.

Cutting, J. (1996). *My family.* Bothell, WA: Wright Group.

Frasier, D. & Compton, C. (1994). *This is my family*. Carlsbad, CA: Dominie.

Friends. (1976). Glennville, IL: Scott Foresman.

Gingerbread boy. (1995). Austin, TX: Steck-Vaughn.

Glazer, T. *On top of spaghetti*. (1993). Glenview IL: Scott Foresman.

Great big enormous turnip. (1976). Glenview IL: Scott Foresman.

Green, S. & Siamon, S. (1992). *Danny's dollars*. Carlsbad, CA: Dominie.

Hollander, S. K. (1976). *Baby monkey*. Glennville, IL: Scott Foresman.

Hunt, R. (1996). *What a bad dog!* New York, NY: Oxford University Press.

King, S. (1989). *Baby's birthday*. Crystal Lake, IL: Rigby.

Lewis, T. P. (1983). *Hill of fire*. New York, NY: Harper Collins.

Lobel, A. (1979). *Frog and toad are friends*. New York, NY: Harper Collins.

Lobel, A. (1983). *Mouse soup*. New York, NY: Harper Collins.

Munching Mark (book based on a story by Elizabeth Cannard). (1995).
        Crystal Lake, IL: Rigby.

My cat's surprise. (1989). Austin, TX: Steck-Vaughn.

Parker, J. (1990). *Look out for your tail*. Crystal Lake, IL: Rigby.

Randell, B. (1996). *Ben's tooth*. Crystal Lake, IL: Rigby.

Randell, B. (1996a). *Father Bear goes fishing*. Crystal Lake, IL: Rigby.

Randell, B. (1996b). *Clever penguins*. Crystal Lake, IL: Rigby.

Randell, B. (1996c). *Hermit crab*. Crystal Lake, IL: Rigby.

Randell, B. (1996d). *Hot dogs*. Crystal Lake, IL: Rigby.

Randell, B. (1996e). *The hungry kitten*. Crystal Lake, IL: Rigby.

Randell, B. (1996f). *Lazy pig*. Crystal Lake, IL: Rigby.

Randell, B. (1996g). *Lizard loses his tail*. Crystal Lake, IL: Rigby.

Randell, B. (1996h). *Me!* Crystal Lake, IL: Rigby.

Randell, B. (1996i). *Tom is brave*. Crystal Lake, IL: Rigby.

Rollins, C. (1976). *Red and blue mittens*. New York, NY: Harper Collins.

Semple, C. & Tuer, J. (1988). *Pancakes for supper*. Crystal Lake, IL: Rigby.

Too Many Bones. (2000). Austin, TX: Steck-Vaughn.

Walker, C. (1993). *Slugs and snails*. Bothell, WA: Wright Group.

Wyvill, M. (1992). *The witch's haircut*. Bothell, WA: Wright Group.

Yuen, R. (1996). *What is red?* Carlsbad, CA: Dominie.